The Games Black Girls Play

The Games Black Girls Play

*Learning the Ropes from
Double-Dutch to Hip-Hop*

Kyra D. Gaunt

NEW YORK UNIVERSITY PRESS
New York and London

NEW YORK UNIVERSITY PRESS
New York and London
www.nyupress.org

Cover photo by Raymond Depardon, © 1998, Magnum Photos.
Title: "USA, 1981, New York City, Harlem District, 110th Street,
Festival for the Police." Originally printed in *Voyages* (Paris: Hazan,
1998).

Library of Congress Cataloging-in-Publication Data
Gaunt, Kyra Danielle.
The games black girls play : learning the ropes
from Double-dutch to Hip-hop / Kyra D. Gaunt.
p. cm.
Includes bibliographical references and index.
ISBN–13: 978–0–8147–3119–2 (cloth : alk. paper)
ISBN–10: 0–8147–3119–8 (cloth : alk. paper)
ISBN–13: 978–0–8147–3120–8 (pbk. : alk. paper)
ISBN–10: 0–8147–3120–1 (pbk. : alk. paper)
1. African Americans—Music—History and criticism. 2. African
American girls—Social life and customs. 3. Rap (Music)—History
and criticism. 4. Singing games—United States. 5. Rope
skipping—United States. I. Title.
ML3479.G38   2005
780'.89'96073—dc22   2005024053

New York University Press books are printed on acid-free paper,
and their binding materials are chosen for strength and durability.

Manufactured in the United States of America

c 10 9 8 7 6 5 4 3 2 1
p 10 9 8 7 6 5 4 3 2 1

I dedicate this book to Jasmine and Stephanie, the twins who inspired the start of this "game"; my mother, Ardell, who trained my four-year-old feet to dance, who propels me and prays for me to be free to do my thang; and my birth father, Norman, whose presence makes life complete. Now, something else is possible. Let me be open to what it brings and what I have to bring to it.

* * *

Dare to be different than the recipe that brought you here.
—Bernice Johnson Reagon

* * *

somebody / anybody
sing a black girl's song.
bring her out
to know herself.   (Shange 1977)

A Zen poet once said: A person who is a master in the art of living makes little distinction between their work and their play, their labor and their leisure, their mind and their body, their education and their recreation, their love and their religion. They hardly know which is which and simply pursue their vision of excellence and grace, whatever they do, leaving others to decide whether they are working or playing. To them they are always doing both.

Contents

List of Musical Figures   xi

Acknowledgments   xiii

Introduction   1

1   Slide: Games as Lessons in Black Musical Style   19

2   Education, Liberation:
    Learning the Ropes of a Musical Blackness   37

3   Mary Mack Dressed in Black:
    The Earliest Formation of a Popular Music   56

4   Saw You With Your Boyfriend:
    Music between the Sexes   89

5   Who's Got Next Game?
    Women, Hip-Hop, and the Power of Language   111

6   Double Forces Has Got the Beat:
    Reclaiming Girls' Music in the Sport of Double-Dutch   133

7   Let a Woman Jump:
    Dancing with the Double Dutch Divas   158

    Conclusion   181

Appendix:
Musical Transcriptions of Game-Songs Studied 188

Bibliography 197

Index 211

About the Author 221

Musical Figures

Figure 1   Cheer "OO-lay, OO-lay." Cyclic model of refrain   33

Figure 2   "Mary Mack" version 1   65

Figure 3   "Mary Mack" version 2   65

Figure 4   OO-lay vs. Oh-la, cheers compared   79

Figure 5   "James Brown" chant   135

Figure 6   Double Forces chant   153

Acknowledgments

This book is the product of various collaborations with friends, colleagues, mentors, coaches, and the social memory and lived experiences of African Americans, both female and male. It has been full of ups and downs, but it is a privilege to bring this work forth to the world.

This would not have been possible without the generous support of faculty summer fellowships from the University of Virginia, a fellowship from the National Endowment for the Humanities, and a postdoctoral fellowship for underrepresented faculty from the Ford Foundation. The Ford Foundation's commitment to not only increasing the number of minority faculty in the professorate, but also offering mentoring and collegial interaction at its annual conferences, is profound and has enriched my academic life immensely.

Thanks to Jasmine, Stephanie, the fifteen women I interviewed and got to know, the girls from a summer writing program in Ann Arbor, Michigan, Candace Ramsey and Bridgette Ramsey in Philly, LaShonda Barnett, and particularly the Double Dutch Divas and the director of the film of the same name, Nicole Franklin. Franklin's film is perennially broadcast on the Discovery Channel. Thanks for the honor. I hope readers are inspired by my thoughts about you all.

Various colleagues, mentors, and staff have assisted me along the way: Judith Becker at the University of Michigan; Ed Ayers, Adria LaViolette, Richard Handler, Jessica Feldman, Cindy Wall, Scott DeVeaux, Judith Shatin, Michelle Kisliuk, Deborah McDowell, and my dear friend, Kandioura Dramé at the University of Virginia; Robin D. G. Kelley, Linda Tucker, Michael Beckerman, Gage Averill, Pauline Lum, and especially Mercedes Dujunco and Suzanne Cusick at New York University; and thanks to various colleagues elsewhere, including Niloofar Mina and Joe Schloss for assisting, supporting, and inspiring me. Your generosity, encouragement, inspiration, laughter, and faith in me I acknowledge here. Your contribution has always been right on time.

Some colleagues are old friends from graduate school at Michigan: Stacy Blake, Guthrie P. Ramsey, and Nancy Hopkins-Evans. As an instructor who's always learning from my students, I want to thank all the graduates and undergraduates from my courses in African American music, hip-hop, popular music, jazz, and ethnomusicology history and theory. I teach because of the greatness you inspire in me and will inspire in others. Additional support on this project was generously given by several of my graduate and undergraduate students, including Amy Daken, Melvin Butler, Brett Pyper, Monica Hairston, Michael Birenbaum-Quintero, Jalylah Burrell, William (Billy) J. Levay, and Yesenia Godoy. If I left anyone out, your generosity is acknowledged in spite of my forgetfulness.

No project of this size or scope could be completed without partnership. I want to thank Corinna Fales, who generously assisted at several stages with editing this project and, finally, Sue Birch, my chaos management coach: You made it so that I could hear my own thoughts and find them later, too.

Close friends gave me insight into who I am beyond being a teacher or scholar: Thank you Myra "Nicky" Anderson, Harry Allen, Tomás Doncker, Lenise Logan, Liza Lopez, Melvin Thomas Brown, Shabbir Kazmi, Toni Blackman, Roxane Butterfly, and my other friends and coaches at Landmark Education who keep the power and magic of life alive and real for me and all people.

Thanks to the Hopkins family in Philly, my immediate family in Rockville, Maryland, and my youngest family members who I am committed will have an education that matters; to Arielle, Aliazah, Amanda, Dakotta, Cheyenne, Elizabeth, and Garrison, all my love, laughter, and support. I am in academia for the opportunity to bring our culture to my students and the world out there so I can bring what people get about us back home. And, to that special man out there for me (perhaps you're already in my life): With the completion of this book I am clear there's plenty of room for you to appear. Come play with me. I got a few other games to share. You bring yours!

Finally, let me thank Eric Zinner, Despina Gimbel, and Emily Park, my editors and assistant editor at New York University Press. I was everything but "coachable" for most of the years it took to complete this project. Thanks for believing in my work from the start to the very end. Thanks for all you did (and didn't do) to cause this to happen. Your time and enduring attention to my work will pay off in ways none of us can predict, but we all can wish for the best. I thank you humbly and joyfully.

All thanks to the creator for bringing me to this moment, and for giving me the courage to persist and play big. Let us cause the next game of life because that's who we all were made to be! *'Cause we're big B-I-G / And we're bad B-A-D / and we're boss B-O-SS B-O-SS BOSS!*

Asé!

Three girls playing jump rope as young boy looks on. Photograph by Katrina Thomas.

Introduction

When we think of the music that drives the popular culture of African Americans, our first thought is not of double-dutch: girls bouncing between two twirling ropes, keeping time to the tick-tat under their toes, stepping out with snatches of song and dance that animate their torsos and release their tongues with laughter. Instead, what comes to mind is hip-hop, neo-soul, go-go, crunk, and R&B. The games black girls play —handclapping game-songs, cheers, and double-dutch jump rope—may not even register as a kind of popular music because the term is chiefly reserved for commercial productions often dominated by men. Commercial popular music tends to exclude or simply incorporate the communal or everyday forms of popular music that cannot be assigned individual authorship or ownership: no royalties for the song-makers of double-dutch.

But everyday, black girls generate and pass on a unique repertoire of chants and embodied rhythms in their play that both reflects and inspires the principles of black popular music-making. This book is about those games: the musical games that are passed down by word of mouth and body, beyond the scope of Billboard charts and Soundscan.

Listen in on girls' daily broadcasts from the playground and you'll hear more than "nonsense." You'll hear a sophisticated approach to non-verbal syllables that mirror the melodic and linguistic approaches found in jive talk, scatting, and the verbal freestyling of hip-hop. Watch their daily routines, which mix colloquial gestures and verbal expressions, and you'll be hooked on their fascinating rhythms, their use of call-and-response from word to body, and their rap-like manipulation of phonics and rhymes just for the fun of it. Feel the finger-snapping, handclapping, thigh-pattin', chest-thumping, and foot-stomping and grasp the friction of their embodied cross-rhythms and social "rhythm sections." Girls be doing it up like they were making the latest hits for popular broadcast.

1

At first it may seem that girls are emulating the music from radio and TV. But what if girls are also initiating the textures that inspire the music we hear commercially? This is a story about the performance and politics of race, gender, and the body in African American vernacular and popular music. It is also a contribution to rethinking the ways we have represented blackness and gender in musicological studies, offering an empowering way to approach it in the future.

If we were to re-examine the aesthetics of African American musical style and practice from the ethnographic perspective of black females' participation, we'd find that African American girls embody the ideals of black music-making in the games they play: syncopation and rhythmic complexity spark handclapping and foot-stomping; call-and-response distinguishes the linguistic and musical interactions between their voices and bodies in group play; and a highly percussive approach to singing or chanting is prevalent.

Drawing upon several years of participant observation, and on my own childhood experience performing African American girls' musical games, I demonstrate how black musical style and behavior are *learned* through oral-kinetic practices that not only teach *an embodied discourse of black musical expression,* but also inherently teach *discourse about appropriate and transgressive gender and racial roles* (for both girls and boys) in African American communities. Based on this premise, I elucidate different aspects of the musical lives of African American girls and the women who affectionately call one another "girl" throughout their lives.

The musical games black girls play offer a unique site for analyzing and understanding how syncopation, sophisticated gestures or everyday choreography, and linguistic, melodic, and rhythmic aspects of improvisation are learned and socialized through "in-body formulas" (Drewal 1992). These formulas, which I call "oral-kinetic etudes," function as lessons in black musical style and taste.

While the embodied musical practices performed by girls are ordinarily visible in African American neighborhoods and urban communities, the appropriation of black girls' musical game-songs by male commercial artists is often overlooked. It makes sense that girls borrow from, say, hip-hop or R&B, or that the folklore of girls' musical play is a repository of ideas from mass-mediated realms of music and dance. But what do we make of hip-hop, an art form predominantly associated with males and masculinity, sampling from the familiar chants and beats of a female musical expression? Are men incorporating the public into the commercial, the feminine into a patriarchal interpretation of keepin' it real, or is there more to the gender politics of this exchange that could enrich our understanding of the politics of authenticity, aesthetics, and taste in black popular music?

The appropriation or adoption of familiar musical ideas is actually the basis of most popular, gospel, and folk music production within black communities. As an aesthetic, it can be linked to African ideals of music-making (see "borrowing" in *Grove Music Online,* http://www.grove music.com). As one scholar notes, Africans bring an ability to "choose eclectically from a variety of sources" in their music-making, and since improvisation is never a "totally new creation," they never "rule out the existence of a good deal of pre-existing material" (Small 1987, 22–23). In this way, improvisation is a compositional method that can be applied by the group as well as the individual. This is one example of the aesthetic practice being developed and fostered through African American girls' musical play.

My analysis of the games black girls play as lessons in black musical style, where performances function as musical scripts for behavior, is the basis of an ethnography that reveals a circular relationship of appropriation and adoption between the rhyming, dancelike gestures, melodies, and rhythms practiced in girls' musical games and in the commercial music of black male artists from rhythm and blues in the 1950s to hip-hop in 2000.

Knowing and Embodying a Musical Blackness

> Whatever else music is "about," it is inevitably about the body; music's aural and visual presence constitutes both a relation to and a representation of the body. (Leppert 1993, xx)

The Games Black Girls Play is an investigation into the epistemology of musical blackness: uncovering ways of knowing black musical aesthetics and black musical identifications through an embodied practice. The expressive realm of "kinetic orality" is the social training ground upon which girls create a background of relatedness to one another; performances of race, ethnicity, and gender are embodied through song, chant, and percussive movement. By kinetic orality, I am referring to the transmission and appropriation of musical ideals and social memories passed on jointly by word of mouth and by embodied musical gestures and formulas. While the oral transmission of words and verbal language obviously sustains the intergenerational performance of handclapping games, cheers, and double-dutch, all this is masterfully linked to musical communication and expression enacted through patterns of handclapping, foot-stomping, and other body-patting leading to a mastery over polyrhythmic expression and social interaction at a very young age.

We cannot interpret the politics of the black body without confronting the stereotypes about race, gender, and intellect concerning African Americans and black females. This too is passed on through the musical practices of girls. But, by studying the gendered black musical body, or girls' kinetic orality, over time and place, I can also reveal a "somatic historiography" of black musical style that captures the social memory of a community in new ways. African Americans inhabit repertoires of kinetic orality intergenerationally and translocally: they embody and archive memories of black social dances and mix them up with various chants and songs from the past and the present, but certain formulas of expression and identity remain.

Paul Gilroy and Cornel West both draw attention to the significance of kinetic orality in black social memory and history. Gilroy discusses it in the context of "post-slave cultures," while West discusses it in reference to "post-colonial black cultures." Each lends itself to my theory about interpreting black girls' musical games as *oral-kinetic lessons* in black musical style and identity. Reading the performance of the body is key to unlocking the somatic historiography of the musical and social life of people of African descent. According to Gilroy:

> The distinctive kinesics of the post-slave populations was the product of . . . brutal historical conditions. Though more usually raised by analysis of sports, athletics, and dance it ought to contribute directly to the understanding of the traditions of performance which continue to characterise the production and reception of diaspora musics. This orientation to the specific dynamics of performance has a wider significance in the analysis of black cultural forms than has so far been supposed. Its strengths are evident when it is contrasted with approaches to black culture have been premised exclusively on textuality and narrative rather than dramaturgy, enunciation, and gesture. (Gilroy 1993b, 75)

Gilroy is pointing to the fact that a whole world of communication exists beyond the analysis and interpretation of song lyrics or people's words, a world that resists verbal language, a world signified instead through the interpretive and dramatic realms of rhythm, gesture, and movement.

Cornel West was first to label this metacommunication "kinetic orality" when he wrote:

> The concrete, everyday response to institutionalized terrorism—slavery or Jim-Crowism—was to deploy weapons of kinetic orality, passionate physicality, and combative spirituality to survive and dream of freedom. By kinetic orality, I mean dynamic repetitive and energetic rhetorical styles that form communities, e.g., antiphonal styles and linguistic innovations that accent fluid, improvisational identities. . . . By passionate physicality, I mean bodily stylizations of the world, syncopations and polyrhythms that assert one's somebodiness in a society in which one's body has no [perceptible] public worth, only economic value as a laboring mechanism. (West 1989, 93)

For many African Americans, the bodily stylizations that assert "somebodiness" have remained a critical mode of expressing our inalienable rights to freedom embodied as social memory and action, even when freedom and democracy were being denied African American citizens in other realms. Think of the role and impact of the protest songs during the civil rights movement.

African Americans, male and female, are constantly contending with imposed stereotypes about our social and musical bodies, our somebodiness, as well as the internalized assumptions we carry and impose upon ourselves and other black bodies. Blackness is often defined by one's dance card rather than one's race card. We are constantly negotiating an artificial split between the mind (supposedly the exclusive realm of the intellect) and the body (the supposed realm of impulse, rhythm, and pleasure, rather than control). But, as recent scholarship by educational psychologist Howard Gardner has revealed, humans possess multiple intelligences and the kinesthetics of the body is one of seven he has defined thus far (1999).

Gardner's study was by no means the first to call attention to the significance of the body. Scholarship on African and African American music has always acknowledged the inseparability of music and dance (Floyd 1991, 1995; Maultsby 1990; Small 1987; Stuckey 1995; Wilson 1985, 1992; see Agawu 1995 and Radano 2000 for a critique of American race politics, rhythm, and the black musical body). Yet previous writing solely alluded to embodiment within the context of race or ethnicity. Rarely was the context of gender and sexuality expressed, for instance, in various social dances.

In a seminal 1991 article about the antecedents and aesthetic roots of African American music found in the "ring shout," namely, a counterclockwise formation of song, shuffling rhythms, storytelling and more, musicologist Samuel A. Floyd Jr. (the founding director of the Center for Black Music Research in Chicago) wrote that black music must be understood "as an *ingredient of,* and *accompaniment to,* dance" (emphasis added; Floyd 1991, 268). But any examples of dance or musical embodiment were eclipsed by the musicological tendency to analyze sound as a text and interpret the compositional intent of composers and seminal artists. By the way, the practitioners of the blues, jazz, and classical music that serve as his representatives of blackness in *The Power of Black Music* are primarily male (1995).

Floyd's 1995 book is one of a few monographs by an African American musicologist or ethnomusicologist in the last ten years that broadly address African American culture (see also DjeDje and Meadows 1998 and Ramsey 2003). In this instance, his thesis was that "dance, drum, and song" should be the basis of "all African American musical analysis and interpretation" (Floyd 1995, 7). Though it would seem that dance would naturally inspire a discussion of gender and sexuality, dance and musical gestures are limited to a few perfunctory remarks and footnotes.

In their essay "Theorizing the Body in African-American Music," musicologists Susan McClary and Robert Walser call attention to their black counterparts' reluctance to critically examining the body, despite the fact that the body is a compelling topic among scholars throughout the humanities and social sciences.

Given the ongoing struggle to have black music perceived *as* music, black culture recognized *as* culture, black people respected *as* people, it is tempting to pursue projects of legitimation that treat the body as a stumbling block in the way of full appreciation of black artistic development. As understandable as this attitude might be, it would be unfortunate if questions concerning the body were to disappear from writing about African-American music, especially at this moment in cultural studies (78). . . . Crucial to theorizing the body in African-American music [is] the fact that physicality and sexuality are tremendously complex discursive fields. That is, to discuss the erotic or bodily aspects of cultural texts or performances is not to *reduce* them [or one's scholarly authority, I would add]. (McClary and Walser 1994, 80)

The tendency to accentuate the "positive" (the *artistic*) and diminish the negative (*embodiment, sexualized dancing, unequal gender relations within black culture*) has led to fixations on the analysis of musical sounds and textures at the expense of the embodied and gendered social relations expressed in black musical practices.

Ironically, almost ten years before McClary and Walser's publication, composer and musicologist Olly Wilson called for a broadened analysis of black music. He stressed the intrinsic relationships between music, movement, and dance in what was, to my knowledge, the first edited volume devoted to the ethnomusicological study of African American music.

Most studies tend to make comparisons on the basis of the presence or absence of specific musical characteristics . . . While this approach is certainly necessary and valuable as far as it goes, *it is inadequate* . . . because this approach deals with foreground aspects of music and not the *guiding background factors which, in fact, determine the presence of these foreground features.* (emphasis added; Wilson 1985, 9)

The background here is the embodied performance or kinetic orality of black music-making, though I doubt gender relations were on his mind. Despite his call, the search for the roots of an African past (Africanisms) prevailed as a mode of racialized discourse that trumped the discussion of gender and sexuality in black music even in Wilson's own subsequent writing. Academic writing always seems to resist dance, resist speaking of the body and its attendant modes of expression. Studying girls' musical games is an opportunity to heed Wilson's earlier call, offering a way to explore the musical and social relations between females and their male counterparts, as well as examining the ways girls encode masculinity and femininity in their embodied and linguistic play.

Originally Wilson specified several key features found in African music which supported a notion that the body and dance were central to the appreciation of African American music and analysis: (1) instrumentalists in African and African-derived genres are often dancers; (2) dance and musical gestures register and project emotional as well as spiritual discourse; (3) percussive materials (rattles, bells, beads) are often attached to the body and its limbs, adding texture and contrasting timbres as a result of embodied rhythmic activity; and (4) musical movement is used to mark religious rituals (ecstasy or gettin' the holy ghost), social and individual work and play (railroad line gangs and girls' games), and other distinct social occasions (protest as well as partying). But little came of this line of thought in musicology or ethnomusicology.

If black movement and gesture actually determine foreground features such as *call-and-response, cross-rhythms, dramatically contrasting timbres, metrical ambiguity,* and *individuality within collectivity*—features outlined in Wilson's subsequent, influential essay on heterogeneous sound ideals (1992), then analyzing black girls' embodied musical play should elicit insights into the dynamics of learning and practicing black musical expression in other contexts.

The Body and Gender in Black Music Research

> The body is where the social is most convincingly represented as the individual and where politics can best disguise itself as human nature. (Fiske 1989, 70)

The kinetic orality of black musical expression is a path to learning ethnic group and gender identity, and is a way of playing with a somatic consciousness that expresses such identifications. Girls as well as boys come to rely upon this embodied consciousness in musical and nonmusical social interactions from childhood into adulthood.

Black girls' public musical experience begins with learning to embody practices passed down by siblings and peers at home, then perhaps at block parties and family reunion picnics, and also at wedding and funeral gatherings. Simultaneously, their musical experiences are influenced by various mediums of mass communication (radio, music television, Walkmans, and iPods). Girls, like boys, become consumers of racialized and gendered commercial products and mass popular performances that may homogenize black popular music, but popular music also becomes an extension of and abstraction from many everyday and local phenomena—

phenomena that may have first been experienced in the black public sphere of African American girls' music-making and play.

The oral and nonliterate expression of black girls' play is not usually thought of as a serious realm of black musical expression, or as a site for learning the ideals of black musical practice that are associated with adult, much less male, African American practice (i.e., syncopation, overlapping call-and-response, musical signifying through appropriation, and musical and dance improvisation). In this book, I put forward the claim that black girls' play is not only indicative of, but central to, understanding African American expressive culture and black popular musical aesthetics.

This reminds me of the expression "heaven is here on earth, but men do not see it." If games are an access to understanding black music, most male and female academics do not see it because "the gender of black cultural identity in African, Caribbean, and African American literature is often assumed to be male despite the use of seemingly nongendered nationalist identifications, such as 'black,' 'African,' 'African American,' or 'Caribbean'" (Olaniyan 1995, 119). The tendency to present black music culture as "nongendered" is prevalent in the most commonly referenced literature about African American music, including *Blues People* (1963) by cultural critic and activist LeRoi Jones (aka Amiri Baraka); the three editions of *The Music of Black Americans* (1973, 1983, 1997) by musicologist Eileen Southern (1973); and other works by Samuel Floyd (1983, 1991, 1995); Portia Maultsby (1990); and Olly Wilson (1974, 1985, 1992).

The musical and social history of the ring shout, spirituals, the blues, soul, funk, and hip-hop, for instance, are too often read or interpreted as if men, women, and children are a unified group. This erasing of sexual difference, differences in power and privilege in dancing, singing, and performing, leaves us with a sanitized interpretation of the black musical past and present, of traditions and innovations shared by both sexes, of improvisation and composition inspired by influential women and groups of children, by individual artists, yes, but more often than not by social practices and conventions shared in communal practice.

Discussions of black music among scholars in other fields—such as anthropology, cultural studies, and American studies—have begun to incorporate gender as a category of analysis, but black music studies has not caught up. Susan McClary, a noted feminist musicologist, acknowledged that generally the discipline of "music lags behind the other arts; it picks up ideas from other media just when they have become outmoded" (McClary 2000, 1285). Influenced by the scholarship of philosopher and gender specialist Judith Butler, feminist musicologists in the early 1990s began to study and write about genders, sexualities, bodies, emotions, and subjectivities among a vast array of musics. But these conversations, conversations that McClary said dominated the humanities for twenty years before arriving in music, have yet to truly penetrate the ideological and academic approaches to the study of black music by African American musicologists and ethnomusicologists. Works by Barbara Hampton (1992), Irene V. Jackson (1985), and Cheryl Keyes (1993, 2002) are among the quiet exceptions.

The study of gender in contemporary music discourse was re-introduced in the late 1980s, though early ethnomusicological study by women in the mid-twentieth century marked the origins of such interests. In historical musicology, *Feminine Endings: Music, Gender, and Sexuality* (McClary 1991); *Gender and the Musical Canon* (Citron 1993); *The Sight of Sound: Music, Representation, and the History of the Body* (Leppert 1993); and *Musicology and Difference: Gender and Sexuality in Music Scholarship* (Solie 1993) are a few of the important edited volumes that contributed to the "new musicology" that emerged in the early 1990s. Embracing the postmodern, the *new musicology* identified gender, sexuality, and social power as key forces in the cultural analysis of music-making.

Among ethnomusicological literature, *Music, Gender, and Culture* (Herndon, Ziegler, and Baumann) appeared in 1990 and was followed ten years later by *Music and Gender* (Moisala and Diamond 2000) and *Music and Gender: Perspectives from the Mediterranean* (Magrini 2003). Of the fifteen female contributors to *Music, Gender, and Culture,* not one author was of African descent, though the music of Africa was represented in an essay. The Moisala and Diamond collection devoted to music in the Mediterranean is relatively the same, though the inclusion of male authors is noteworthy. Still, men or women of African descent are absent, though their inclusion was perhaps unlikely given the region of interest.

Outside of music, black women authors have been doing the "real" work that music scholarship has yet to catch up with, arguably the most notable of which is the theoretical work of Patricia Hill Collins on the foundations of a black feminist thought and standpoint. (For a range of critical work in black feminist thought or gender relative specifically to music, see Carby 1990, 1991, 1992, 1998, 1999; Cole and Guy-Sheftall

2003; Crenshaw 1991; Davis 1990, 1998; Griffin 2001; hooks 1990; Kernodle, 2004; Kirk-Duggan 1997; Mahon 2004; Morgan 1999; Perry 1995; Rose 1991, 1994, 1996; Wallace 1990). Other, non-African American scholars have contributed significantly to this conversation. American studies scholar Sherrie Tucker's *Swing Shift: "All-Girl" Bands of the 1940s* (2000) offers one of the most insightful analyses of gender where race *and* music are concerned.

Today, race continues to be disassociated from gender in most contemporary literature. One recent musicological text reveals the way race continues to trump gender. In Ronald Radano's *Lying Up a Nation: Race and Black Music* (2003), gender doesn't even appear as an index topic in a book that critically challenges the distinctiveness of black music. Though he focuses on musical practices and issues in the nineteenth century, the exclusion of such analysis and discourse reifies a patriarchal interpretation of the black musical past. A notable exception to this is Guthrie Ramsey's *Race Music: Black Cultures from Bebop to Hip-hop* (2003), an excellent example in which the author, a black male scholar, incorporates gender relations into his readings of black community theaters and subjectivities.

Music scholars are compromised by the fact that our training tends to exclude analyzing choreographed movement, embodied percussion, and dance, not to mention gender and sexuality, in our interpretations of musical performance. Musical analysis tends to be about sound, texture, and a composer's or a performer's intention. But, by doing this, male (and many female) scholars have been "invisibilifying" (Lott 2000, 75) girls and women in histories of African American music and in attention to contemporary styles of performance. Now, we must begin the difficult task of rendering gender, sexuality, and other embodied expressions of difference visible in critical analyses of African American musical practice and discourse. That means we'd have to allow ourselves to feel the sexual politics of power and gender at work in musical performances. It is fitting that we begin to discover this through the in-body formulas and oral-kinetic etudes of black girls' musical games.

> If bodily performances can be both constitutive of gender and metaphors for gender, then we who study the results of bodily performances like music might profitably look to our subject as a *set of scripts for bodily performances which may actually constitute gender* [or other dimensions of identity] for the performers and which may be recogniz-

able as metaphors of gender for those who witness the performers' displays. (emphasis added; Cusick 1994)

The study of black music is more than the appreciation of black musical traits, styles, and genres devoid of attention to the lived and embodied experiences of being male and female. Analyzing African American musical practice in the everyday, rather than from recordings, begs us to examine the sexed bodies, the sexual relations, and the politics of power exemplified by race and gender (on and off the dance floor, at home and in public, at work and at play). Music-making accompanies all these modes of identity and social interaction openly and behind closed doors. Like other cultures, black popular music has rested upon symbolic representations of patriarchy and a "necessary repression of feminine aspects" that "introduces conflict into the opposition of masculine and feminine" (J. Scott 1999, 39). This is evident in both communal and commercial popular music-making from double-dutch to hip-hop. But what if girls and women are both resisting as well as sustaining this hegemonic order?

By focusing on a dimension of everyday music culture associated with African American *girls* instead of boys, and by providing a *gendered* interpretation of an ethnic music practice, I invite students and scholars to broaden their analysis and interpretation of black musical experience to include the interpenetration of race, gender, and the body. I ask them to dispel a myth of unanimity between males' and females' musical experience under the public label of "blackness." Focusing on girls and their musical games complicates these things. It makes the inequalities within music and culture transparent in ways that ordinary readings of black music and culture have not.

Getting to the Heart of My Own Musical Games

There is a space between the concrete and heaven where the air is sweeter and your heart beats faster. You drop down and then you jump up again and you do it over and over again until the rope catches on your foot or your mother calls you home. . . . You mambo back and forth, it's like dancing. When you *do-around-the-world,* it's like a ballet dancer's pirouette. In the rope, if you're good enough, you can do anything and be anything you want. (Chambers 1996, 2)

As a child moving in and out of the black neighborhood where my mother was also raised, I believed I didn't have the skills to jump double-dutch. In my imagination, all the other girls were athletes. I was not. All the others had it down. I didn't. They knew just what to do when. They made it seem so . . . natural, off-the-cuff, unrehearsed, magical, like watching Michael Jordan fly on the basketball court. Many people marvel at Jordan's skills as a basketball player, but most fail to remember that Dean Smith, his college coach, claimed that he was a mediocre player when he began college. This means he worked at what he achieved on the court. Like musical talent or basketball prowess, double-dutch is learned and requires daily practice to make it feel and look second nature. I was never able to master double-dutch as a child, but I got the music anyway, through other kinds of musical play, namely handclapping games, cheers, and their accompanying chants, not to mention the dozens of dances I learned.

In an interview with Paul Gilroy, Toni Morrison located the innermost secrets of African American folk culture in its music: "Music provides the key to the whole medley of Afro-American artistic practices" (Gilroy 1993b, 181). Morrison also remarked:

> Black Americans were sustained and healed and nurtured by the translation of their experience into art, above all in the music. That was functional . . . My parallel [as a writer] is always the music, because all of the strategies of the art are there. All of the intricacy, all of the discipline. All the work that must go into improvisation so that it appears that you've never touched it . . . The major things black art has to have are these: it must have the ability to use found objects, the appearance of using found things, and it must look effortless. It must look cool and easy. If it makes you sweat, you haven't done the work. You shouldn't be able to see the seams and stitches. (Ibid.)

Once I began to observe the kind of games I used to play among a younger generation of girls, I found myself compelled to examine the ins and outs of a popular African American musical culture from the standpoint of the embodied and gendered musical practices of black females at play. I became intrigued by the idea that black girls' musical play offered insight into the *learned* ways of being that foster and reflect individual and group identity within African American communities.

Musical play is a vital environment within which black folks, not just girls, learn to improvise with what it means to be dominant and subordinate in musical and nonmusical relationships. Black female practice is a significant but often neglected part of a larger social economy that constitutes social taste and appeal in black popular music. To ignore the sounds and relationships that link dominant African American expressions and ideology to the lived phenomena of race and gender is to ignore the everyday communal events that make up and contribute to a mass popular-music culture from R&B to hip-hop to jazz.

My intent throughout this book is to transform the usual assumptions about race, gender, and music that African Americans and people writing about black music have tended to bring to their readings of the culture. Girls' musical games may even reveal a new way of reading the often-disparaged musical aesthetics of hip-hop sampling. What if sampling is nothing more than an extension of kinetic orality of girls' games, and girls' musical play is one of the earliest musical contexts shared as public music culture within black families and communities?

Ultimately, what can these games tell us about how female members of black culture learn, share, sustain, and reject meanings about their racial and musical identity? What does all this have to tell us about gender relations within an ethnic community? What might it tell us about the role that gender and embodiment play in shaping a communal sense of blackness and a black "national" or communal taste for the latest performances of African American popular music?

The Games Black Girls Play is about how African Americans learn the "rules" of black social identity and musical practice beyond the dance floor and the music video. It reveals the not-so-obvious connections between girls' handclapping games, cheers, and double-dutch, and contemporary styles of black popular music such as hip-hop. I assert that there is a whole world of insight about racial and gender socialization and ethnic identification within African American culture that is hidden within the seemingly trivial maneuvers of games like double-dutch.

The Research Process

Let me share a bit about how I collected the data for this research. I conducted fieldwork from 1994 to 2002, collecting a broad repertoire of game-songs from assorted settings, including a traditional and a blues-based version of "Miss Mary Mack" from a set of twins in Ypsilanti, Michigan, and several games from a group of black and biracial adolescent girls and boys participating in a summer writing workshop for homeless children in Ann Arbor, Michigan. Composed by a much younger generation, these game-songs were unknown to me. I had left playing girls' musical games behind at least thirty years earlier, in my teens, to sing popular music and think about boys.

Versioning, such as the examples of Mary Mack, are quite common in girls' games, and I encountered an interesting regional version of a game I had first collected in Ann Arbor, which is actually practiced in Philadelphia, New York City, and many other locales. But this recent version, performed by my ten-year-old African American cousin in 1995, had the flavor of Latino culture, transforming "oo-lay oo-lay" to "o-la o-la." Arielle brought it with her when she visited from Denver, Colorado, where it was one of the chants she performed as part of a cheerleading squad at a Southwest middle school.

In addition to collecting specific games, for which I offer close readings of the embodied lessons learned through their performance, I also videotaped several games that were played on the periphery of an international double-dutch competition I attended. At this competition, which was held in North Charleston, South Carolina, and sponsored by the American Double Dutch League, I was able to observe the ways that girls' musical practices are monitored and policed to fit into the male-centric and Westernized view of sports—where music and dance are usually separated or divorced from athleticism. In ice skating, for example, one would never find an athlete singing while they perform their triple Lutz or death spiral. Would that heighten the dramatic impact or confuse the interpretation of a sport? In double-dutch street play, music and athleticism go hand-in-hand.

Along the way, I also picked up glimpses of handclapping games, cheers, and double-dutch chants practiced by black girls with whom I serendipitously interacted (musicologist Guthrie Ramsey's daughters Candace and Bridgette were important contributors), as well as those remembered by adult African American women I interviewed during the course of my research, shared my work with, or those who attended my colloquia.

I interviewed seventeen African American women who ranged in age from eighteen to sixty-five, and who were working and/or studying at the University of Michigan. I needed a context from which to interpret the games I was studying, and I wanted that context to be shaped by black women's voices, memories, and lived experiences. These women shared their life stories through black musical interactions with females and males, which made quite a difference in the ways I read my analysis of black girls' musical play and gender relations in black culture.

I invited each "sister" to share her earliest memories of learning to be musical, and how she learned to dance and with whom. I also invited all of them to recall their participation in everyday life and mediated musical activities with parents and siblings at home, with their childhood playmates in their neighborhoods, or with relatives in other places.

All of the women I interviewed traced their lineage to Southern states, rather than to locations outside the United States in Africa or other parts of the African diaspora. For the sake of managing the data, I decided to limit my attention to these women, instead of women of Caribbean or recent African extract. I am clear from my interactions with other blacks from the Caribbean and Africa that our orientations to handclapping and singing are not the same, though we borrow from one another in many instances. For example, many Jamaican and Trinidadian handclapping game-songs tend to accent beats one and three in a four-beat meter rather than accenting beats two and four with clapping and finger-snapping. (For a rich study of race, gender, and music in transnational culture, see Melvin Butler's dissertation, 2005.)

The eldest of the women I interviewed was born in 1938, and the youngest was born in 1982. Six of them had grown up in metropolitan areas and suburbs surrounding Detroit (the home of Motown), including Highland Park, Ann Arbor, and Washtenaw County. Others hailed from Chicago, Memphis, Shreveport (Louisiana), Pittsburgh, Baltimore, and Washington, D.C.

The Unfolding of the Ropes

In the first chapter, I introduce girls' games as a site for exploring race, gender, and the body as a musical text expressing African American approaches to pitch, timbre, and various rhythmic and metrical ideals. Girls' games teach and sustain ideals of black music-making through "in-body formulas" (Drewal 1992) employed later in other musical and dance contexts, including admiring the music, but not the lyrics, of hip-hop.

Chapter 2 explores how music captures an ethnic identity of a group to create a context for understanding how the body represents both ethnic and gender identity through music. African Americans are stereotypically considered to be great dancers and singers, and that belief often collapses notions of race and ethnicity. In this chapter, I distinguish the idea of a musical blackness as a social paradigm, not a racial or essentialist construction of identity. I discuss how black musical style is a function of a process of musical socialization that begins at a very young age, debunking the myth that music in black culture is biologically determined, and challenging views that African Americans over-essentialize their ethnic affiliations defined by music.

Chapter 3 offers several close readings of handclapping games and cheers to show how individuals become aware of their ethnic and gendered identity through both the lyrics and the embodiment performed in girls' games.

Chapter 4 brings a gendered perspective to my analysis of the appropriation of girls' musical games by male artists in the music business, and the borrowing of popular tunes by male artists from young girls composing communal games. This fourth chapter concerns ideology, gender, and power—unveiling the ways that girls are acculturated into an androcentric ideology. In appropriating from girls' games, male hip-hop and R&B artists and composers are, in essence, admitting that they view girls and girls' games as part of African American culture, but girls and women are limited from participation in the world of music. Girls, on the other hand, tend to borrow from popular jingles and male-voiced songs, yet as popular artists once they reached adulthood, they avoid borrowing from the female realm of music-making they formerly occupied in their youth. They do not view it as a source for generating popular taste as male artists appear to do. This chapter offers a way of understanding how girls' musical games help them learn to identify with men (rather than women), to view men and masculinity as powerful, and to view heterosexual relations as the norm.

Chapter 5 discusses the different notions of games that exist, from girls' games to hip-hop culture. "The game" is a dominant metaphor in hip-hop that speaks to the power plays involved with negotiating a record deal in the music business, and maintaining longevity as a popular artist. The discourse of these power plays is highly gendered. I tease out the gendered constructions of lyrics that lead to the separation between the musical play of black girls' games and the "game," or business, of hip-hop.

This is followed by the voices of women speaking about their musical lives and the importance of their own musical games.

Chapter 6 is devoted exclusively to observing double-dutch as an institutionalized sport, as opposed to its street play, at the 1995 annual competition of the American Double Dutch League. In this context, double-dutch is no longer music or musical. The nonperformers who preside over the rules and regulations of the competition—adults and justice officials—seem to "police" the expression of a sport where girls are supposed to rule the day.

Chapter 7 focuses on adult women and double-dutch. The Double Dutch Divas are a group of women ranging in age from about thirty to fifty, many of whom have returned to their childhood play and re-invented it to accommodate adult womanhood. They respond to the ways that men maintain their childhood play and turn it into an occupation for life. Although double-dutch initially represents girlhood, for these adult women it represents a maturity of style and identity that reflects the musical values found in black popular styles of music like hip-hop (i.e., mixing, sampling, and improvising through the body and rhymes).

This chapter shows how relations of power are woven into performances of womanhood and blackness. Women can subvert and blur those relations, but this cultural labor is often done out of sight in the popular sphere of the everyday.

Now, to the games: Let's get on the playground and *shake it to the east, shake it to the west, shake to the very one that you love the best.*

1

Slide

Games as Lessons in Black Musical Style

What if black girls' musical play was a training ground for learning not only how to embody specific approaches to black musical expression, but also learning to be socially black? When I was trying to pin down a topic for my dissertation, I wanted to find a way to privilege women's musical participation in African American popular music. I didn't want to write about the misogyny and sexist lyrics that emerged with the L.A. style of hip-hop in 1988 when N.W.A.'s "Straight Outta Compton" went gold and put gangsta rap on the map. When I was searching for a topic in 1994, Coolio ("Fantastic Voyage"), Warren G and Nate Dogg ("Regulate"), and Snoop Doggy Dogg ("Gin and Juice") broke through to the mainstream pop charts. Their videos were dominated by images of late-night parties with dozens of women captured with their "bootys" bobbing in the air by the down-low gaze of a male cameraman's eye, while Snoop delivered his dope-ass rhymes. There was not much room around those sights and sounds to privilege women's musical contributions to hip-hop or black popular music except where their bodies might be concerned. Female rappers Salt-N-Pepa were the exception that year, flipping the script by featuring male dancers as "video hos" in their top-forty hit single and video "Shoop," featuring the female vocal quartet En Vogue. What if there were earlier musical experiences that gave women access to participating in a musical style consistently dubbed misogynist and sexist?

In a discussion with Judith Becker, my dissertation advisor, I explored the possibility that there might be a musical angle to reading women's participation in hip-hop. I, along with many other African American women between the ages of eighteen and thirty, listened and danced to the music and a critical number of us knew and sang along with all the lyrics. It seemed to me that the *beats,* the distinct rhyming, the rhythmic patterns, and the polyphonic textures that made girls' musical games sound and feel "black" were connected to hip-hop. Settling on studying African American girls' games serendipitously became a real possibility while I was at an academic conference devoted to ethnomusicology.

Conferences about music are rarely about playing games or music in the literal sense. "Players" at conferences devote endless hours reading papers littered with references to this theory or that scholar with few visual aids, little or no eye contact with their "opponents," and very few cases of actually creating music or having fun. The best game you can hope for is scoring points shooting down the other "players'" intention or inspiration during the Q&A session. "There always seems to be a need, in the academic arena, to score points against your opponent by submitting his every move to an ideological litmus test, or by targeting her for . . . an intellectual drive-by shooting" (Fox 1997, 13–14).

At the reception following the "scoring," I heard the snap, crackle, and pop of a handclapping game being played down the hall. It reminded me of the sound of caps, those long, red strips of paper dotted with gunpowder, struck against the pavement of playgrounds with some small rock we found in the corner of a gutter. There were two girls rapt in the intentions of their percussive hand gestures. They executed uneven patterns combining clapping and chanting that didn't fit the usually square, four-beat phrases of most games. Their rhythmic patterns slid back and forth between meters ambiguously. Both syncopation and metrical play were present. So too were the metrical ambiguity of cross-rhythms in their clapped patterns and the easy polyrhythmic embodiment of lyrics, syncopated melodies, and beats.

The black girls were fraternal twins accompanying their mother, Rose, who was freelancing as the caterer for the reception. By day, she was my classmate in my voice studio with George Shirley, the longest reigning black tenor with the Metropolitan Opera. Jasmine and Stephanie were nine years old and Rose had recently adopted them. When there's nothing better to do or when the time or place limits what's possible, handclapping games can do the trick.

> Miss— Ma— ry—
> Mack, Mack, Mack all dressed in
> Black, Black, Black with sil- ver
> Butt'ns, Butt'ns, Butt'ns all down her
> Back, Back, Back

The twins played a version of Mary Mack that had completely different melodic phrases than what I had known when I was a child. It sounded funkier, like a blues melody with handclapping punctuating the fourth beat of each line. In the third line ("Diamonds all down her back") there was a distinctive nasalized bending of pitches into a descending blues scale characteristic of African American sacred and secular singing.

> Ma- ry Mack (clap)
> Dressed in black (clap)
> Diam'nds all down her ba- a- a- ck (clap)

Soon the twins introduced me to a series of games I had never learned before. I wanted to know them! After all, these were *black* girls' games, right? Although the oral nature of transmission allowed handclapping games like this and others to be found in integrated schoolyards, on *Sesame Street,* and as background footage in popular films, this game-song was part of a broader repertoire of games that featured nasalized blue notes syncopated against percussive movement and language that signified African American social dances, and that's what made them "black." I wanted to add these games to my repertoire of music (not just games) and run home to tell my girls about the latest music I had heard. To be a girl again, a black girl stepping on the cracks of my mama's back. Playing all day. Ripping and running. Singing and chanting. But black girls may not know they are learning how to be musical through such play. It was just a game, right?

"Slide": Embodying the Language of a Black Music

Handclapping games often feature a melodic tune, or chanted lyrics, that resemble an approach to rapping not only prominent in hip-hop culture, but one that has existed in African American music-making since slavery. For example, juba-patting, an embodied practice of handclapping, finger-snapping, thigh-and-chest slapping, and foot-stomping accompanied by a rhymed patter known as juba-rhyming, was an improvised nineteenth-century practice shared among slaves of African descent. This musically embodied practice was recounted in a travelogue about a visit to a Maryland plantation in 1859:

As soon as she joined the throng, Clotilda, without a moment's pause, whirled herself among and through the crowd of dancers . . . and began to recite the following verses in a shrill sing-song voice, keeping time to the measure, as Ike had done, by beating her hands sometimes against her sides, and patting the ground with her feet. An interval of some seconds afforded time for the dancers to follow the direction given in each; but the beating of the hands and feet continued without intermission. (Hungerford 1859, 195–96)

The author James Hungerford captured the lyrics of Clotilda's performance rendered under the song title "Juber Dance" as follows:

> Laudy! how it make me laugh
> Ter see de niggers all so saf' [soft];
> See um dance de foolish jig,
> Un neber min' de juber rig.
>   Juber!
> [Negroes dancing every one after his or her own fashion, but keeping time to the beat.]
> *Juber lef' and Juber right;*
> *Juber dance wid all yo' might*
> *Juber here an' Juber dere,*
> *Juber, Juber, ebery where.*
>   *Juber!*
> . . .
> *Dere's ole Uncle Jack*
> *Hab er pain in his back;*
> *Ebery time he try ter skip*
> *Den he hab ter get er limp.*
>   *Juber!*
>
> *Guess I knows er nigger gal—*
> *Dere she is, her name is Sal—*
> *Un she hab to min' de baby,*
> *Show us how she rock de cradle.*
>   *Juber!*
> [A variety of swaying motions, intended to represent cradle-rocking in a ridiculous view. All, a daughter of Aunt Kate, and a nurse of a baby sister, indignantly, "I alwus said Clotidly wus crazy!"] . . .

Try de Juber reed again;
Try yo' bes', un try to win.

Juber forrud, Juber back;
Juber dis way, Juber dat;
Juber in, un Juber out;
Juber, Juber, all abbout.
      Juber[!] (Hungerford 1859, 198)

This excerpt highlights many of the lyrical features and social dancing associated with African American popular music and dance styles from the early twentieth century to the present. This kind of embodied music-making played a central role in social music during slavery and continues to play a role in formulating social experience in black communities today. For example, rhyming extemporaneously on topical subjects, calling instructions for the dance (like the line dancing of the Electric slide and the Cha-cha slide in contemporary settings since 2000), and embodying the percussion that accompanies the rhymed chants which are clearly linked in sound and behavior to the beat-boxing and rhyming of hip-hop culture.

There is one game-song from my childhood that I'll always remember. "Miss Lucy" is a provocative game that includes all kinds of sexual innuendos about boys and having babies.

Mi-ss . . .
Lu-cy had a ba-by (clap clap)
She named it Tiny Tim (clap clap)
She put him in the bath-tub (clap clap)
To see if he could swim (clap clap) . . .

I vividly remember playing "Miss Lucy" at the bus stop on my way to elementary school: the linguistic play of double entendres and elisions created when certain syllables and words are just about to mean something sexual or scatological and then they suddenly shift into some benign reference that made "Miss Lucy" (the game and the ideas of a woman) fun and sexy to play with.

Be-*hind* the elevator (clap clap)
There *was* a piece of glass (clap clap)

Miss *Lu*-cy fell upon it and it *went* straight up her
Ask me no more questions (clap clap)
I'll *tell* you no more lies (clap clap)
The *boys* are in the bathroom (clap clap) pulling up their
Fly me to the O-cean (clap clap)
(and so on . . .)

Back to the unknown game the twins first introduced to me. I said earlier that it wasn't like "Mary Mack" nor "Miss Lucy." The shifting meter of this game was more rhythmically complex than those. *Slide* or *Numbers*, as it is called, didn't feature a song or chant except for the counting out loud that marked certain shifts in the clapping patterns and in time.

ONE (clap) . (clap) . (clap clap)!   [1]
ONE (clap) two (clap)! ONE (clap) two (clap)!   [2]
ONE (clap clap) TWO (clap clap)!

What stood out were nuances of their intonation, the articulation and in-flection of each phoneme of the numbers was the song.

So much of African American languaging expressed in music, sports, play, and everyday social discourse is inflected and made meaningful through nonverbal linguistics and percussive enunciations of pitch and timbre.

If, as in the colloquial greeting, "Wha's UH-up, girrl??!!!" one finds musical elements that intensify the meanings of words (such as lengthen-ing sibilant and liquid consonants: *esses* and *elles*), nasalizing or chang-ing the quality of a sound (timbre), or undulating the pitch within a syl-lable or word, why wouldn't such an approach dominate nonverbal ex-pression in musical contexts? The twins' expressive chanting of the numbers had more of a story to tell me about embodying the structure of musical expression than I might have imagined.

ONE (clap) two (clap)! ONE (clap) two (clap)!   [2]
ONE (clap clap) TWO (clap clap)! .
ONE (clap) TWO (clap) three (clap)!   [3]
ONE (clap) TWO (clap) three (clap)!
ONE (clap clap) TWO (clap clap) three (clap clap)!

The pattern of beats seemed to be expanding, while it also seemed to transform the earlier stated rhythms moving from a duple to a triplet feel and from duple to triplet meters and back again. The downbeat seemed to constantly shift, causing me to wonder if these games might offer some access to thinking about not only how syncopation is learned and unfolds, but how a metronomic sensibility—a strong sense of pulse and tempo—so often remarked upon about African and African American musical behavior, gets developed through ordinary practice.

Anthropologist Edward T. Hall asserted that nonverbal communication is the "essence of ethnicity . . . rooted in how one experiences oneself as a man or a woman" (Hall 1981, 82). Ethnomusicologists have failed to take embodiment and visual perceptions of embodiment, not to mention gender, into account in our analyses and inquiry into African American musical and social practice. What has tended to dominate the discussion is rhythm, not gendered bodies making and embodying rhythmic language and other musical expressions. If dance informs the surface features of music, as African American musicologist Olly Wilson asserted in 1985, where is the analysis and study of sounds and bodies as musical experience? The body language Stephanie and Jasmine expressed offered more clues for rethinking not only how we learn black musical aesthetics, but also how we learn to relate socially and identify with one another ethnically, through musical behaviors that reflect those concepts.

In nearly all handclapping games, there is a base from which all other movements seem to stem: each player claps separately on beats two and four, serving as the link between other gestures. Slapping the chest as if crossing the heart (what I call the "criss-cross" gesture) is another gesture generated individually. Slapping the upper thighs usually follows, with all this reminiscent of another earlier African American style of embodied play known as *hamboning*. Hamboning was prominent by the middle of the twentieth century, with several popular songs and lyrics making reference to the practice as "hand-boning" or "hand jive" during the era of rhythm and blues and rock 'n' roll.

The game Slide or Numbers has a simple goal: carry out the complex and expanding pattern of gestures up to ten without messing up. In young girls' interactions, it is common to label the levels of play: *ones-eez, twos-eez, threes-eez, fours-eez,* and so on. This kind of linguistic play is found occasionally in double-dutch and more often associated with playing *jacks*. In the latter, each code (*ones-eez*) signals how many jacks you need to pick up after each bounce of the rubbery ball. Though this language is rarely present in handclapping games, I use it to evoke the linguistics of girls' play as I recall the delivery of performing Slide as I demonstrate my analysis of it.

Stephanie messed up. She forgot where they were in the game. The girls were supposed to be doing their *fives-eez,* but Stephanie clapped one too many, or one too few, times. So the twins started over, which gave me the opportunity to see the game from the beginning. Facing each other with one palm up to the sky and the other toward the ground, they clapped their palms together—then immediately slid them apart. At the same time, the slithery sound of the word "slide" rolled off their tongues, commencing with the sound of their clap and tracing their coordinated movement from the heels of their hands to the tips of their fingers—sliding movement, sliding language, and sliding sounds creating a synergy of onomatopoeia. The preparatory move reminded me of a conductor tapping her baton on the podium's stand as a signal to the orchestra—and to the audience—that a performance is about to begin.

The girls' individual claps were framed by the sounds of "high fives"—first between their right palms, and then their left. Altogether, these gestures created four even beats, reflecting a typical four-four measure of written music. Instead of counting "one-two-three-four," they simply counted "one." Then I could see how they embodied and created the triplet I had heard earlier: after making an individual clap in unison, the backs of their hands slapped together in mid-air, followed immediately by a clap shared by their palms. Here was the sense of two against three. For just a moment, a sense of polyrhythm or polymeter emerged before they started the pattern of their gestures over again. They maintained a steady pulse all the while.

The sound of the different claps—individual claps in unison, shared claps between opposing right and left palms (*criss-cross*), and the alternation from back to front between both opposing hands (*back-front*)—evoked timbres of sound that implied a subtle percussive melody. This added to the sense of the shifting meter in the game when the structure began to expand. In other words, the stronger sounds of the individual claps had a pitch that was relatively lower (suggesting downbeats) than the other two, higher-sounding types of clapping: the *criss-cross* pattern and the *back-front* gesture. And the criss-cross pattern of beats was stronger in emphasis than the back-front, which distinguished the difference between the sounds even further. Thus, certain phrasings or units of beats sounded like the alternation between a bass drum and a snare, as two beats or triplets in a quadruple meter. But further rhythmic complexity was created at subsequent levels of the game, such as at threes-eez, fours-eez, and fives-eez.

It had become clear to me, with the aid of the verbal instructions from Jasmine and Stephanie, that the basic structure of this handclapping game involved applying a rather simple and logical pattern—what was, in essence, the embodiment of an *algorithm*: the repetition of a formula or operation to accomplish some end. The embodied formula was composed of eight beats of clapping created from combinations of three basic moves.

The formula applied to these eight beats, which were divided into three units of movement, was to add an extra beat to every subsequent unit until you reach ten. In other words, doubling, tripling, quadrupling, etc., each of the three units, until the tenth level was reached and completed.

Once you understand and learn to master the motor skills involved in this "algorithm," putting the game into motion with even strangers would be easy. On the first level, eight beats are performed, suggesting quadruple meter broken into a pattern that most would hear as 2 + 2 + 3 (+ 1), with the last beat feeling somewhat like a rest in the music. At level two, 15 beats are broken into 4 + 4 + 6 (+ 1). And at level five, 51 beats are broken into 10 + 10 + 15 + 15 (+ 1).

Since it gets complicated to even write out correctly, imagine how complicated it would become to count all this out. Even without counting, it is really easy to get lost in the flurry of gestures at the breakneck speed most girls apply to the performance of Slide. So, in comes the chanting: a mnemonic device to remind you where you are as you play.

Jasmine and Stephanie were counting the repetition of beats for each unit of gestures, minus the final clap that appears to serve as a kind of cadence—a point marking the end. When they performed their fives-eez, I could hear certain tones and inflections in their voices that accompanied their moves. As the form lengthened, so did their tones when they chanted the numbers: the enunciation of the words began to glide more and release more emphatically, more percussively. As they criss-crossed five times, meeting each others' hands in the space between their bodies, their counting began to sound less like chanting and more like singing. The girls sustained the tones of certain numbers for as long as the units of gestures lasted, whereas they cropped the last number enunciated in the level. This, they punctuated, signaling the end of that level with a sharp, spiking intonation, no matter what the number.

Emphasizing or stressing the final number in this manner contradicted the sense of the first beat of each phrase as the downbeat. In these algorithmic formulas based on even, odd, and prime numbers, the emphasis is rarely on the count of "one," but on multiple levels of awareness in the moment.

This incrementally expanding and additive rhythmic formula contributed to the sense of shifting downbeats and unexpected syncopations. Syncopation, usually expressed as a singular noun, is typically and loosely defined as the accentuation of beats other than those found on the downbeats (one and three, in four-four time). The *Merriam-Webster Dictionary* (1999) defines syncopation as "a temporary displacement of the regular metrical accent in music caused typically by stressing the weak beat" or "a syncopated rhythm, passage, or dance step." If the "regular" downbeats are unpredictable, one might sense that there is no form, or assert that the idea of a downbeat, in Slide, is movable rather than fixed. Instead, it is defined by the context of each segment of clapping, and (according to my senses), may actually feel and sound like different kinds of syncopation: either anticipating a downbeat, closely following one, or falling right in the middle of a downbeat and a so-called weak beat.

Given all this, syncopation has to be understood in a context—within a musical game, for example. Then it has to be experienced across a number of different musical games. In the context of Slide, girls may be learning how to play with repositioning their sense of keeping a beat or having rhythm, as well as learning how to understand syncopation in a variety of ways.

In Search of and Learning Black Musical Ideals

Unlike Slide, many other handclapping games tend to have three or four basic gestures, or units, repeated again and again. This more typical embodied *groove*—three- or four-beat patterns—usually accompanies songs and chants with four beats to the measure. But they tend to be broken up into the asymmetrical units found in the handclapping gestures of Slide. Learning to negotiate a three-beat pattern of handclapping against the feel of a song in quadruple meter seems as good a way as any to groom a sense of a polymeter and polyrhythm during childhood. Games such as Slide, where the *body* follows ambiguous rhythms and meters, provides superb training for black musical sensibilities related to polyrhythm and polymeter: the sensitivities fostered in this way create a strong ability to feel and hear rhythmic complexity in song and dance, as well as the tendency to improvise in the expression of both.

This kind of embodied practice produces *cross-rhythms,* a Western European term used to define the aurally perceived rhythmic tensions and ambiguities that arise when fewer points of unity (no longer the squarely recurring downbeats) connect two distinct rhythms or *beats* (as they are called in everyday popular-music discourse). In these ways, girls' hand-clapping games may generate an embodied subjectivity—an African American musical identity—that signifies an African sensibility. Only through the combined rhythms does the music emerge, and the only way to hear the music properly, to find the beat, and to develop and exercise "metronome sense" [often clapping or dancing the metrical undercurrent that is the basis of other parts], is "to listen to at least two rhythms at once. . . . [Following] Hewitt Pantaleoni and Moses Serwadda . . . The African learns the whole simultaneously with the parts. . . . He is not 'thrown off' by hearing mis-accentuation, but by the failure of some . . . part of the ensemble to occur at the right time" (Chernoff 1979, 51).

Girls' handclapping games are an example of the lack of dependence on an externalized beat (such as tapping one's toe). Rhythmic sensibilities are developed and sharpened as part of play, not separate from it; neither are Jasmine and Stephanie's movements caught up in thoughts about making music or keeping time.

At the very least, Slide may train girls to perform at least two different rhythmic orientations at once. Imagine how strong one's inner sense of metrical and rhythmic complexities can become from hours of playing this and other embodied musical games. The experience left me thinking about the importance of embodiment in the art of "reading" black music —interpreting, feeling, and knowing it in a classroom.

Girls' handclapping games, therefore, are as much a social and phenomenological formula as they are motor-rhythmic formulas that contribute to musical events. The games put into motion another ideal of black music-making: the art of having rhythm, of being able to be in sync with others while dancing and/or singing, without the aid of an external conductor or timekeeper.

From my confusion about Slide and my subsequent analysis of it, I gleaned a few valuable lessons about how black musical style or ideals are learned. One is that syncopation is embodied through playful and competitive patterns of behavior between two girls (in this case). Each maintains what early scholarship about African and African American musical sensibilities referred to as a "metronomic sense" of meter: neither girl conducts or leads the rhythmic play. Instead, each embodies the additive complex of patterns and manages a reliable and interdependent sense of timing or flow. This is essential to the practice of syncopation, and the foundation to learning a variety of beats and dances that will be accumulated over time.

I infer that this view of syncopation actually points to tension between multiple rhythms, rather than the usual definition: accentuation of an off- or upbeat—tensions that develop between two rhythms embodied by independent limbs or acts, tensions created between the rhythms we create by clapping versus stomping versus chanting, or tensions between bodies, say, for instance, in call-and-response (which is not present in this game, but is in many others). Slide allows girls to play with a shifting "downbeat," a sliding sensibility of time, while also learning how to maintain a steady beat over a shifting rhythmic pattern, an invaluable lesson for a social dancer or a possible jazz musician.

Another lesson I learned is that timbre plays a significant role in the way one perceives and understands rhythms in black musical practice, and mirrors a similar approach in black linguistics (the use of intonation and inflection to emphasize words and meanings). Often syncopation accompanies intonation and inflection in the chant.

A simple musical structure of three or four beats can become more complex by variations in the distinct timbres created by each type of clap, as well as the accompanying vocal dimension of sound. These sonic gestures parallel the percussive textures created from the distinct timbres of a drum kit in various styles of contemporary R&B and hip-hop, for instance. Do the embodied gestures of girls' games mirror the timbres of the snare, bass drum, and high-hat, or do those embodied timbres mirror rhythms formerly embodied by both men and women from earlier times in unequal ways? Boys actually mock girls' gestures and chants, while girls are mastering their musical play. Yet, girls often leave their games behind before they mature into women. Could hip-hop be their next generation of musical play?

Similar approaches to shaping rhythm through timbres in children's music-making can be found among black boys, but they are usually expressed in the form of drumming with sticks or hands on the bottom of buckets, on tabletops, or in the performance of verbal dueling (i.e., playing the Dozens). Beyond the elemental expectation of keeping the beat (the oft-cited *metronomic* sense), embodying rhythms with a concomitant sensibility about timbres (high-mid-low, or other variations) is key in African American musical expression, both in vocal and dance behavior.

The phenomenon of sensing tuned pitches in speech, melody, or percussion reflects what African musicologist Meki Nzewi calls a *melo-rhythmic* approach (Nzewi 1991): one hears melody in rhythms, and rhythm in melodies. This is analogous to the *percussive approach to linear expression* that Olly Wilson outlines in his article about heterogeneous sound ideals in African American music (Wilson 1992), and is, at least in part, what makes the sounds *sound* musical and the *music* of the game sound *black*. The patterns mirror conventions found in popular styles of black music and, broadly speaking, American popular music.

One may ask which came first, the girls' games or the popular music. The answer is that these musical practices are in dialogue with one another, and have been for generations.

Another lesson (or, perhaps, insight) is that black girls don't ever need to stop and think about how to break down the music of their games into meter, rhythm, or melo-rhythmic dynamics. It would be abnormal to see kids stop and think about something other than the moment of the play; there is no interest in, or need for, the big picture about how musical skills, race, gender, and communal values are learned, or how their games mirror and teach sociomusical values and ideals of behavior and sound.

Nevertheless, analysis is at play. Black girls' analysis occurs simply as criticism, or a critique of the play, right there on the court of the action. If someone messes up, interrupts the flow of the game, or can't make it even to their *fives-eez* after several tries, it will be "analyzed" or, as we say, *read* with some neck-poppin', teeth-suckin' attitude in the name of determining *who did it*—who stopped the flow of the game (or the music). No matter who the culprit was, the answer to "who dunnit" is always, "*You* did!"

Another lesson: the "we," the collective participation of the moment, can never be performed if one player is not in sync with the coordinated body formulas of the play. The mistakes allow for a critical moment in learning the social discipline of black music-making: *you gotta be together*. All of this happens in the name of the freedom of play, which later offers the potential, and may actually lay the foundation, for more sophisticated forms of musical improvisation in musical and nonmusical contexts.

Although there is little need for *post-performance discussion, analysis, and theorizing* (cf. Schechner 1992, 281), the "analysis" that does occur during girls' play—analysis of *social practice and interaction*—can add dimension to the forms of sonic or formal analysis practiced in the music classroom, or may serve as music theory homework.

In Slide, the markers of difference do not necessarily lie within the embodied musical dynamics or the lyrics that are performed by non–African Americans. Rather, they may lie in the way embodiment is deployed in the service of social music-making within an ethnic culture, where difference has been marked on and by the body.

One might think that difference is expressed inherently within the rhythmic orientation. In appreciating the shifting sense of patterns and punctuations, I could suggest that the game sounds like it is based on a *timeline,* such as an African bell pattern. Indeed, another game I collected and later analyzed has a more distinct "timeline" sensibility that drives its embodied performance. The refrain of this handclapping game-song, known as "OO-lay-OO-lay," reveals a more percussive sense of time, and a more complex sense of meter than a basic four-beats-per-measure kind of game.

> OO- . lay-OO-. lay . na-OO-tay-. stay back that's me .
> OO- . lay-OO-. lay . na-OO-tay-. stay back that's me .

Timelines would be relevant here because they are circular in nature and allow for the change and shift of one's sense of syncopation in any context, depending upon where one feels oneself to "be" in the cycle. Oddly, I've never heard Africans talk of syncopation. Nor would I say I felt I was performing syncopations in the African traditions of music and dance in which I have participated. I performed cross-rhythms and polyrhythms, but syncopation feels distinctly African American to me because that's where it's talked about most.

However, one could hear the reiterated "OO" sounds in the above refrain as a series of emphases that create an asymmetrical feel more commonly found in African timelines than, say, black girls' musical games. Or one might simply hear those articulations as a form of syncopation in a fairly straightforward eight-beat phrase. The stresses in and atop the structure, as well as the different kinds of timbres that are evoked by the different vowel sounds woven together in a performance, create a musi-

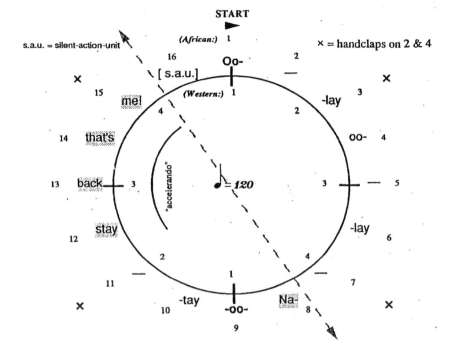

Cheer "OO-lay, OO-lay." Cyclic model of refrain.

cal texture that is distinct and rich in many examples of black musical expression in the public sphere.

It would be easy for me to argue a strong association between the performance of Slide and the rhythms of West Africa: subtle dimensions of an African sensibility are embedded within black music still today. But once you actually see Jasmine and Stephanie or other girls performing Slide, what is drummed into your consciousness is the nostalgia for *African American* social culture (rather than a tangible and often imagined "African" heritage). Many listeners from the United States would perceive Slide as part of American culture—as part of the West, where European colonialism and African social sensibilities merge into a unique phenomenon reflecting Creolization, miscegenation, and cultural exchange (forced and mutual). These games carry the rhythms, moves, and linguistic expressions of the everyday and the communal. A popular African American musical sensibility, clearly informed by African sensibilities that we are learning to reclaim, is embroidered within the fabric of the everyday, through the embodied formulas of the games black girls play.

Representing Musical Embodiment and Difference

Whenever ethnomusicologists try to translate the sonic and embodied data of musical performances into linear narratives of experience, we will always confront the problem I encountered that day during the reception. This is the problem of perceiving an embodied experience primarily as sound, and attempting to translate this incomplete, disembodied information into literate objects of thought and communication. When the body is finally rendered visible in such accounts, I worry about how such narratives might be complicated by the cultural misdirections of racial discourse, especially in the reception of black bodies in mainstream discourse. The question is how to translate blackness into a musical transcription, and what form would permit the reading of such a transcription as something of "blackness," "American-ness," *and* female gender?

Part of what I wish to convey in relating my own thinking as I encountered the twins' "performance" as a representation of black musical experience is the uncertainty and inarticulateness of such a translation. How do we convey the multiple sensory behavior and awareness that become so unified in a single moment? And how do we learn to translate and transcribe the many sounds and meanings that occur in the same instance?

The only way I can think of to do this is to show the messiness of one's thinking and the different ways we translate sound, musical behavior, and meaning, according to the various training and socializations we bring to any observable moment of interaction. The embodiment of ethnicity, particularly relative to blackness, is absent from transcriptions that capture references to sound, which key into the outcome of physical and encoded behaviors that result in music.

We can no longer permit such an omission of the *embodied* linguistic data from our analysis. It is essential that scholars interested in reflecting the social sensibilities of African American musical practice attend to the body and the musical, social, and cultural role it plays in making music meaningful in practice.

Could these games be the "DNA," or part of the "genetic material," that shapes black musical style and behaviors, asked a performance theorist reading an earlier version of this manuscript? While the idea of girls' games as the cultural DNA of black musical style or aesthetics is provocative, I am no longer willing to evoke anything akin to an evolutionary model of culture and civilization relative to black identity. The application of such a metaphor or trope of cultural recognition not only privileges a stark difference between the so-called races, it also privileges a view of gender as natural and biological, an ideological construct that is not effective relative to determinations of race.

In the early stages of this study, I was intrigued with the idea that the use of musical games by black girls reflected an *embryonic* stage of musical blackness: "embryonic" conjures up the *primordial, unconscious,* or *instinctual* aspects of an individual's behavior. But it is not the *forms* that manifest the style of musical behavior. Similar games, or versions of these games, do not precipitate the same musical aesthetics and social meanings for girls from other ethnic groups. What matters are the meanings of these social interactions that are passed down from generation to generation and are found wherever black girls are in African American contexts.

My attention to the games *black girls* play represents what Gayatri Spivak calls "strategic essentialism" (quoted in Hall 1992, 29), and although this may not meet the desires of readers in search of a more cross-cultural, multi-ethnic investigation of the games girls play, this study is centered within the social and musical economy of black culture, behavior, and ideology.

The study of black culture would be null and void if it were always assumed to be essentialist. As Stuart Hall asserts, "the essentializing moment is weak because it naturalizes and de-historicizes difference, mistaking what is historical and cultural for what is natural, biological, and genetic" (Hall 1992, 29).

Therefore, I hope to unravel how the "black" and what is "popular" in black musical culture is historical, cultural, and negotiated through gender roles and meanings. "We are always in negotiation, not with a single set of oppositions that place us always in the same relation to others, but with a series of different positionalities . . . [that] are often dislocating in relation to one another" (ibid., 31).

I left the reception that day considering the possible connections between what black females learn and what's going on in mass-mediated styles of African American music. Are the rhythms, chants, and dances of black girls' play elementary forms of adult musical practice? Do they reveal how we learn how to be musically black, and how to understand the culture that surrounds what we do musically?

I don't think the difference between children's and adults' music in African American culture is significant. Subsequent generations share similar approaches to moving the body, to making music "feel" black or African American, favoring certain textures (such as an affinity for feeling the weight—the "bottom," figuratively and literally—of bass textures). The chants may orally evolve with each generation, but we share musical behavior and use it as a kind of ideology *across* generations, even if individuals in certain generations are not conscious of its presence in children's musical play.

2

Education, Liberation
Learning the Ropes of a Musical Blackness

How can we talk about a musical blackness when the very notion of "race" is currently contested? While it is assumed that Western classical music is learned through disciplined practice, many still assume that for African Americans musical practice is "natural" (or unlearned). This belief afflicts many musics that rely on dance and other embodiment to convey its meaningfulness, often excluding the significance of literacy. These musics have persisted without academic instruction. Based on myths of biology, the musical discourse of African American people is believed to require little or no thought, "schooling," or skill, seemingly leaving all explanation to realms of mystery and fantasy. But in a book devoted to understanding how gender is important in conversations about African American music or how women and girls contribute musically to male-dominated popular musics like hip-hop, it is imperative that we address the issue of "race."

Race, as debunked by the American Anthropological Association, is not a biologically determined marker of differences in intellect, power, musical expression, and sexual appetite. Yet any use of a term like "musical blackness" tends to call up the notion of race-as-skin-color rather than standing as a vernacular code for ethnicity among certain groups of people of African descent in the United States. In the remainder of this chapter I trace several of my own experiences as a musical being and as a scholar that call attention to matters of ethnic difference that remain important to discussions of African Americans and their popular musics. This chapter will challenge notions of essentialism and authenticity that others and African American men and women themselves may hold about black musical behavior and African American musical identity.

While rhythm had always been associated with African and African-American musical performances, [at the turn into the twentieth century it] seemed to overtake other aspects, identifying what many believed to be the music's vital essence. . . . Among African-Americans, moreover, hot rhythm frequently perpetuated the same racial myths while providing a means of affirming positive identities in an egregiously racist, national environment. The primitivist orthodoxy of "natural rhythm" afforded a new sense of racial pride that was ironically reinforced by white supremacist assumptions of a bestial Negro instinct. (Radano 2000, 459)

Blackness is neither innate, as essentialism would have it, nor entirely fabricated and irrelevant, as infers anti-essentialism. . . . Anti-anti-essentialism considers that there exist identifiable elements of blackness, and that these elements are transmitted and transformed within the cultural exchanges of the diaspora. (Gilroy 1993b)

My stance is that musical blackness is a culturally transmitted set of practices, communications, and traditions, where embodied language and orality (kinetic orality) play a significant role in the social construction and knowledge of being African American in a sphere of culture and identifications that is dominated by music. "Though [racial/ethnic subjectivity] is often felt to be natural and spontaneous, it remains the outcome of practical activity: language, gesture, bodily significations, desires" (Gilroy 1993b, 102). In other words, racial subjectivity is "the product of the social practices that supposedly derive from it" (ibid.). The experiences relayed below reveal this very process in my own life.

As a teenager, I dreamed of becoming a singer. Growing up in the Washington, D.C. area, I dreamed through nightly broadcasts of the original "Quiet Storm" with host Melvin Lindsey on Howard University radio (WHUR-FM) in the mid-1970s. I sang along with the love raps of Barry White, the soulful coloratura of Minnie Riperton, and smooth choruses of "Summer Madness" performed by Kool & the Gang. *Who* I dreamed of being was Chaka Khan. She represented an emerging fusion of R&B, gospel, and rock vocals, and I wanted to be that. We had lots in common. She was dark-chocolate, like me. She was a former Catholic, like me. Her luscious lips and healthy legs strapped in thigh-high boots were not too much for me. I wanted to be like Chaka with her wild, sexy hair on the cover of the album *Rufusized* (ABC Records, 1974) with a band of black and white musicians swarming around me.

I was captivated by, and could imitate, the way Chaka strutted across the stage, and her interpretation of melodies and lyrics ignited funky dance grooves I played over and over again: "Once you get star-ted / Oh! It's hard to stop / Yes, I just, just, can't stop." Chaka could lull you into a spiritual affair: "Roll me through the ru-shes / Just like Mo-ses on the Nile." Or soulfully rock you into a slow drag even with no partner: "I wish you were my lover / But you / Act so undercover. / To love you chil' my whole-life long / Be it right / Or be it wrong." I embodied those songs. I came of age behind their emotion and their subtly Afrocentric lyrics. Inhaling her matchless voice, I imagined I could inhabit who she was when I first saw her live in concert at D.C.'s Warner Theater.

I believe these recollections are a significant part of my subjective identity as a black female musician, but are they "real"? Speaking about the "different rhythm of living and being" that is part of the process of racial identity construction in the African diaspora, Paul Gilroy wrote: "a precious sense of black particularity gets constructed from several interlocking themes that culminate in this unexpected time signature. They supply the accents, rests, breaks, and tones that make the performance of racial identity possible."

In an age full of accusations that blacks are segregating themselves from others and that race no longer matters in black popular music (swap Eminem as the new Elvis), "authenticity" in black musical experience is a dirty word. But what about the phenomenological experience of living that musical difference as a social phenomenon, not merely as an individual memory like mine above? Gilroy could be read as if he is suggesting that the preciousness of musical blackness is *woven out of time* (constructed out or from past moments; a product of an improvisation). He writes: "The discourse of The Same . . . helps to fix and to stabilize the boundaries of the closed racial community. . . . [drawing] the line between past and present which is so important in black expressive cultures." Music, he asserts, is the critical sphere of cultural activity out of which black expressive culture and identity are shaped (Gilroy 1993a, 202).

Before I began this project, I rarely questioned such beliefs. African Americans had "soul" in ways that other Americans did not. As an African American, it felt good to *possess* that difference, to be empowered by it, within a racially biased culture that privileged the learned "white" ways of thinking, feeling, believing, and behaving whether in literature, business, education—and, relative to my years in higher education—music. Education is more obviously a process by which we learn to avow and remember certain knowledges and devalue and forget others. We grow up repudiating the local and personal in favor of what will get us ahead and away—this coming of age in an intellectual field that by no means arbitrarily creates disinterest and oversight in some areas while directing desire elsewhere (John 1989, 55, quoted in Visweswaren 1994, 103).

The idea of actually studying how musical blackness is learned, or how the disciplined art of black musical identity may be constituted, was not possible until the traditional icons of American music—Billie Holiday, Miles Davis, Laurie Anderson, Ozzy Osbourne, and, to my amazement, the hip-hop group, Public Enemy—were introduced in my third year of graduate study in classical voice. The year was 1990.

Not much older than some of the graduate students in the course, the instructor strolled into the first day of class with an electric guitar, promptly plugged it into an amp, and before uttering a word he cranked it up and played a few power chords; heavy metal was his introduction. He also highlighted his scholarly interests and performance chops as a trumpet player in classical and jazz in addition to playing heavy metal guitar. Thank you, Rob Walser.

This was the first course involving contemporary popular music since I began studying music formally in 1979. It was my first course in music to raise the issue of segregation and the politics of race and gender, which had always been a matter of importance in my life though rarely addressed in my formal education. Midway through his course, I experienced what I would call a breakthrough insight. It was OK for me as an African American to be "black," to think and write about blackness and music in the classroom and possibly be a scholar writing about black popular music and culture from an African American perspective.

I had never heard of or seen anyone—white or black—teach contemporary popular music, much less probe issues of race *as well as* gender with scholarly authority, with the intellectual and social integrity of a classroom full of a variety of "racial" subjects. I thought to myself: if a white man with classical chops can study and teach heavy metal, why couldn't I do the same with regard to African American music? My classical chops might come in handy in ways that might be beneficial to interpreting African American music culture.

A discursive space opened up. I wanted to teach black popular music. I wanted to offer a perspective on black music culture that revealed its everyday sites of production rather than its commodified peripheries and that also addressed race, gender, and the body. By 1991, I had switched my studies from voice to completing a Ph.D. in ethnomusicology. The move came from a revelation that classical voice was never really what I wanted to do in the first place. I realized I wanted to teach African American music from a cultural perspective. I was free to bring my people's music to the table, but I was not free of certain ideas about race.

Members of any multicultural society may be privy to a broad array of musical styles and influences from the cradle to the grave (cf. Kubik). Despite this hybrid context, their musical tastes and interests in any given moment may be to identify with one cultural group or cluster of styles attributed to one people defined by roots or place. They may practice and identify with distinct styles of performance and methods of appreciation in variable patterns of use and meaning but that speak to one community. The idea of a musical blackness attempts to grasp this.

In the United States, the practical and interpretive moves that constitute our musical identities are fraught with the underexplored politics of power that signify differences that arise in corporate boardrooms, local churches, private homes, and community playgrounds. In other words, we dance, sing, chant, perform, and rehearse who we are, through multiple and shifting alliances; through expressions of agency characterized by our notions of gender, nation, race, class, sexuality, religion, age, ability, and disability; and through other modes that signify the *interdependence* (the dialectics) of the self and the social.

For the purpose of my ethnomusicological investigation, I apply the term *musical identity* to the subjective and dynamically shifting process of the self and the social. Like other identities, musical identity is not biologically determined, nor is it simply a matter of choice. The notion of "trying on identities," according to anthropologist Kamala Visweswaren, "obscures the fact that identities, no matter how strategically deployed, are not always chosen, but are in fact constituted by relations of power that are always historically determined" (1994, 8).

In this age of anti-essentialism, the singular usage of the term *musical identity* may cause alarm, possibly suggesting stasis instead of an experience or process. The meaning I intend here is the latter, for lived identifications with African American musicality involve a *learned and interdependent dynamic of the self and the social;* the individually learned ways of thinking, feeling, believing, and behaving musically are inherently *so-*

cial acts (cf. Volk's definition of culture, 1998). Music, after all, not only *expresses* and *communicates* the human condition to one's self, it does so to and for others as well (cf. Davies 1999; Jackson 1996; Visweswaren 1994). And as a noted ethnomusicologist reminds us, "Processes of enculturation are in principle lifelong" (Kubik 1998, 223).

As we begin to accept that race is a social construct—that skin color is a pigment of our imagination, and that all humankind is a single species or "race" (see the statement on race by the American Anthropological Association, available online at http://www.aaane.org/stmts/racepp.htm)—I want to resist tipping the scale in the opposite direction of assuming universals about people and music. On the other end of the spectrum, one might hear a recording of Stevie Wonder singing, "music is a world within itself, with a language we all understand" (from "Sir Duke" on *Songs in the Key of Life,* 1976) and uncritically embrace a broad-sweeping notion about music where all Americans participate in it *equally*—America as simply one nation under a groove. Note the first verse of the song:

> *Music is a world within itself / With a language we all understand*
> *With an equal opportunity / For all to sing, dance and clap their hands*
> *But just because a record has a groove / Don't make it in the groove*
> *But you can tell right away at letter A / When the people start to move*
> Chorus:
> *They can feel it all over / They can feel it all over, people* (repeat)

Ultimately, there are multiple and overlapping ways of being musical in American culture, not to mention interpreting what music means, and these *lived* differences should not be denied. Even though many people from the United States and around the world can also construct their identifications from the language of black music, every ethnic *body* does not learn the *embodied language* of African American musical discourse, and the people whose subjectivities shape that musical discourse—the everyday folks out of which emerge recording artists like Stevie Wonder —are largely ignored in ethnomusicological and musicological scholarship.

I am interested in understanding the African American matrix of musical embodiment that is constituted through gendered and nongendered social and musical phenomena. The musical games that black girls play offered an unusual site for examining the intersections of race, gender, and embodiment, as well as the everyday ways a gendered musical blackness is socially constructed or *learned.*

As certain commodified traditions, histories, and performances primarily associated with African Americans enter the "mainstream" in the curricula of music schools and departments (namely, jazz, blues, rhythm and blues as rock 'n' roll, and to a lesser degree, spirituals, gospel, contemporary R&B, rap, hip-hop, and black classical music) one finds few musicological or ethnomusicological investigations exploring the *kinds of experiences and practices* that contribute to learning the mosaic of traditions associated with African American musical identities and communities. Though African American or black musical identity is lived and imagined by many as a distinct and divergent way of embodying musical expression and communication, it now infiltrates other *national and international* identities.

At the national level, hip-hop, for example, converges with white Southern musical identity and identifications with certain black musics by a host of ethnicities. At the international level, it converges with African and African diasporan identities, as well as Japanese, Bosnian, British, Finnish, and Indonesian identifications with certain black musics mediated by the global music industry. Nonetheless, what are the early experiences that are *inhabited,* and what are the social practices that are *conditioned* to become black musical sensibilities among members of African American communities in the United States (cf. Scott 1999)?

From my standpoint as a professor, students of various national and international backgrounds constantly seek an answer to discrepancies about who can "really" perform black music or who is authorized to "play" [an] African American musical identity in my classroom or in the media. Can Vanilla Ice perform black music? Is it okay for Eminem to rap? Can Mariah Carey, who is biracial, sing it, or did she learn it? What of 'N Sync, Santana, Bonnie Raitt, or Johnny Mathis, who possess different degrees of blackness (see Rudinow 1994)?

The question marks here are not meant to indict any of these icons one way or another, though they may invoke an unsettling reaction in some readers (see Reed 1998). I intentionally included figures outside the usual black and white orientation of such discussions: given the function of race as a marker of difference, not simply color, whiteness is not the only identification implicated in discussions of racial authenticity and blackness. But the "invisibility" of others besides whites works against reading "race" with the cultural complexity it requires. Even African Americans' "authentic" blackness is implicated by my questions: who gets musical blackness "right"?

These tougher questions we rarely ask are about the role that power and privilege have played in the unequal distribution of labor and capital —historically along racial lines—in the domestic and international recording industry. Arguably, these questions and answers have their roots in commercial practices that divorce musical sounds from the body. As feminist musicologist Susan McClary writes, "Western musical thought has been devoted to defining music as the sound itself, to erasing the physicality involved in both the making and the reception of music. . . . The advent of recording has been a Platonic dream come true, for with a disk one can have the pleasure of the sound without the troubling reminder of the bodies producing it" (1991, 136).

Radio, cassettes, LPs, compact discs, downloading mp3s, and iPods feed this pleasure. And now that 'N Sync, the Backstreet Boys, and Britney Spears have mastered the art of black musical embodiment, the troubling reminder of difference is lost in that pleasure. The most recent technology of downloading mp3s and iPods has contributed much more than compact discs to divorcing consumers from the visual and embodied lives and cultural contexts of "racialized" performers and performance, giving me a completely new insight into the assertion my students often make that "race" or ethnicity no longer matters. But a lot of lessons about musical difference happen merely in day-to-day conversation.

A Conversation: The Exception Proves the Rule

In graduate school, I was one of two black students in the musicology program, which encompassed both historical musicology and ethnomusicology. Once, as we wrapped up a summer reading course meeting held in the backyard of a professor's home, the other African American student shared an observation that his youngest daughter *did not* have rhythm like the rest of his family. I don't recall how the subject came up, but he added, "I know it's not genes, 'cuz my daughter don't have no rhythm!"

The senior ethnomusicology professor hosting the session interjected, "Yes, but the exception *proves* the rule," to emphasize the rule of culture, rather than biology, over the ethnic behavior of rhythm and dancing.

Since becoming a professor myself, I've reiterated her response to my students on several occasions.

Years later, I can bear witness to the fact that my associate's daughter grew to be an exceptionally rhythmic dancer, with an exceptional affinity for music-making, which illustrates a critical part of my thesis: black musical identity is learned. At the time, however, the words of that professor seemed so empowering, not only because she was considered an expert on people making music in/of culture as a senior ethnomusicologist in the field, but also because I perceived her to be a discerning thinker. There she was, defending the lived meaningfulness of a *musical blackness*. It definitely mattered for me, in that moment, that this "voice of reason" was that of a white person.

In an open letter published in the journal *Popular Music* (vol. 8, no. 3), musicologist Philip Tagg, who proclaims himself to be a "white, middle-class intellectual," attempts to raise a constructive discussion on music, race, and ideology by questioning the needs that give rise to terms such as "black" or "European" music (Tagg 1989, 285–98). He writes:

> We are all implicitly expected to know exactly what everybody else means and to have clear concepts of what is black or African about "black music" or "Afro-American" music, just as we are presumed to have a clear idea about what is white or European about "white" or "European" music. I just get confused. Very rarely is any musical evidence given for the specific skin colour or continental origin of the music being talked about and *when evidence is presented, it usually seems pretty flimsy to me from a musicological viewpoint.* (emphasis added; also see http://www.theblackbook.net/acad/tagg/articles/opelet.html)

There seemed to never be any justification, particularly among many white music scholars in print, for a "black" musical experience in the emerging deconstructive, anti-essentialist climate of U.S. academic discourse in the early 1990s.

That day, on the deck in the professor's backyard, was the first time I had witnessed such a defense in my, then, ten-plus years of "formal" music education. It happened in an informal classroom setting outside the university grounds, after the serious discussions had taken place.

While these incidents suggest that it matters who is speaking about difference or who has the authority to shape discourse, it points out the lack of discussion about African American subjectivity within musical institutions of higher learning. Until recently, I had never stopped to think critically about how the expression "the exception proves the rule" worked to satisfy my need to legitimize my own experience. However, this expression was not the best intervention against biological assumptions about musical blackness. Biological determinism lurks deep within the imagination of the American public when it comes to African American musical ability. *Rhythm* and *soul* are the main examples many "experience" as biological differences between the races. While "having rhythm," as it's referred to in African American musical discourse, may be a cultural "rule," this so-called rule must first be *learned* to be followed. African Americans must learn to discipline their kinesthetic sensibilities and their highly social musical embodiment. But how?

Black musical behavior is embodied through a learning process we take for granted. Prior to this realization, all I had known, for better or worse, was that *most* African Americans had rhythm, *most* sang, and *most* identified with and expressed themselves through contemporary African American styles of music and dance. *How* we got rhythm or soul —how we acquired these musical skills or how these skills served our self and group identity—was never investigated.

I began to ponder how I feel at home *in* my musical identity—how my identification with African American musical experience seemed an eternal and ancient "changing same" (cf. Le Roi Jones, aka Amiri Baraka), to borrow an expression that perpetually crops up in academic discussions of black music (as if classical and other musics do not subscribe to the same "changing same").

I have always felt and come to know myself to be a great dancer. Throughout my life, I've always had rhythm. I have even imagined I could intuitively figure out earlier styles of black dance that precede my birth just from hearing the music that might have accompanied it. I sensed a changing sameness, a sense of being connected to previous generations, through interactions with my mother, from TV and vintage films of black music-making, and from recordings of shouters and songstresses I heard that reflected the recent or distant past. I experienced the past in what I saw and what I did as a black dancer.

That illusion was shattered when my mother told me that she had taught me how to dance—that, in essence, she had taught me how to have that "different rhythm in living and being" that Gilroy mentioned. My mother shared her observations of my toddler years: "Your first experience (of moving to music), I could see it. It was like you were on the wrong side of the beat" (personal communication, August 11, 2001). She expressed fear upon discovering that I didn't have a good sense of rhythm on my own. "So," she told me, "I danced with you a lot."

That was not how I had recalled it. I vividly remembered my four-year-old feet struggling to stay afloat on my mother's Lindy-hopping toes. But I had no idea it was because I *didn't* have rhythm—I didn't have a "metronomic sense" of dancing along with the beat of the records she played every Saturday night on a stereo that doubled as a credenza in our living room. I merely assumed, in hindsight, that she had been teaching me specific choreographies (like the Lindy) and other dances I actually did learn from her, which she had acquired before I was born. I learned the Twist, the Funky Chicken, the Australian Slop, the Tight Rope, and the Tighten Up (which we danced to the song of the same name by Archie Bell and the Drells). I even learned how to do the Freak from my mother, a single partying parent, when I was a teenager in the 1980s.

My kinesthetic memories of dances and the music that went along with them were vivid. Before my mother gave me another explanation, I created one in my head: I figured she was passing on local and national popular traditions that had been more closely connected during segregation. I believed I had the right sensibilities to put everything into action, and that my African American body came with rhythm in it. My mother was just teaching me the choreographies. I wasn't wrong about that.

Believing self and group identity come naturally is part of the customary phenomenology of black musical identity politics. We want to believe who we are is fixed, set, and complete—a belief that is especially common in the collective consciousness surrounding black experience. Even while recognizing that I *learned* how to have rhythm, my sense of my musical blackness—my sense of belonging and being socially affiliated with a distinct African American culture—remains. So there must be some cultural, rather than biological, need for this subjective (and spiritual) feeling that is both about the self and about being a part of the social experiences known as "African American" that are, as a rule, learned.

I am well aware that presumptions about fixed conceptions of ethnicity, culture, and subjectivity, as well as generalities about singular black musical identity, are viewed as problematic, given current anti-essentialist discourse forwarded by the likes of Gilroy, whom I quoted above (Radano 2000, 4; Frith 1996, 108). However, I see what I am doing here as contributing to a vacuum in our discourse about African American musical identity. Showing her vision back in 1990, bell hooks warned:

> Criticisms of directions in postmodern thinking should not obscure in-
> sights it may offer that open up our understanding of African American
> experience. This critique of essentialism is useful for African Americans
> concerned with reformulating outmoded notions of identity. . . . [How-
> ever,] this critique should not be made synonymous with a dismissal of
> the struggle of oppressed and exploited peoples to make ourselves sub-
> jects. (1990, 28–29)

There is a radical difference between a repudiation of the idea that there
is a black "essence" and recognition of the way black identity has been
specifically constituted through experience (29).

In the wake of deconstructing purely imagined identities, music scholars have lost sight of the phenomenology of African Americans' everyday
musical experience. In my assessment, this oversight is complicated by a
lack of attention to the ways musical blackness is learned and experienced. Some of us need to continue to understand and investigate how
black musical discourse and black musical subjectivities in African American culture are learned through *everyday* social practices.

The musical subjectivities of African American males and females are
not a "blind recapitulation of givenness" (Jackson 1996, 11). We develop active relationships with what has gone before and what imagi-
natively lies ahead, to make a future, or a *home,* out of the "sedimented
and anonymous meanings of the past" (ibid.). These sedimented and
anonymous meanings are boundless; they are not confined by race or
sex, though they tend to be bound on the surface to things American (as
is exemplified, generally speaking, in hip-hop culture and, as I will
show, in black girls' musical games). The cognitive moves to deny *phenomenological* musical experiences do not take into account "how people immediately experience space, time, and the world in which they
live" (Jackson 1996, 12). As anthropologist Michael Jackson goes on to
say:

> Use, not logic, conditions belief. That the phenomenologist is loath to
> essentialize such terms as nature, femininity, or Aboriginality does not
> preclude an appreciation that a separatist, essentializing rhetoric is often
> an imperative strategy for besieged groups and ethnic minorities in lay-
> ing claim to civil rights and cultural recognition. . . . Ideas can be mean-
> ingful and have useful consequences even when they are epistemologi-
> cally unwarranted." (13)

Home and Homelessness: Rethinking Musical Blackness

I am proposing an alternative to the ways we have conceived the musical subjectivities of African Americans. Given the economic and social histories of African Americans—from being considered "property" to struggling to define their own worth through musical discourse in contemporary culture—black musical identity or musical blackness might be more usefully viewed as a kind of "home-lessness" or, perhaps, a kind of "homework." The notion of homework also came to me as I began to think of my own fieldwork as homework from a "native" ethnographic perspective. The concept of belonging is problematic even within spaces thought of as home (see Davies 1999; Visweswaren 1994). In other words, musical blackness is an imagined "home," constructed to represent a place of return, a place of social and political comfort. It is a *learned* place of inhabitance; an *embodied* dwelling that might be viewed as a protection from real and imagined threats. This kind of musical homework is not simply about a return to contemporary Nigeria or ancient Yorubaland imagined or constituted by the descendents of African slaves living in the United States.

African Americans are embodying "home," performing their affiliation and identification with the collective experience of blackness, as a result of perpetually confronting a kind of "homelessness" in this so-called New World dominated by descendents of Europeans, who themselves embody an imagined "home" in America at the expense of native Americans, who experience homelessness in a land that was their own. "What seems to lie about in discourses of race concerns legitimacy, authenticity, community, belonging. In no small way, these discourses are about home" (Morrison 1997, 5).

We must realize that the practices and ideologies that socialize African American children or acculturate adults into "black" ways of being musical are never mechanical reproductions of a distinct and unitary black musical identity. "Black" ways of approaching singing and chanting, moving and dancing, talking about and composing musical ideas (from lyrics to melodic and rhythmic improvisation) are a contemporary project. This project is always and already shaped by multiple, arbitrary, and shifting experiences—past and present—that are narrated as if sprung from one root, one point in time, one parent culture. Since the phenomenological experience of being *musically black* continues to register for African Americans, scholars cannot, and should not, seek to erase its presence, because anti-essentialist rhetoric wants to throw the baby (African American cultural identifications) out with the politically incorrect bath water (racial essentialism).

We don't need another set of stories that usurp race as the myth producing African American alliances—following an argument by philosopher Kwamé Anthony Appiah—but we do need more intersecting narratives that overlap with ones that privilege the most expressive and emblematic, the most emergent, and the historical experiences of musical blackness as predominantly male and masculine. While group solidarity is an important force with real political benefits, "it doesn't work without its attendant mystifications. . . . You cannot build alliances without mystifications and mythologies" (Appiah 1995, 106).

While black group solidarity through music has been a real and powerful agent in forging alliances—for example, to combat racism—it has rarely forged to combat sexism against African American women within black communities, popular culture, and the larger society. Subjugation of women's gender politics stands in contradistinction to the fact that specific approaches to embodying *rhythm* or *soul* are *primarily allied around the embodied public discourse of black musical bodies* of men and women. But mythologies concerning *male* gender dominance in everyday life, as well as musical performance, tend to eclipse female participation and denigrate the feminine, so that even girls and women tend to overlook their own contributions and participation in sustaining the social practices that constitute black musical identity. Women and girls are not included among the master drummers or griots or, for example, the corn shuckers to whom Roger Abrahams devotes an entire book. In his *Singing the Master* (1992), he attempts to trace the origins of African American national or cultural identity through musical practices associated with male slave labor. Often the exclusion of women and girls is not so overt.

My concern for the ways gender and the experiences of girls and women intersect with masculinist readings of history and culture came about from my first teaching assignment in women's studies. The year before I started assisting with the teaching of Western art music for nonmajors, I taught my own course titled "African American Women and Feminism." That year, "diversity" was instituted into the undergraduate curriculum, and white fraternity members who were "inspired" by the mandated, university-wide requirement, opted to enroll in a women's studies course (rather than Russian history or black studies, which were among the other options). They expressed that it would be an easy way to fulfill the diversity requirement at the University of Michigan. Many of the black male students probably opted for African American or African studies rather than women's studies, which was perceived to be primarily about white women. Few of either group of men opted for my course on African American women and feminism.

Aversions to dealing with issues of women, gender, and race disturbed me when I began teaching African American music, primarily because of my own gendered musical experiences as an African American woman fascinated with studying hip-hop culture—perceived to be a predominantly male and masculinist culture. From various "nonmusical" experiences in the classroom, I became convinced of a need to uncover the ways in which black musical identity as "black" or "male" is not a pure or finished product.

Gilroy states that gender and sexuality have played a significant role in reducing the "untidy patterns of differentiation" to *black masculinity* as the primary, if not sole, signifier of *race* in mass popular culture.

> Sexuality and gender identity are the other privileged media that express the evasive but highly prized quality of racial authenticity. Their growing power in configuring contemporary notions of blackness raises once again the critical issue of how the complex dynamics of race and gender come together. In a situation where racial identity appears suddenly impossible to know reliably or maintain with ease, the naturalness of gender can supply the modality in which race is lived and symbolized. . . . The popularity of [Jamaican] slackness and the more misogynist forms of hip-hop can be used to support this diagnosis. The chief effect of this unhappy situation is that today's crisis of black social life is routinely represented as a crisis of masculinity alone. The integrity of the race is defined primarily as the integrity of its menfolk. (1993a, 7)

Thus, we tend to remember the authenticity of the blues through Robert Johnson and Leadbelly, but rarely through blues women, possibly because their association with the mass mediation of "race" records would be read today as "selling out" to the commercial side of music. But remembering blues women would require us to think of critiquing race *as well as* gender in our analysis of music and the recording industry.

The masculinist focus of dominant jazz, swing, and hip-hop histories may, in fact, stem from a long-standing white fascination with perceptions of black masculinity. If the appeal of mainstream music histories is their ability to dispense models of black masculinity to white consumers through information and anecdotes about black men who play jazz and white men who successfully play black music, then it is no wonder that all-women bands, both black and white, find themselves the subjects of separate histories with limited readerships.

Black identities are more complex than the hegemonic, often masculinist, interpretations of tradition deployed to re-produce and remember the liberating moments of black freedom during the twentieth century, such as playing "the Dozens." It has never been enough to chant, "Say It Loud (I'm Black and I'm Proud)," if you were transcending a racial self-loathing alongside feeling female, gay or lesbian, bi- or transsexual, or a number of intersecting vectors of social identity signaling religious, cultural, sexual, socioeconomic, national, or international affiliations within African American culture. This is why theorizing the intersection of race, gender, and music is essential in contemporary African American musical discourse.

Ingrid Monson has insightfully observed that ethnomusicologists and musicologists had "an interpretive habit of viewing ethnic identity and gender as relatively independent cultural variables rather than as two components of multiply-determined cultural processes that continually inflect one another" (Monson 1997, 24–25). A critical mass of distinguished scholarship representing the intersectionality of ethnic and gender identity in the study of African Americans and their performance in blues, swing, jazz, rhythm and blues, gospel, rock, house, Latin dance musics, and hip-hop have emerged in the last four to ten years from various disciplines primarily outside music (see Ake 2002; Bowers 2000; Carby 1990, 1991, 1998; Cole and Guy-Sheftall 2003; Crenshaw 1991; Davis 1990, 1998; Griffin 2001; Keyes 1993; Kirk-Duggan 1997; Mahon 2004; Pelligrinelli 2000; Porter 2002; Pough 2004; Ransby and Matthews 1993; Rose 1991, 1994; Stein 1998; Tucker 2000; Ward 1998; Wong 2000). Much of this work is expanding musical discourse by engaging issues of class, sexuality, sexual orientation, and other ethnicities as well (Aparicio 2000; Fikentscher 2000; Hunter 2000; Neal 2002; Rivera 2003; Zoloth 2001). An edited volume titled *Sexing the Groove* devoted to popular music and gender does not include anything relating to African American women musicians, their musical tastes, or the popular music by people of African descent (Whiteley 1997). Such omissions reinforce the notion that white women's "feminism" and "gender" are sublimated in matters of race (i.e., whiteness). It tends to exclude black women, their issues, and the impact of patriarchy and whiteness upon them in its political agendas and social critiques.

It is imperative to now extend the discourse of rhythm and soul, as well as other black musical discourse, to recover and include the lived meanings of gender in black musical experience—of women and children—before we toss aside black musical identity. We need to explore the gendered embodied practices and social ideologies that produce the phenomenology of black musical subjectivities. These explorations are a guiding force behind my analysis of the role that girls' musical games play in constituting and building gendered black alliances (whether among men, among women, or between the sexes). What are black females learning through these social practices that can help us better understand how men and women, girls and boys, negotiate a gender-biased black community that is not necessarily satisfying to those of the "lesser" sex?

The musical games black girls share are an important avenue (among others) of enculturation that is marked by an embodied musical identity: the embodiment of social interactions that produce musical events is a primary site for discovering how black musical aesthetics are learned and communicated as self and social experience. The musical performance of race *and* gender is characterized *through* embodiment. If mass music is locked in a dialectical relationship with local traditions of music-making produced and shared in black communities, then black girls' and women's practices offer a critical site for the study of black musical identity as a relationship between the sexes, and the gendered roles associated with them.

Conclusion: Girls as Masters of Musical Knowledge

Studying girls' games need not, therefore, be confined to traditional *folklore* or vernacular studies. They, too, are part of contemporary and popular culture, and should not be relegated to the "other" categories of study and analysis that lie outside the artistic and the popular. Black girls live in the same technologically mediated and global world of communication that adults do—in some cases, more so. It would be misleading to simply categorize them as *folk* or vernacular music: as I will show, there is ample evidence of contemporary popular songs and dances within their games. There is evidence that contemporary recording artists, mostly male, are tapping into this music as a resource for their copyrightable texts, suggesting overlooked gendered relationships within African American culture and within mass cultural forms.

Like folklore-oriented studies, this project does not feature a large collection of data where oral examples from the past and present represent the historical significance of a cultural form through quantity and classification, although girls' games are pervasive enough to occupy such a collection (see Abrahams 1969; Brady and Eckhardt 1975; Merrill-Mirsky 1988; Riddell 1990). Unlike the earliest folklore studies of children's games (Gomme 1894), I resist the usual antiquarian impulses to collect significant quantities of games to help preserve the past (i.e., presenting the games as remnants of *primitive* vs. *complex* customs and beliefs).

Children's (and girls') culture is too readily equated with the *pre-modern,* the *pre-technological,* the *pre-adult*; all designations that invoke "otherness" deny the complexity of phenomenology that, whether studied or not, contributes to the social construction of culture and identity. The games and the girls who play them have much to tell us about the processes of black musical enculturation and the phenomenological conditions of *embodying* musical blackness; I want to resist the patronizing impulses to "other" or exoticize children's music culture by treating it as less modern or primitive, less complex, or less serious in comparison to popular commercial music, adults' music, or written genres of music. If children are relegated to otherness like primitives, because of their age, because their behavior is considered simply imitative of adults, or because their practices seem to represent the past, then their reliance on the body —given the cultural abnegation of the feminine—could exclude black girls from any consideration as complex subjects of black musical identity. Just because girls' games take place in the realm of play, and because they are transmitted primarily as oral and embodied communication, we shouldn't disregard the complexities of their musical and social phenomena, for they live among and within dominant realms of culture.

Accepting the fact that children's music is as complex as any, merely analyzing the lyrics, melodies, and rhythms of girls' play to discover its complexity is insufficient. Rather than focusing solely on black girls' games as a collection of texts to be analyzed as black music, I also focus on the social interactions of gendered musical bodies at play. I want to demonstrate (through the process of *defamiliarization*) the complexities of children's everyday music-making as other studies have shown (see Blacking 1967, Kartomi 1991; Campbell 1998; Agawu 1995b). I am fascinated by the ways the embodied discourse of music in these games may "insure the operation and maintenance of culture or social systems" (Seagoe 1970, 139, quoted in Brady and Eckhart 1975, 2): Not just an ethnic system, but also a system where music, race, and gender intersect. The ethnography of experience I offer here is as important as what I uncover from my experience with black girls and their games, the most important of which is the argument I make about this sphere of musical play. Girls' games are the first such public sphere of musical activity that most children of either sex will encounter outside their family and immediate home, which is the subject of the next chapter.

3

Mary Mack Dressed in Black
The Earliest Formation of a Popular Music

Studies of handclapping games, cheers, and double-dutch have documented African American play in major urban cities in the Northeast (Philadelphia, D.C., and New York City), in the South (Texas and Alabama), and in the West (Los Angeles). Black girls as young as three and as old as fourteen practice these games, which dominated urban play as early as the 1960s. By 2001, the games black girls play turned up just about anywhere American children are present or represented.

Like everything else, these games were globalized through sonic, visual, and musical mediums. And they continue to be globally transmitted to places outside everyday practice, through commercial print and audiovisual media, the Internet, and even face-to-face interactions between children speaking different languages, whether in domestic contexts or abroad (i.e., overseas bases of the armed forces in Germany, Japan, and now perhaps Afghanistan and Iraq).

Domestically, these games are accessible as a result of contact with commercially marketed field recordings of *skip rope games, play party tunes,* and *Negro folk songs* produced by Smithsonian, Folkways, New World Records, and the Library of Congress (see recordings of Bessie Jones); books for children; 1980s commercial television ads featuring images of black girls handclapping to the beat of a McDonald's jingle advertising Big Macs; "window-dressing" scenes in Hollywood films and made-for-TV movies in the 1990s (i.e., the film *Big*, with Tom Hanks); and featured clips of black girls' play on PBS's *Sesame Street* and Nickelodeon's *Gullah Gullah Island*.

Despite the mass mediation of these practices, handclapping games, cheers, double-dutch rope play, and the chants and songs that accompany them, continue to represent a unique set of meaningful social practices—a complex of verbal and nonverbal acts and events among African American female peer groups from ages five to fourteen—that feature the expressive aesthetics of black music-making, shared more or less with boys and adults.

The musical games black girls play are a unique and under-examined ethnographic site of black musical experience contributing to two important insights about African American musical culture. First, handclapping games, cheers, and double-dutch operate as *oral-kinesic lessons,* where girls (and even boys) learn the "in-body formulas" of African American musical and social aesthetics through group play (Drewal 1992).

Second, the acquisition of this embodied phenomenology has implications beyond the same-sex youth interactions of girls' play into adulthood. These embodied games socialize girls into behaviors, tropes of feeling (soul, rhythmic complexity, and group identification), and musical interaction (mirroring a hip gyration across from a partner) that shape communal interpretations of race and gender roles in musical and nonmusical contexts. Girls' everyday practice contributes greatly to a sense of a black musical identity. It serves as a cultural resource for establishing and remembering the individual and social body as it reflects ethnic group cohesion and solidarity despite national, geographical, and socioeconomic differences among African Americans across time and place.

As the earliest public sphere of black social practice and popular discourse among African American girls, this chapter explores the obscured musical and social connections and interconnections in these games. The kinetic orality of African American musical aesthetics that girls learn to inhabit through these games points to a lived phenomenology of a gendered blackness as well as a complex web of relations that suggest an "ethnographic truth," the "spirit of the local and situational quality of knowledge and experience . . . positioned within the experiences of specific historical actors" (Ramsey 2003, 41).

The Body as a Technology

After my initial encounter with the nine-year-old twins, Jasmine and Stephanie, I decided to conduct an ethnographic study of these games. Dating back to the early decades of the twentieth century, the phenomenon of learning to play girls' musical games from generation to generation continues to drive a translocal knowledge of popular musical culture among African American girls. "Translocal" refers to the ways in which vernacular practices transcend divisions of geography, and thereby class, age, national origin, and migration. The result is a national sense of black communal memory and experience (or identity) defined by musical practices that involve key strategies of black linguistic play and musical movement. These are black girls' first public interactions in rural and urban communities.

Participation in these formative "lessons" constitutes one of the earliest musical and cultural formations that could be called a "black popular culture": the games are passed down from older girls to very young ones, with little or no direct formal "teaching" or education from adult members of the community. In this early sphere of public and popular activity, girls perform identifications with dominant interpretations of blackness, musical blackness, and black femaleness from a hegemonic African American perspective.

In handclapping games, cheers, and double-dutch, the musical and social agency of black girls rules the day. The style of black girls' embodied play reflects dominant characteristics of African American music and dance: the use of bent notes to inflect meaning; the playful and dramatic use of call-and-response; and the use of hip and pelvic gestures, as well as the percussive and rhythmic complexity and improvisational tendencies of oral and kinetic expression that are found in African American sacred and secular performance. Within this expression, I discovered ways that African American musical ideals and social values are learned and enacted. The medium expressing these musical and social ideals—where these values are played with, enacted, and constituted into a sense of being—is the site of the body.

The mimicry and dramaturgy of language expressed by the body—its physical movements as well as its linguistic gestures—are constituted through the social interactions and meanings of games black girls play. They learn to map or embody the media of a musical blackness—the ordinary practices and social discourse that transmit and symbolize a social way of being musically black—in the context of African American play.

Samuel A. Floyd wrote in his 1995 study, *The Power of Black Music,* that the subjective concept of cultural memory is "connected to cultural *forms*—in the present case, music, where the 'memory' drives the music and the music drives the memory" (Floyd 1995, 8). This tautological construction leaves little room for understanding how this process works and what actually constitutes the music and the memory—the gendered bodies of African Americans.

In this way and others, the body is a *technology* of black musical communication and identity. *Merriam Webster's Dictionary* defines "technology" as "the practical application of knowledge, a manner of accomplishing a task (i.e., identifying with blackness, the African diaspora, Africans), using a skill or craft, a method or process" (1999). Extra-somatic instruments (drums, flutes, violins, steel pans, and, arguably in some circles, turntables) are acceptable media of *artistic* technology. The social body as a tool or method of artistic composition and performance, however, continues to be overlooked in the study of music, just as the black vernacular body continues to be overlooked in dance history.

Drums or any other forms of musical "technology" are but extensions of things the body and voice can do. The striking of body parts and cavities, the resonating of the singing voice, and use of verbal and nonverbal language, manufacture codes, identifications, and ideas about music and life through the "systematic" (re)production of an embodied phenomenology.

At an early age, therefore, black girls learn to embody a "social process through which traditions [and identities] are elaborated and made perceptible" (Coplan 1994, 30). While orality tends to be the primary focus of discussions about the transmission of vernacular traditions and cultural identifications, it is a conjunction of orality *and* kinetics—what Cornel West calls "kinetic orality"—an underexamined phenomenon in studies of black musical identity and performance. Through the practical activities of musical play, girls actually inhabit "in-body formulas" (Drewal 1992) that construct their consciousness of themselves as black and female members of a subculture, in contradistinction to the traditions and privileges of the dominant culture, relative to race and gender (among other factors).

Linguistics, lexical meaning (lyrics), and musical sound are as important as the textual and verbal dimensions of musical experience, but embodiment, particularly social embodiment, is equally significant in its power to carry, pass on, and connect the core values and ideals of a musical tradition from the past, and project it into the future as a memory. Because of the early development of girls' social knowledge and skill, the consciousness that arises from participation in the musical games black girls play is eventually "naturalized."

Training in this context is a matter of conditioning. It is informal, but it is training nevertheless. Because the training is so subtle, the outcome often seems like second nature (Malone 1996 in Caponi 1999, 227).

While music scholars tended to overlook the musical sensibilities of embodied behavior, girls and the social process of learning how to be musical in black communal and popular contexts were also discounted.

Both African Americans and those who write and teach black music have tended to operate as if black musical style and identity were a given, rather than a learned phenomenon of social relations and musical affiliations, enacted through embodied practice and social memory. Acting on behalf of an *anti-anti-essentialist stance,* Gilroy reminds us that "though it is often felt to be natural and spontaneous, [identity] remains the outcome of practical activity: language, gesture, bodily significations, desires. . . . racialized subjectivity is the product of the social practices that supposedly derive from it" (1993b, 102; cf. Foucault). In other words, the black musical body is a social mnemonic device that exhibits the inhabited and learned embodied knowledge, as if it were second nature.

The relationship between orality and kinetics is rarely explored as a path to disciplining (or learning) black musical ideals. It begs analysis that is no longer "premised exclusively on textuality and narrative, rather than dramaturgy, enunciation, and gesture—the pre- and anti-discursive constituents of black metacommunication" (Gilroy 1993b, 75).

All this invites critical attention to the significance of "kinesics" in African American social and musical experience. Kinesics was introduced by R. L. Birdwhistell in 1952 and rose to prominence through the early 1970s. It is an area of linguistic study that analyzes body motion and gesture, "visually sensible aspects of non-verbal interpersonal communication," and "the vocal qualifiers" that accompany kinetic activity. Gestures and motions are not thought to be instinctive human nature in this area of study, rather they are considered "learned systems" (dictionary.oed.com, s.v. "kinesic"). Kinetic orality is one of the primary ways that African Americans learn how to *feel* part of their socially constructed identities; this is through a "passionate physicality" of "syncopations and polyrhythms that assert one's somebodiness" (West 1989, 93).

Studying performances of the musical body and shared experiences uncovers the "somatic historiography," or the embodied social memory, of musical blackness. Embodied practices—including dramaturgy, gesture, and dress—can re-present, re-member, and re-perform the historical as well as the contemporary ways that class, region, ethnicity, nationality, and citizenship have shaped what it means to be "African" and "black" in American society and African American culture. This may produce a sense that musical blackness is always already there, rather than socially enacted and embodied from the earliest moments of one's life.

We can appreciate the significance of these sites of musical meaning-making by focusing attention on the conjunction of *orality and kinetics*: the flowing together of sounds, behaviors, and concepts passed down by word of mouth and invested in body language. Witnessing Jasmine and Stephanie perform the handclapping game Slide set in motion my investigation of black girls' oral-kinetic musical lessons. I wanted to discover what they can tell us about the social construction of black musical aesthetics, social identity, and even the dominant culture of popular music.

Previous musicological scholarship has called attention to the significance of African and African American children's musical performance (see Blacking 1967 [r1995]; Courlander 1963; Small 1987; Harwood, 1992, 1993; Kartomi 1991; Coplan 1994; Agawu 1995b; Campbell 1998). Ethnomusicologist John Blacking, ethnomusicologist David Coplan, and musicologist Kofi Agawu write of the ways African children learn to master everyday musical life at a young age, often as part of play among their contemporaries. Folklorist Harold Courlander writes:

> Negro children brought [to play songs] musical concepts derived from the mainstream of Negro musical tradition. They endowed the songs with a distinctive imagery, and often gave the postures and motions of the accompanying action some of the characteristics of Negro folk dancing. Responsive singing, to the accompaniment of rhythmic (often syncopated) handclapping, sometimes approximated the effects of adult game songs or church songs. (1963, 148)

Agawu, in particular, acknowledged a dialectical relationship between children's and adults' music while also noting that children's forms of music-making mirror adults more or less, though with no less complexity. "Childhood and adulthood are not separated by a firm boundary but are rather linked in a continuum. And since the child's musical language is, at least in part, an imitation of adult language, it is more accurate to say that child and adult languages are locked in a dialectic in the production, revision, and consumption of musical ideas" (Agawu 1995b, 63).

In localized contexts of African American play, game-songs constitute a crucial means by which girls learn to enact black musical interactions and social aesthetics. In learning these games, they inhabit or embody the formulas of black musical identification or stylistic expressions at a time when learning is intuitive rather than systematic, oral rather than written, and disciplined through competitive and cooperative play among peers, rather than as a set of rules defined by those outside of play. Through these games, girls learn to play with the convergence of oral-vernacular conventions from speech to song, and the "grammatical syntax" or logic of *embodied* musical language—coded gesture, movement, and dance. African American girls socially learn themselves into "popular" forms of musical blackness through ordinary social play.

Once we attend to the underexamined role of "kinetic orality"—the conjunction of orality and embodied language and meaning in black musical discourse—the role of the lived phenomenology, or subjective embodiment as musical expression, will become apparent. The use of embodiment to participate in music, and to create complex and socially produced sound textures and vocal expressions, explains why one can literally *feel* part of a phenomenology—of an experience of being musically black—not only as some imagined musical past, but as a lived musical present that refashions an "African" past to re-present a new way of being "African" in contemporary U.S. culture.

While all this sounds provocative and interesting, some readers may be unaware of the musical dimensions, as well as the kinetic orality of these games, that speak to the critical role of the body in black music-making. So let me introduce the performance practice and levels of competency at work in black girls' play. The remainder of this chapter will explore two of the three types of musical game-songs that define black girls' play— handclapping games and cheers. Double-dutch will be addressed in greater detail in subsequent chapters.

Handclapping Games

Handclapping games are the first type of embodied musical play that tends to occupy girls' attention, beginning as early as age four or five. They may be recognized as *handclaps, clapsies* (Ehrenfeld 1988), and even *cheers* by some participants (Ruqaiiyah from Detroit, interviewed March 16, 1995).

This play begins with two girls rhyming chants while accompanying themselves with a pattern of percussive sounds they create with their bodies: choreographed body percussion. The percussive embodied timbres involved include high-pitched finger-snappin' and handclappin', which articulate the backbeat on beats two and four (four beats per measure) and lower-pitched body-slappin' or pattin' upon the chest or the thighs. The combination of these embodied beats recalls earlier African American expressive practices or forms of body percussion: juba-pattin' and rhymin' in the antebellum period and *hambonin'* (from hand-bone) or *hand jive*.

Handclapping games represent the simplest form of girls' musical games. The game-song "Miss Mary Mack" is the most common hand-clapping game in the English-speaking world, and the most familiar in the black repertoire.

Roger Abrahams (1969) found variations of this game-song in Kansas (1940), Missouri (1947), North Carolina (1948), Arkansas (1949), Pennsylvania (1959), Texas (1963), Indiana (1966), and New Zealand (1959). He linked the performance to region, and did not include any information about the ethnicity of the performers. According to Abrahams, the first lines of "Mary Mack" are based on a riddle for "coffin" that has origins in English oral practices (Taylor 1951, 234, quoted in Abrahams 1969, 120). In black girls' play, "black" may be symbolically associated at some level with one's ethnic identity—dressing oneself in blackness, so to speak. As a child I often assumed that "Miss Mary Mack" referred to an older black woman like the woman of the house that I was accustomed to addressing as Miss Joanne and Miss Almeda. Meanings and ideas in handclapping games, as in any folk practice, can be read within the frame of local relationships. "Mary Mack" is one of the earliest game-songs I played in elementary school.

Within Jasmine and Stephanie's extensive repertoire of handclapping games were two contrasting versions of "Mary Mack." The first was the common version of this handclapping game-song, with its syncopated reiteration of the rhyme in each phrase:

> Miss– Ma–ry– /
> Mack Mack Mack all dressed in /
> Black Black Black with silver /
> Butt'ns Butt'ns Butt'ns all down her /
> Back Back Back . . .

The most common version of this game-song is a simple diatonic melody in a major mode featuring repetitive stepwise motion up and down the scale. The twins, however, performed a contrasting version that occurred as a diminished scale. Its lowered fifth scale degree (flat-5) suggested the blues inflections found in popular songs.

The influence of a black approach to singing or playing music, namely the blues, clearly informs the twins' second version of "Mary Mack." Though blues was not the popular music of two nine-year-olds in the mid-1990s, this version reflects the use of the blue, or "bent," pitch found in earlier and contemporary styles of vocal performance, from the blues to contemporary R&B and gospel singing.

Girls are playing with forms of pitch inflection that shape meaning, and in many cases they compose new ideas based on these formulas. This is a compelling argument for the role and power of girls' games as a vehicle for learning ideals of music and social identity, and a decent example of the ways a simple handclapping game conveys a cultural process of musical transmission in children's play.

My discussion of these melodies thus far does not begin to reveal the musical and kinesthetic relationships at work in "Mary Mack." In playing the first version, four basic gestures are performed in this order: (1) arms cross your heart, and both hands pat your chest; (2) pat your thighs; (3) clap your hands; and (4) clap alternate right or left palms with your partner. These handclapping gestures occur as eight equidistant pulses subdividing every four beats: the lyrics always begin as a pickup that anticipates the downbeat. The rhyming word at the end of each phrase is syncopated.

In the second, fourth, sixth, and eighth measures of the first version of "Mary Mack," individual claps on beats two and four serve as the backbeats for the rhymed sequence of phrase endings ("Mack," "black," "buttons," and "back"), until the last syncopated ending cadences on an offbeat. It is the embodied polyrhythmic complexity established between the narrative phrases and rhymes, and the rhythmic sequence of the percussive gestures, that engender a practical understanding of syncopation as more than a concept of accenting the unstressed beats. Girls are producing syncopation between their coordinated percussive gestures and chanting a different rhythm or beat.

In *African Rhythm and African Sensibility,* John Miller Chernoff describes how the flexible and dynamic relationships between multiple rhythms allow "different points of unity which the other rhythms share with the first rhythm." Musicians keep their time steady rather than following a stressed beat (1979, 51–52).

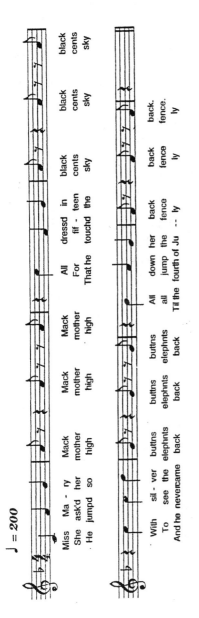

First version of twins' melody in the handclapping game-song "Mary Mack."

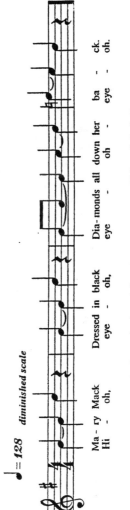

Second version of twin's melody in the handclapping game-song "Mary Mack."

The emergent relationship between the body and the voice produces syncopation as a process of setting up and disrupting rhythmic expectations in a linguistic manner, like embodied poetics; the patterns of clapping gestures that accompany any rhyme or game-song are inseparable from, and integral to, understanding its musical structure. Even the high and lower-pitched timbres of the percussive gestures help shape one's sense of what syncopation is, and how it can be articulated effectively.

There is another version of body-patting to "Mary Mack" that I participated in as a child. It involved a slightly different set of body-patting gestures (including patting your chest in a "cross your heart" manner, and patting your thighs) in a different combination against the lyrics. In another case, the same combination of percussive handclapping gestures found in "Mary Mack" accompanies the game-song "Miss Lucy," known for its flirtatious linguistic play with "dirty" words and reference to sexualized body parts. The gestures that are foregrounded when the chant breaks are underlined in the following example to highlight changes in the relationship between the cadence of the chant and the handclapping patterns. This game-song begins with onomatopoeic words that sound like the opening movements across the chest and down to the thighs: the players are describing what they are doing while they do it. The fourth type of percussive gesture is created between the right ("pat-r") or left ("pat-l") hands of the two partners.

1	Cross	down	Miss	Lu-	cy	had	a	ba-
	chest	*thighs*	*clap*	pat-r	*clap*	pat-l	*clap*	pat-r
pulse orientation:	6	7	8	1	2	3	4	5
2	-by		His	name	was	Ti-	ny	Tim
	chest	*thighs*	*clap*	pat-r	*clap*	pat-l	*clap*	pat-r
	6	7	8	1	2	3	4	5
3			She	put	him	in	the	bath-
	chest	*thighs*	*clap*	pat-r	*clap*	pat-l	*clap*	pat-r
	6	7	8	1	2	3	4	5
4	tub		To	see	if	he	could	swim
	chest	*thighs*	*clap*	pat-r	*clap*	pat-l	*clap*	pat-r
	6	7	8	1	2	3	4	5
5	Cross	down	be-	hind	the	el-	e-	va-
	chest	*thighs*	*clap*	pat-r	*clap*	pat-l	*clap*	pat-r
	6	7	8	1	2	3	4	5
6	-tor		There	was	a	piece	of	glass
	chest	*thighs*	*clap*	pat-r	*clap*	pat-l	*clap*	pat-r
	6	7	8	1	2	3	4	5

Line	1	2	3	4	5	6	7	8	9
7			Miss	Lu-	cy	fell	up-	on	
	chest	*thighs*	*clap*	*pat-r*	*clap*	*pat-l*	*clap*	*pat-r*	
	6	7	8	1	2	3	4	5	
8	it	and	it	went	straight	up	her		
	chest	*thighs*	*clap*	*pat-r*	*clap*	*pat-l*	*clap*		
	6	7	8	1	2	3	4		
9	Ask	me	no	more	que-	stions			
	pat-r	*clap*	*pat-l*	*clap*	*pat-r*	*chest*	*thighs*		
	1	2	3	4	5	6	7		
10	I'll	tell	you	no	more	lies			
	clap	*pat-r*	*clap*	*pat-l*	*clap*	*pat-r*	*chest*	*thighs*	
	8	1	2	3	4	5	6	7	
11	The	boys	are	in	the	bath-	room		
	clap	*pat-r*	*clap*	*pat-l*	*clap*	*pat-r*	*chest*	*thighs*	*clap*
	8	1	2	3	4	5	6	7	8
12	Pull-	ing	down	their					
	pat-r	*clap*	*pat-l*	*clap*					
	1	2	3	4					
13	Fly	me	up	to	hea-	ven			
	pat-r	*clap*	*pat-l*	*clap*	*pat-r*	*chest*	*thighs*	*clap*	
	1	2	3	4	5	6	7	8	
14	*Fly*	*me*	*to*	*the*	*moon*			*The*	
	pat-r	*clap*	*pat-l*	*clap*	*pat-r*	*chest*	*thighs*	*clap*	
	1	2	3	4	5	6	7	8	

[and so on . . .]

Timbre (the quality or difference between sounds), and a relative sense of the highness and lowness of the pitches created from the gestures, accent or stress certain beats in the flow of the chant. The chest slaps vibrate the cavity above the breast, hinting at a bass-sounding drum as the lowest sound created by the gestures in "Miss Lucy." The shared pats between right or left palms occupy a mid-range, and the individual claps are akin to a treble or snare-drum sound. A kinesthetic syntax of sounds emerges, which articulates a sense of quadruple meter and inflects a sense of syncopation throughout the game-songs.

As in all the game-songs discussed, the syllables are expressed on equidistant pulses, but the breaks or pauses in the verbal part are often filled with the patting of thighs (line 2), or other patterns of patting or clapping (compare lines 1–4 with 7–10). By line 9, following the first play on meaning away from the use of a "bad" word ("and it went straight up her . . . Ask me no more questions"), there is a distinct shift in placement of the "cross down" chest-patting gestures from the beginning of the phrase in lines 1–4, to the end of the phrase in lines 9–11, where the gesture serves as a cadence, or punctuation, at the ends of lyrical phrases and ideas ("Tell me no more lies"). This re-orients the shape or feel of the musical expression to fit the linguistic and cadential needs of the verse and narrative.

While these embodied expressions punctuate the linguistic meaning of provocative phrases, their presence also suggests that black girls are learning how to play with multiple and different orientations to time, which precipitates a strong sense of maintaining a steady pulse, and being able to accommodate polyrhythm and polymeter above that pulse orientation.

In the 1950s, folklorist Harold Courlander documented several game-songs also known as "play-party songs," including "Mary Mack," "Sally Walters" (a handclapping version of the ring game "Little Sally Walker"), and "See See Rider," among the best-known African American singing games in western Alabama. All live on in the realm of adult popular music. "See See Rider" (aka "C. C. Rider") lives on as a popular folk lyric that has been sung by a range of folk, popular, and blues artists (including one of my favorite versions by the black, female a cappella group Sweet Honey in the Rock). "C. C. Rider" has been recorded almost 200 times. Among those who performed it were Ma Rainey, Leadbelly, Big Bill Broonzy, Chuck Berry, King Curtis, Ray Charles, Wayne Newton, The Everly Brothers, Dakota Staton, Joe Sample, The Grateful Dead, and Jewel. "Little Sally Water" also appeared as a popular recording by the nine-piece house band known as the Savoy Sultans at the Savoy Ballroom in 1938. And "Mary Mack" became the basis of a song called "Walkin' the Dog" by Rufus Thomas in 1963.

The lyrics of the musical games black girls play circulate between the dominant three types of play found in girls' games. For example, the lyric and melody of "Mary Mack" occur as a handclapping game-song and as a jump rope chant. Additionally, these same lyrics and melodies operate within a wider musical system that includes the blues and other styles of popular music typically associated with adults.

The partner style of handclapping, with only two girls, gradually expands to a type of handclapping game known as "bridges." The most popularly known handclapping bridge is "Tweedle deedle dee," based on the melody and lyrics of "Rockin' Robin," Michael Jackson's first hit single as a solo artist, and his first departure, in 1971, from the Jackson Five on Motown Records.

All around the periphery of the American Double Dutch League Competition girls spontaneously share a moment of play including the handclapping bridge "Rockin' Robin," performed inside the local arena where the competition took place in North Charleston, South Carolina, in the summer of 1995.

"Rockin' Robin" was a cover of the 1956 single sung by African American R&B artist Bobby O'Day. Michael's version sent his spectacular singing and James Brown–like stage presence soaring among his teenage fans (of which I was one, at the age of thirteen, growing up in Rockville, Maryland). My cousins and I played the game "Mystery Date" with the Jackson Brothers in mind: Michael was a "dream," and Jackie and Tito were "duds."

Jackson's version featured a guitar solo reminiscent of Chuck Berry on Chess Records, and other "rock 'n' roll" guitarists of the 1940s and '50s, reflecting the regeneration of earlier R&B instrumentals in the youth-oriented, backbeat-driven sounds of Motown since the mid-1960s. While black girls in the mid- to late 1990s performed a translocal expression of black popular culture shared across regions, they also (re-)performed and (re-)embodied the kinetic orality of a social musical blackness marshaled from the 1970s era of integration and black power (and even further back, the 1950s era of a segregated black past).

Young girls at play are unaware that they are socially performing the embodied memories of a black musical past, but this explains the sub-conscious links between the generations of youth, and between youth and adults, over time. Paul Gilroy says that there are particular elements of narrative rituals and musical performance that serve a mnemonic func-tion in black expressive cultures, and that direct "the consciousness of the group back to significant, nodal points in its common history and its so-cial memory. The telling and retelling of these stories plays a special role, organising the consciousness of the 'racial' group socially and striking the important balance between inside and outside activity—the different practices, cognitive, habitual, and performative, that are required to in-vent, maintain, and renew identity" (Gilroy 1993b, 198).

In other words, girls are telling stories through their embodied play: dramatizing the "infinite process of [African American and black musi-cal] identity construction" (ibid., 223) by practicing and performing the mnemonic rituals of a kinetic orality; this represents "a non-traditional tradition, an irreducibly modern, ex-centric, unstable, and asymmetrical cultural ensemble . . . [that even as] an adjunct to the sale of black popu-lar music . . . [forms] a direct relationship between the community of lis-teners . . . [and] the living memory of the changing same" (ibid., 198).

Gilroy identifies music as the most important locus of ethnic identity construction or play. He particularly emphasizes the ritual practices of call-and-response as a primary vehicle in the formation of individual and group-related identities where "the performer dissolves into the crowd" (ibid., 200).

Extending Gilroy's line of thinking to my interest in the role of the body and kinetic orality in the social construction of a hegemonic and gendered musical blackness among African Americans, embodied ver-nacular practices like handclapping bridges publicly ritualize social mem-ory as a somatic musical history that nurtures "a caste of performers [and listeners] capable of dramatizing" key rituals that engender an embodied feeling of group solidarity. These games are an example of "the identity-giving model of democracy/community that has become the valuable in-tersubjective resource that [Gilroy calls] the ethics of antiphony" (ibid.).

By examining the musical activities and connections involved in the games black girls play, we begin to appreciate how an African American or black musical identity is repeatedly being socially constituted, subjec-tively embodied, and communally performed into being, within gendered contexts that contribute to a black and alternative public sphere—a black popular musical culture that lives in- and outside of the commercial realm, and begins at a very young age.

I encountered another case of a handclapping bridge exemplifying this socially embodied process while doing some consulting at the Harlem PAL Center on October 18, 1999. The PAL (Police Athletic League) patrolled and assisted in the regulation of children's play in New York City from the early 1900s through at least the 1970s, when double-dutch was instituted as a sport by a couple of Harlem police officers. By the time of my visit in 1999, the five PAL centers located in Manhattan and the Bronx were no longer affiliated with the NYPD. Whether by coincidence or a remnant of their past affiliation, however, these centers are in close proximity to existing precincts.

In my capacity as an educational consultant for children's programming at TV station WGBH-Boston, the producers enlisted me to find some girls playing games in New York City, to be featured in segments for the debut season of a new series called *Between the Lions,* slated to begin airing in April 2000. The mission of the series, which emulated the fun-filled lessons of *The Electric Company,* was to teach literacy to kids aged three to seven. The innovation of the show was the merging of two approaches to teaching literacy that schoolteachers often pitted against one another: whole language and phonics. The producers wanted me to locate chants that featured the words *star, dream, hen, cap, man, chap,* and *trick,* or any parts of these words.

After surveying the girls present at the Harlem PAL's after-school program, we created quite a stir by inviting five or six eight- and nine-year-old girls to run through their repertoire of games for the new television show. But I soon realized that the short, vowel-sound words highlighted in the target words were not showing up in the games these black girls tended to play, nor any I could think of.

As is the case in other forms of musical expression, black girls' games tend to favor combinations of words and phonics that feature dramatically contrasting timbres in their chants, songs, and even their everyday colloquialisms. These performances may emphasize various linguistic events modified by musical effects: (1) *hard or bright vowels* with an undulating pitch (the "a" sound in the elongated exclaimed affirmation "Hey—!"); (2) *diphthongs,* or a *melismatic range of sounds in a single syllable* that may or may not ordinarily be present in standard pronunciation ("He's fine" becomes an elongated "He's so faw-een!"); and (3) the percussive and rhythmic accentuation of initial and final consonants

("What's up, girl" or "Cute, cute, cute, too cute"). The short vowel sounds found in the target words we sought for the producers that day were absent (dream, hen, cap, and chap).

In an attempt to salvage the afternoon, I, along with Vinny Straggas, the coordinator directing the shoot, selected a couple of the girls to make up chants using the words *star, trick,* or *man.* Girls do "compose" or add, interchange, and revise elements of their chants in the sense of the extemporizing, versioning, localizing, and borrowing that takes place in any oral practice and tradition. But this ordinarily happens spontaneously, not on demand. After several tries, the girls came up with corny formulas that sounded and looked inauthentic, and they were quickly losing interest. The lure of being on TV was fading behind our attempts to orchestrate a good shoot.

As I stood outside with the all-white camera crew, pondering whether I should teach the girls a song featuring one of the target words—the chorus to the popular song "Shining Star" by Earth, Wind, and Fire would do ("You're a shining star / No matter who you are")—a middle-aged black man in an aging van passed by the street corner. He sat watching at a red light at the corner of West 114th Street and Manhattan Avenue, and when the light turned green, he peeled off, pointing his words at me as if on a drive-by shooting: "You're selling our *culture* to the white man!"

WGBH may have been able to afford to pay royalties for "Shining Star," but would it still be a black girls' game? Though I was still a black girl, in the communal sense shared by women, would my intervention as an adult and a scholar working with a white camera crew and a predominantly white production staff at WGBH change things? The members of the camera crew either ignored the driver's remark, or perhaps never heard it, since it wasn't targeted at them. I turned my focus back to the girls, and five of them were in a circle surrounded by cameras and a sound boom, occupying the smallest area of a humongous fenced-in black-topped playground.

"Lights, camera, action!" The girls began chanting the lyrics and melody of the opening lines of "Candy Girl." I recognized the song immediately and was titillated at discovering a game-song that showed a relationship between recent popular music culture and the ongoing tradition of creating girls' games from it as a resource.

The girls patted hands with the girl to either side of them, creating an alternating current of contact around the circle. I was witnessing one of the latest bridges based on the early 1980s "bubblegum soul" of the group New Edition. This game would have preceded these eight- and nine-year-old girls by ten years: they were born in 1991 and 1992. ("Candy Girl" was New Edition's first hit single, and it became the title of their first album released in 1983.)

New Edition was promoted as the Jackson Five of the eighties. Its members, Bobby Brown, Ralph Tresvant, Michael Bivens, Ronnie DeVoe, Ricky Bell—and later, Johnny Gill—became one of the most popular groups appealing to the youth market, and as solo artists and splinter groups, they contributed to the fusion of hip-hop and R&B/funk known as "new jack swing" in the early 1990s. Bobby Brown was the first to leave, with his popular hit "My Prerogative." The group Bell Biv DeVoe (Ricky Bell, Michael Bivens, and Ronnie DeVoe) rose to fame as a spin-off group, with their 1990 breakaway hit "Poison" ("Never Trust a Big Butt and a Smile"). "Poison," from the album of the same name, reflected the misogynist lyrics and lyrical refrains that became increasingly popular in mass-mediated R&B and rap, as well as underground hip-hop, during the early 1990s.

The girls' handclapping, bridge version of "Candy Girl" highlighted the borrowing of popular dances from the recent past: it featured the Jamaican Pepperseed, marked by the alternating movements of the torso from left to right on *one two three and* (hold) *four / one two three and* (hold) *four*. With arms spread out to the side, the movements of the torso on *one two three and* (hold) *four* transferred wavy currents of motion from one arm to the other, causing the arms to look and feel like they were treading water. The game featured the late 1980s dance the Running Man, popularized by bad boy Bobby Brown of New Edition. This dance involved the funky locomotion of lunging forward on alternate feet while thrusting your chest out and pulling your fists back by your sides. The dance was all about the subdivided timing of strides marking the offbeats between *one and two* and *three and four,* while your feet executed a sliding action and a slight scuffling sound after each forward lunge, emulating a running man (or woman).

I recognized one other dance within the formulas of "Candy Girl": the Fight from the early 1980s, which accompanied a chant about Mike Tyson. It involved mimicking a flurry of jabs, hooks, and punches timed to the downbeats of the music, and I often deployed it when I was on the dance floor at a club or a party with a guy who was getting too friendly —too close for comfort. (These were the guys that wanted to turn even a fast song into an intimate slow dance or a grind.)

The girls had fit these three dances, and others, into the kinetic orality accompanying the lyrics. They repeated the game-song for the camera.

> Can-dy Girl / You <u>are</u>- my world
> Look- so sweet / <u>Spe</u>-cial treat

Following this was a section of show-and-tell, an embodied call-and-response of a sort, where the conjunction between word and the body, between individuals and the collective, became apparent. As they sang of doing the Janet Jackson, they danced the Pepperseed. As they sang of doing the Mike Tyson, they did the Fight. As they sang of doing the Bobby Brown, they did the Running Man.

> This the way you do— the Janet // Jackson ["Pepperseed"]
> This the way you do— the Mike // Tyson ["the Fight"]
> This the way you do— the Bobby // Brown ["the Running Man"]

Calling out the names of prominent African American stars that they would have been familiar with as popular icons in the media, the girls dramatized a salient feature of these figures' personas, or image, through kinetic orality. One could assert that the girls were performing the communal discourse, as well as a musical grapevine of blackness, through the body and their in-body formulas.

Traditional African American children's games revolve around dance, and its influence can be seen in almost all physical activities. Song and dance are an integral part of storytelling, for example. Cheerleading becomes dance, double-dutch rope jumping becomes dance, and so do the agile exertions of athletes from the end-zone to the hoop. Play serves as the training for performance. Through interaction, we learn fair play. That is, we learn the ethics of a culture and we learn to identify good play, which is similar to learning how to recognize good performance. The determining factors have to do with personal creativity, styling, and aesthetics. Thus, play becomes performance (Malone 1996 in Caponi 1999, 226).

The expressive interplay, the intertextuality of musical sound and motion, and their dramatic or theatrical embodied musical play, mirror popular culture, music television, and the composition of popular songs that tap into a community of listeners and a body of black vernacular traditions. I watched those Harlem girls on the playground at West 114th and

Manhattan Avenue revel in the synesthesia of communal memory and musicalized drama that comments on the contemporary and the past, and gives life to a black sense of musical identity.

George Lipsitz, a scholar specializing in American studies, once critiqued British sociologist Simon Frith for understating the importance of musical and historical traditions inspired by black music in the construction of rock 'n' roll and American popular music in general.

According to Frith, black music's popularity depends on its "immediate and democratic" nature, which he claims means that listeners "need no special training or knowledge to appreciate it," because "the qualities that are valued in spontaneous music-making are emotional rather than technical" (Frith 1981, 16–17, quoted in Lipsitz 1990, 106).

Girls' musical games offer empirical evidence of the "special training" to appreciate black music that leads to the "immediate and democratic" feeling of black music. As Lipsitz writes further:

> Children's rhyming games provided the lyrics for Lee Dorsey's 1961 "Ya Ya" and Shirley Ellis's 1964 "The Name Game" and 1965 "Rubber Dolly." Cheerleaders at a football game in Florida yelling "Our team is red hot, your team ain't doodley squat" gave Billie Emerson the inspiration for his 1955 hit "Red Hot," a song covered a year later by rockabilly artist Billy Lee Riley. Bo Diddley's 1959 "Say Man" and "Say Man, Back Again" drew upon the street-corner insult game, the dozens. . . . Songs with references to familiar folk tales and sagas or to everyday speech or street-corner games tended to include listeners in a community of improvisation and elaboration. The songs came from life and easily blended back into it. As members of the audience [or black communities] remembered and repeated, they ritualistically confirmed the commonality of everyday experience . . . These folk retentions survived because of their appeal as narratives, but also because they marshaled the resources of the past as part of defining identity in the present. (Ibid., 114–15)

It is the orally as well as kinetically transmitted resources found in girls' games that "educate" listeners and dancers into a "technical" knowledge of black music-making and black musical aesthetics, as well as the social construction of a black musical identity. While Lipsitz stated that "the presence of sedimented historical currents within [recorded] popular culture illumines the paradoxical relationship between history and commercialized leisure" (1990, 5), it is the embodied "media" found in black girls' games, not an electronic mass media, that interests me. This is the media that shapes a relationship between history or collective memory and African American musical identity relative to the social construction of a musical blackness.

Cheers

Cheers are the second type of play that occupies girls' musical and social play. They are also known as "scolds" in Memphis, and in urban centers like Philadelphia, as "steps." The latter links the practice of cheers to a competitive tradition of group identity, known as "stepping," that was practiced by black, Greek-lettered fraternity and sorority members throughout much of the twentieth century. It involves creating in-body formulas that represent the unique identity of each group, by sampling and re-composing aspects of black vernacular style and expression as well as moments of popular recorded song from gospel to hip-hop, from preaching to playing the Dozens. Competing groups try to outdo one another by choreographing a funky routine of embodied percussive beats and chants, collectively enacted by the group that names individual members, while also signifying their unique group identity (i.e., individuality within collectivity). Stepping began at predominantly white universities, where many of these black "Greek" organizations exist, as well as at historically black universities and colleges (HBCUs).

This practice occurs with several girls gathered in a circle or a row, reminiscent of ring games like Little Sally Walker. Together, the girls synchronize their individual performances of percussive choreography—based on a more polyrhythmic and multi-limbed sequence of hand-clapping gestures, thigh-slapping, and foot-stomping. While cheers and handclapping games share percussive gestures, cheers feature a greater degree of difficulty relative to physical coordination and musical expression.

In performing cheers, girls must learn to create the embodied percussion of the gestures separately; there is little or no contact with others to produce percussive sounds and gestures, as was the case in handclapping games. In order to transition from performing handclapping games to cheers, girls must learn to navigate a sea of embodied sounds they had initially produced in tandem with another person and move to perform individually, yet collectively, in concert with others, rhythmically.

Who keeps the beat among the crew? Who synchronizes the timing of their collective gestures and moves to avoid cacophony and disarray? Everyone keeps the beat simultaneously, and no one person, per se, conducts the music-making. This is one of the earliest examples of the development of the so-called *metronome sense* frequently alluded to in musicological literature about African and African American aesthetics.

A metronome is a small, clockwork-driven, mechanical device used by classically trained musicians to establish and maintain musical tempo during their individual practice sessions. A. M. Jones (from 1930s to 1960s) and Richard Waterman (1952) were the first researchers to postulate the structure of this concept and the inner experience, respectively (Kubik 1998). Some African American musicians detect the absence of an internal rhythmic sensibility when they hear a "stiff" maintenance of a metronomic sense of the beat. Deborah Wong discusses this as the "hearing of race" by African American musicians in jazz or the "racialized conditioning of bodily and musical behavior," particularly among non–African American musicians (Wong 2000, 71).

Following my interactions with the twins, Stephanie and Jasmine, I learned and collected a few handclapping games and cheers in the summer of 1995 from a group of black and biracial girls (ages 10–15) participating in a summer writing workshop for current or formerly homeless girls and boys. The program was held at Community High School in Ann Arbor, Michigan. And because boys were constantly lurking around when the girls were demonstrating their games during recess, this site elicited some interesting observations about female–male relations, in what often resembled scenes from commercial popular culture in reverse (i.e., boys dancing to the rhythms created by the girls' play).

One of the games I most enjoyed learning at Community High was a cheer performed by Tomika and Laura (ages 10 and 11) that began "OO-lay, OO-lay / na-OO-tay / Stay back that's me," and culminated with an antagonistic call-and-response: Call: "Oo! She thinks she bad." Response: "Baby, baby, don't get me mad." This game-song initially reminded me of an African timeline, with its pulse orientation through phonic manipulations of assonance (the long vowel "oo"). Later that year, as I mentioned earlier, I happened upon a variant of the same cheer performed by my cousin's daughter, Arielle (age 10). Arielle grew up on an Air Force base in Denver, Colorado, a region influenced by Mexican heritage. And her version may reflect an adoption of Hispanic local practice or may parody it (*Oo-lay* in Tomika's version was pronounced *Oh-la* in Arielle's). Arielle learned her version from her membership on a cheerleading squad in junior high school ("O-la, O-la / Now who thinks they're bad!").

Arielle's version seemed less sophisticated and less complex, not as "funky" as the body of musical games I participated in and observed during my upbringing and research in black settings. Though the rhythm of the vocal dimension was initially the same, there are key differences between the two versions. Tomika's emphasizes more of the ideals associated with musical blackness. Here is a list of specific events that signal this difference:

1. the prominence of hard versus soft vowel sounds (oo-lay vs. o-la);
2. the prominence of diphthongs ("lay") mirroring a kaleidoscopic ideal of sound found in black music; the presence of nonverbal expression ("na-OO-tay" rather than "now who thinks");
3. the internal complexity of rhyming within a phrase that suggested the syncopated delights of polyrhythm and polymeter. In Tomika's version, a seven-beat phrase occurs with the iterations of "OO-lay" plus a nine-beat phrase of linear polyrhythms occurs to the end of the refrain "na-OO-tay / stay back that's me";
4. the strong cyclic feel or sense of a groove, which is not present in Arielle's version; and
5. the filling in of space at the end of refrain ("stay back that's me") that mirrors the percussive fills of a musical break found in blues, funk, or hip-hop.

All these exemplify ideals of black musical sound in various ways. All of these sub-intentional events suggest a richer musical complexity, and a more rigorous kinesthetic experience in Tomika's version. (See figure 1 on page 33).

Cheers offer a more polyphonically-embodied percussion that involves all four limbs, creating additional timbres from finger-snapping, hand-clapping, thigh-slapping, and foot-stomping. They tend to feature more syncopation, swinging of the beat, and rhymed linguistic play, facilitating a competitive nature within such play (more of an emphasis on individuality within collectivity). The fun of performing cheers is the synchronization of voiced chants and the uniformity of embodiment, signaling a

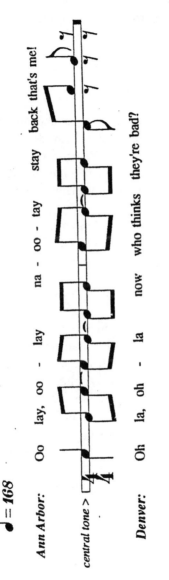

♩ = 168

Ann Arbor: Oo lay, oo - lay na - oo - tay stay back that's me!

central tone >

Denver: Oh la, oh - la now who thinks they're bad?

Comparison of OO-lay version by Tomika (Ann Arbor) and Oh-la version by Arielle (Denver).

team or group effort, even while many cheers internally feature antagonistic narratives of self-assertion within the group, often through call-and-response structures. All of this becomes apparent in the act of naming the self, and claiming to share a group identity that is black and female.

"Jig-a-low" and Michael Jackson

"Jig-a-low" is a cheer I learned from Jasmine and Stephanie that reveals a different aspect of the relationship between girls' games and popular songs by male artists. In this case, the artist is the young, emerging soloist Michael Jackson. And the aspect highlighted here concerns the use of kinetic orality, or transmissions of movement or motion that are used to key into an older dance.

Michael Jackson is referenced in other girls' games, directly and indirectly. His aura as a teenage idol is signified in the handclapping bridge called "Tweedle deedle dee" (involving four players), which is based on "Rockin' Robin" (performed by Michael Jackson in 1971). This was not the first incarnation of this song; R&B artist Bobby O'Day originally performed it in the 1950s.

The expression "jig-a-low," which sonically resembles the word "gigolo," features call-and-response between two or more girls, with opportunities for each player to "do their thang": show off their individual dancing and identity. I imagine that the "jig" in "jig-a-low" refers to dancing, or perhaps even "getting down," in its colloquial meaning in black dance. Definitions of "jig" in the *Merriam Webster's Collegiate Dictionary* include "to move with rapid jerky motions," and "to dance in a rapid lively manner of a jig" (1999). These meanings are not lost here.

Note the lyrics of the latter part of the game-song, which describe the action that accompanies how to "jig-a-low":

> *Well, my hands up high / My feet down low*
> *And this the way I jig-a-low*
> *Well, her hands up high / Her feet down low*
> *And that's the way she jig-a-low*
> Refrain:
> *Jig-a-low / Jig-jig-a-low*
> [repeat the refrain until the next girl introduces herself]

Simple claps on beats two and four accompany the refrain, while the call-and-response sections lack any significant body-slapping, clapping, or finger-snapping. In that sense, this is an unusual cheer. But movement is not lacking here: dance or dancelike gestures are privileged in this game-song, following its name.

In introducing herself, each player inserts her name into a scripted verse of call-and-response, in dialogue with the other girls (one or more) playing the game. In the table below, you will find (line-by-line from left to right) a representation of the patterns of call-and-response unison chanting shared by Jasmine and Stephanie, and the exchange of their roles as they are executed throughout the performance (from caller to responder, or vice versa).

This cheer actually explores contemporary "street" dance styles. When I first observed this game-song between the twins—Jasmine and Stephanie's performance of the then-popular dance I had participated in, in Detroit nightclubs and house parties, and had witnessed on the locally televised, black dance show—it was striking. It was particularly prominent on Detroit's televised *New Dance Show,* which featured local African American teens and young adults dancing in their hottest club attire to the latest hits and re-mixes. (Local dance culture in Detroit is distinguished by a fast-paced, thump-oriented music known as "bass," which originated as a style in Miami.)

At that time, I wasn't familiar with the name of the dance. Though it was easy to recognize, it was performed to the name of an earlier dance, the Robot. The juxtaposition of a popular 1970s dance and a popular 1990s dance suggests both continuity and change in a curious way: while the name was orally transmitted, the dance was not. Instead, the latest style replaced the out-of-style dance practice.

Assuming that the term is actually a remnant of the former style of dance, the use of a contemporary style evident in the Detroit area, alongside the verbal articulation of a formerly popular dance, the Robot, also suggests that its contemporary practitioners adapted the movements and dance found in "Jig-a-low," making them suitable to the present. Girls create variations within their orally and kinetically transmitted texts that reflect both the past and the present, embodying a social memory of black style.

The Robot was the national dance craze of my youth, and I remember watching Damita Jo Freeman, a popular *Soul Train* dancer, skillfully perform the moves every week, often to the sounds of "Dancing Machine," by the Jackson Five (1973).

TABLE I *"Jig-a-low": Call-and-Response Structure (see Appendix, Ex. 2)*

Line nos.	Call	Unison	Response
		Refrain	
1		Jig- a-low-, jig- jig-a-low-	
2		Jig- a-low-, jig- jig-a-low-	
Part 1			
3	Jasmine: Hey *Stephanie*!		Stephanie: Say *what*?
4	J: In-tro*duce* yourself!		S: Know *what*?
5	Jasmine: In-tro*duce* yourself!		Stephanie: OK!
6	Stephanie:	[They exchange roles here]	
	My name is *Ste*-phanie		Jasmine: Yeah!
7	S: I got the *mu*-scle		J: Yeah!
8	S: To do the *hu*-stle		J: Yeah!
9	S: I do my *thang*		J: Yeah!
10	S: On the video *screen*		J: Yeah!
11	S: *I do the*		*J: She do the*
	ro-, ro, ro-, ro-,		*ro-, ro, ro-, ro-*
	ro-bot [punctuates each		*ro-bot [Jasmine imitates*
	syllable with Do Do Brown]		*Stephanie's version of the*
			dance]
		Refrain	
12		Jig- a-low-, jig- jig-a-low-	
13		Jig- a-low-, jig- jig-a-low-	
Part 2			
14	S: Hey *Jasmine*!		J: Hey *what*?
15	S: Are you *ready*?		J: To *what*?
16	S: To *jig*?		J: Jig-a-low?
17		Jig *what*?	
18			Stephanie: A-*low*
19	Jasmine: Well-,	[Exchanged roles again]	Stephanie: Well-,
	My *hands* up high my		my *hands* up high my
	feet down low and		*feet* down low and
	THIS's the way I		*THIS's* the way she
	jig-a-low		*jig-a-low*
	[Jasmine creates a		[Stephanie mimics
	stylized move on "THIS's"]		Jasmine's stylized
			move on "THIS's"]
		Refrain	
20		Jig- a-low-, jig- jig-a-low-	
21		Jig- a-low-, jig- jig-a-low-	

The Robot featured the funky mechanization of the dancing body to signify a collective response, not only to the driving force of funk and soul music, but also the mechanical (assembly line) practices and technological innovations that were emerging in labor, science, and the science fiction of the day. More than any other black social dance practiced by both women and men, the Robot was concurrent with, if not a precursor to, emergent styles of dance associated with rap and hip-hop culture (most notably the art of *popping, locking,* and *pop-lock* dancing often associated with popper Fred Berry, aka Rerun, of the black television show *What's Happening*).

The actual dance that Jasmine and Stephanie performed in place of the Robot in "Jig-a-low," was the Do Do Brown. This dance involved a rapid locomotive action, popping one's pelvis or booty, back and forth—a style of movement my former jazz dance instructor called a "funky backer and a funky upper" (referring to the alternation of pelvic thrusts, or torso contractions, back and forth). It accompanied the song from which its name was taken: "C'mon Babe [Do Do Brown Version]," recorded by Miami-based entrepreneur Luther Campbell (aka Luke Skywalker) and his *Banned in the U.S.A.* (1990) by 2 Live Crew (*All Music Guide,* http://allmusic.com, accessed May 7, 2003). The style of music to which this song "Do Do Brown" belongs has many labels, including *Southern rap, party rap, dirty rap, bass music, booty music, a booty phat classic, a club re-mix classic,* and *a strip club classic.* It remained a classic in clubs for over a decade, from 1989 to 2002 (www.allmusic.com). The alternating pelvic thrusts and torso contractions occurred every eighth-note pulse in the fast-moving tempo of "Do Do Brown" (130 beats per minute or more) (see Luther Campbell's website at unclelukesworld.com/about.htm).

Because of the accentuated, popping action of the booty, females were primarily associated with this dance, though men performed it as well. This association explains the name of the style or genre of this music: "booty" or "bass" music. In this case, "bass" doubly signifies the *low end* of the body, particularly black women's bodies, and the aesthetic ideals of feeling and emphasizing the *low end* frequencies of the music.

Unlike the interconnections between old and new songs and games found in "Down, down baby," "Jig-a-low" demonstrates oral and kinetic interrelationships between black popular social dancing and the rhetoric about the performance of musical embodiment ("I do my thang / On the video screen"). Connections to hip-hop are still evident, and an interplay between the sexes is still at work. In this case, there is a connection between social dances that may signify conventional sex roles in popular culture. For females, it may be signifying their dominant (or subordinate) role as dancers in hip-hop videos, which were receiving a great deal of critical and negative attention in the mid-1990s, when Jasmine and Stephanie were playing this game. For males, the music referenced "bass" or "booty" music sung by male artists, and the idea that female fans responded to their voices suggests a patriarchal control over women's bodies through music.

Actually, the performance of "Jig-a-low" involves learning to master styles of embodiment and social interaction (i.e., delivering call-and-response effectively). It highlights an example of "auto-sexuality" (Miller 1991) in girls' play, where the performance is an expression for themselves, by themselves. It is explicitly about the gaze of men, but it does involve mastering styles of movement and gesture—what might be considered sexual or erotic display. Whether the serpentine wiggle or the jig-a-low, there are issues of sex identity, gender relations, and embodied significations that are suggestive of, but do not explicitly allude to, sexual behavior and erotic gesture. These are entwined in a deeper understanding of the power of black music across time and space. Such information tells us more about the power of the popular than we care to know, or are able to unravel, because it requires a subjective involvement in the social and embodied memory of black music and dance.

Whether girls are conscious of it or not, "Jig-a-low" is linked to the historical popularity of the song "Dancing Machine," the dance the Robot, and the rising star of Michael Jackson, when his popularity in the black community exceeded his popularity in the mainstream by a nose (pun intended). "Jig-a-low" is linked to black girls' fascination with boy singers, like Jackson, as teen idols; linked to youthful trends in black dance, and girls' significant participation in it; linked to girls' imitations of mediated black popular culture "on the video screen," from the Supremes to doing the Robot, as I once did.

As an only child with few social outlets, I learned the dance from watching Jackson perform it on *American Bandstand, Soul Train,* awards shows, and his appearance with his brothers on late-night variety shows. Obviously, this transmission was not limited to black television sets. Others also imitated his dances through this medium, but the larger social framework of living with African American people, values, and simply desiring to learn how to be African American, made a world of difference in the quality and meaning of what I learned, as opposed to what non-blacks gained from it.

Most sports spectators define cheers as a sideline activity, where a girl stands by her man giving his all on the field. But the performance and participation in cheers does not begin on the playing field with boys. It begins within the sphere of neighborhood, same-sex play. Girls use cheers to broadcast their local identities to themselves first, and later to boys on and off the playing field, in the name of heterosexual courting. The "get bad in a minute" cheer, from my younger days, was part of the everyday practice of girls in my neighborhood back when it was cool—sexy even —to talk about being "bad" without actually being so, or needing to be delinquent to prove it. A little embodied defiance was enough.

Later we transplanted this cheer, bringing some musical life to an otherwise square cheerleading squad, once integration was accepted on our cheerleading squad in high school in the late 1970s. In the segregated recreational football league, we black girls chanted and tossed our hips, not only to represent black female agency in the public sphere, but also to represent black group identity in the lingering experience of racial segregation in our "All-American City" of Rockville, Maryland. In high school, I was not a cheerleader. That was too visible for me. But many of my black girlfriends at school were. There, they represented the black race and us. It would have been misleading to think the black girls on the squad were there merely to be near the boys—black or white. Black girls were representing their own multiple and often contradictory identifications with race, gender, and power, representing their power and identifications through their bodies. But they did it through a socially significant, culturally embodied politics of musical blackness and black empowerment that was mistaken for mere sideline fun in a predominantly white environment.

Through the rhythmic and timbral patterns created from handclapping and finger-popping, body-patting and foot-stomping, jumping and dancing, all three types of play—handclapping games, cheers, and double-dutch—operate within the everyday musical landscapes of language, rhythm, sound, and gesture of black female experience. One also finds games based on commercial jingles, for instance. I remember a complicated combination of percussive gestures too difficult to transcribe. There are a few key gestures that any player would recognize as a symbol of this choreography. The cyclic pattern of more than eight gestures begins with each player holding her palms together while slapping the backside of each other's hands together. This leads to a climbing-a-ladder action, created through an alternating series of clasps between their right and left hands, moving from low to high. This choreography accompanied the popular 1970s jingle for Oreo cookies:

> Do you know exactly how to eat an Oreo
> Well to do it

You unscrew it
Very fast
'Cuz the kid'll eat the middle of an Oreo first
And save the chocolate cookie outside for last.

The same choreography accompanied the lyrics and musical refrain from the SOS Band's "Take Your Time (Do It Right)," which was a platinum No. 1 R&B hit single that climbed to No. 3 on the pop charts in 1980:

Baby we can do it / Take your time
Do it right / We can do it, baby
Do it tonite.

It's also used to accompany a McDonald's jingle that I remember from the 1970s:

Big Mac / Filet o' Fish
Quarter Pounder / French Fries . . .

Laura (b. 1976, New York City) remembers playing "Baby We Can Do It" as a handclapping game-song when she was about seven or eight years old (about four years after the song was released). She recalled:

There was one girl and she knew all of the cheers. So we kinda like learned from her. She was also older. I think as I did more and more we all learned and we all led. I had friends from school so I would learn things and then from the neighborhood I'd learn them. So like whatever I learned in the neighborhood I'd bring to school and whatever I learned in school I'd bring back to the neighborhood. Everybody was doing that 'cause whenever somebody got a new cheer it was like *Ooh! Ooh! we gotta go downstairs* away from our parents. (Interviewed October 6, 1995)

Though children's games have long been the study of folklore—and, more recently, music education—black girls' musical games were overlooked as an ethnographic resource, particularly in black music studies and relative to the study of popular music culture.

They have been overlooked for a number of "logical" reasons: it's play, therefore not "serious" music—children, not adults, produce that.

Also, the agents of the play discussed here are female rather than male. As musical expression, these games represent contemporary and common culture rather than the sought-after practices of the middle- or high-brow that reflect tradition and define the significance of a legitimized past.

An equally compelling and unconscious explanation is that this arena of black musical experience, perpetuated by girls as play in everyday culture, is facilitated by modes of nonverbal communication and systems of female embodiment that do not fit the conservative musicological treatment typically found in most black music scholarship. Treatments have tended toward legitimizing blacks as classical composers from the distant or near past, toward tracing histories of jazz as a black and interracial, predominantly male occupation, and toward historicizing the regional and cultural production of dominant genres of black music (often, where men dominate) in New Orleans or Kansas City.

What occurs as too cautious and conservative from my standpoint as an ethnomusicologist and a black feminist is the continual disregard of (1) everyday musical practices, including dance, which discounts ordinary musical people in the present; (2) female contributions to black music-making and communal practice; and (3) the embodiment of sex, gender, and sexuality as it relates to understanding and analyzing both historical and contemporary music-making. Game-songs, like the black vernacular practice of playing the Dozens or rapping, are generally considered *oral culture* and *folklore,* rather than *popular culture* or *mass media,* by the people and for the people.

The origins of the discipline of folklore lie in German Romanticism with Johann Friedrich Herder, who believed that the true spirit of a race or nationality resided in the artistic productions of the lower classes, particularly in ethnic folksong (Wilson 1974). Folksong, the music by the people, for the people, would have been "popular" culture back then— meaning the music of the common folk.

Centuries later, *oral culture* and *folklore* tend to encompass "the uncanonized and signifying practices which lie outside the control of institutions such as schools and universities" (Franco 1999), and popular culture tends to label the dismissive, market-defined products of industrial culture, rather than people's culture. We need to reinvest that latter meaning with study of the former, for they are dialectically related, as girls' games are connected in important ways to mass popular culture. People's culture and mass-mediated or commercial musics are constantly in dialogue, perpetually borrowing from each other and talking back and forth to one another.

Someone once asked me if I was arguing that the alternating foot-stomping, finger-popping, handclapping, and thigh- and chest-slapping that accompany the chants and percussive gestures of girls' musical play are an antecedent to the predominantly male culture of male artists in mass-mediated genres, such as hip-hop. Hip-hop fuses and reclaims oral and written knowledge or communication, mixing and blending musical fragments of oral and composed texts and textures to the "nonstop" loop of an alternating kick-and-snare drum, which closely resembles many aspects of production and performance shared with black girls stepping to the beat. But is this not a matter of arguing which came first: girls' games or hip-hop and its boyz?

What I ultimately want to suggest to readers is that black popular culture operates in a dialectical "production, revision, and consumption of musical ideas" (cf. Agawu 1995b, 63) that often draws on the subcultures of girls' musical games. There is something inherently gendered, or even patriarchal, about this drawing from the cultural well, for female artists are not drawing from their own forms of musical expression as they become popular singers and musicians to the degree that has been happening among male artists.

In the next chapter, I examine several cases, from Memphis R&B artist Rufus Thomas's 1963 "Walkin' the Dog," to rapper Nelly's 2001 "Country Grammar," to examine more closely what can be learned from the connections between handclapping games and specific previously recorded songs.

While girls' contemporary practices illustrate a continuity of embodied approaches to musical behavior and communal interaction that can be traced back to similar nineteenth-century antebellum practices, such as rhymin' and pattin' juba, as well as the early-twentieth-century practice of hambonin' or playing hand jive, what is most fascinating is considering the shared-though-unequal practice of embodied percussion and chant among males and females throughout the twentieth century. The processes of musical as well as social enculturation, enacted through performance, are what propel my examination into the not-so-fixed worlds of race and gender in African American popular music on the local and mass-mediated levels.

4

Saw You With Your Boyfriend
Music between the Sexes

Eeny meeny pepsadeeny / oo-pop-pop-sa-deeny
Atchi-catchi liberatchi / I love you, tu-tu, shampoo
Saw you wit your boyfriend, last night
What's his name / Andy White
How do you know?
I peeped through the keyhole, New—sy!
Wash those dishes, Laz—y!
Gimme some candy, Stin—gy!
Jumped out the window, Cra—zy!
Eeny meeny pepsadeeny / oo-pop-pop-sa-deeny
Atchi-catchi liberatchi / I love you, tu-tu, shampoo

> —Girls' handclapping game-song practiced in Philadelphia
> during the 1970s; see appendix for musical transcription

In this chapter, I explore the hidden connections between girls' musical game-songs and popular songs recorded by male artists. These separate, gendered spheres of musical activity are in conversation with one another, forming a bridge between children and adult culture, and vernacular and popular culture. Here, I will unveil these connections, providing insights into the social and distinctly gendered constructions of taste in black popular songs.

Let me begin by discussing "Eeny meeny pepsadeeny" (above). This game, like several others, features so-called nonsense language. This language is marked by dramatically contrasting timbres, or the nonlexical manipulation of vowels and consonants—"atchi-catchi liberatchi." This is a linguistic code for "education liberation" like the code known as pig-Latin that masks everyday speech among children and adults (Merrill-Mirsky 1988). The dramatically contrasting timbres expressed are further nuanced by the presence of assonance (internal rhymes) within each phrase. These same linguistic features are consistent with certain "novelty" dance tunes recorded by male artists: the jump-band jive of the Savoy Sultans in the 1940s, doo-wop of the 1950s, and R&B or early rock 'n' roll during the 1950s and 1960s. The opening flurry of language in Little Richard's "Tutti Frutti" ("A-wop-bop-a-loo-bop-a-lop-bam-boom") is probably the most well-recognized example of playful speech.

I collected the version of "Eeny meeny pepsadeeny" shown above during my interview with Nancy (b. 1963, Philadelphia). Nancy and I were best friends in graduate school. I was so excited when she taught it to me. It was different than most handclapping game-songs. It had a new set of percussive gestures. Instead of using both hands to create the underlying percussive texture accompanying the chant, the two girls performing the game use only their right hands to create a four-beat cycle, featuring three distinct hand- and body-slapping gestures. First, the pair slap the fronts (on beat one), then the backs of each other's right hands (on beat two), followed by a thigh slap (on beat three), and a finger snap (on beat four). This four-beat pattern repeats, creating a timeline of diverse timbres heard as a melodic or tonal pattern of high-, middle-, and low-pitched sounds (clap-clap-thigh-snap = mid-mid-low-high). The kinesthesia between what's heard and what's spatially felt (high-mid-low) is key here.

After presenting this game-song at the University of Pittsburgh meeting of the Society for Ethnomusicology in 1997, ethnomusicologist John Miller Chernoff recognized the chant from a doo-wop recording he owned. On the cassette copy he sent me, I discovered that a similar version of "Eeny meeny pepsadeeny" opened the recording sung by a Philadelphia-based doo-wop group known as Lee Andrews and the Hearts. In the online *All Music Guide,* this group is recognized as "one of the finest R&B vocal groups of the 1950s," and is further categorized as "Philly soul."

The group had two major hits. They hit number 11 on the R&B charts in 1957 with "Long Lonely Nights," on the Mainline label. Then, in 1958, they had their biggest hit: number 4 on the R&B charts, with their release of "Teardrops," which was picked up from Mainline for wider distribution on the Chess label (*All Music Guide,* http://www.allmusic .com, accessed May 5, 2003). They were promoted in Philadelphia by disk jockey—and later, manager—Jocko Henderson on WDAS-Philadelphia and WWOV-New York as early as 1957, so it is possible that the Philadelphia-based song titled "Glad to Be Here" (United Artists), the B-side of "Why Do I?" preceded and influenced the composition of the girls' game-song practiced later by Nancy during her childhood in Philly (Gribin and Schiff 1992). Or did Lee Andrews and the Hearts imitate an earlier version of a locally popular game-song that was known long before Nancy and her girlfriends performed it during the 1970s? Compare the opening lyrics from "Glad to Be Here" to the chant above:

> Lee Andrews (lead):
> *Say, Eeny meeny distaleeny / gooah my de comb-a-lee-na*
> *Ratcha tachta boom-a-latcha / alla-ya-loo*
> *That means we're glad to-a be here*
> The Hearts (chorus):
> *(We're really glad to be here)*
> All:
> *Ladies and Gentlemen, a-children too.*
> *Here's a five boys to do a show for you*
> *We're gonna turn all around/ gonna touch the ground*
> *Gonna shim-sham shimmy all around*
> *Gonna shim-sham shimmy all over the stage*
> *We gonna shim-sham shimmy when we get paid . . .*
> *Eeny meeny distaleeny you are my da-comb-a-leeny*
> *Ratcha tachta boom-a-latcha alla-ma-doo*
> *It means I'm really glad to be here*
> (Lee Andrews and the Hearts, 1957)

While the songwriting credits are attributed to Calhoun and Henderson (perhaps Royalston "Roy" or Wendell Calhoun, who were members of the group, and disk jockey/manager Jocko Henderson), two other striking connections are present within these lyrics relative to girls' musical play, which opens the door for a discussion of the compositional influence of girls' games on popular recorded songs, and the converse. First, the phrases "We're gonna turn all around / we're gonna touch the ground" are a common chant accompanying double-dutch and single-rope play. Second, "shim-sham shimmy" recalls a segment of a handclapping game-song known as "Hot dog" or "Down, down baby," which I will discuss later. It also recalls an important dance of the same name, the "Shim-Sham," ritually performed by swing and tap dancers. Perhaps the "traditional" or public domain performance of girls' games could be credited as the source of this song, performed or sampled by Lee Andrews and the

Hearts. Coincidentally, Lee Andrews (born Arthur Lee Andrew Thompson in 1938) is the father of a prominent member of the live, true-to-the-art-of-sampling hip-hop band known as The Roots. Drummer Ahmir "Brother ?uestion" Thompson is Lee Andrews's son. This suggests that popular music long before hip-hop was incorporating everyday, found sounds, or folklore, into its compositional processes and begs a closer look at hip-hop as an extension of earlier black practices.

What might this oral and kinetic intertextuality between girls' musical games and black popular songs by male groups say about the role of gender in the social construction of popular musical taste (and other dynamics of power between the sexes), if, for example, girls' games were found to be influencing the compositional choices and production of male performances of black popular music from rhythm and blues to hip-hop? This is the subject of my inquiry throughout this chapter.

For a moment, I want to assert that the unnoticed resemblances in musical approaches to speech-play and beats (like a rhythm section), as well as the repetition and revision that define both the kinetic orality of girls' games and the cutting, mixing, and sampling practices of hip-hop DJs and producers, who tend to be male, are an extension of a trail of musical interactions that signify how race and gender "continually inflect one another" (Monson 1997, 25).

Girls' approach to rhymed verse, which occur in unison choruses as well as in individual expressions of identity within call-and-response formulas, are equivalent to the largely male, rhymed speech-play known as rapping and emceeing in hip-hop though the contexts are completely different. Even the kinetic orality of creating, mimicking, and mixing familiar beats, performed as embodied percussive gestures in girls' games, are equivalent, or at least analogous to, the primarily male technological practice on the turntables or in digital studios, where DJs and producers sample percussive breaks, familiar vocal hooks, and beats or grooves, from previously recorded songs to create new compositions in a communal, as well as commercial, context.

But how does this connection get hidden from view? The way that gender constitutes social relations and metaphorically signifies relationships of power in black culture has a great deal to do with this blind spot.

In a dissertation on singing games in Los Angeles, Carol Merrill-Mirsky asserts that children's music is influenced not so much by schooled learning, or the direct involvement of adults, but rather by an informal network of learning to be musical, which is found in everyday and popular culture (Riddell 1990, ix). Thus, analyzing the intertextuality between separate spheres of gendered musical activity can reveal significant processes that are in dialogue between everyday and popular culture, which are not so obvious to us.

I am uncovering a hidden intertextuality of vocal expression and musical embodiment that has been overlooked because the discourse travels between, and is separated by, the local and the mass popular spheres. This offers a new way to think about the production of popular musical taste through the lens of the relations between the sexes, which is rarely examined. Most studies focus attention on the performance of gender by one sex or the other, rather than examining the dialectical relations of power and performance *between* females and males in musical contexts.

Hip-Hop, Gender, and Community

The interpretive connections I discovered (and trace in this chapter) emerged from moments of serendipity during my fieldwork and my subsequent research and writing. It is a compelling story about the not-so-obvious oral and kinetic correlations between elements of African American girls' musical play and elements of African American popular music performed by men from popular 1950s rhythm and blues songs to chart-topping hip-hop songs.

I stated earlier that the everyday practice of girls' games trains or socializes them into an embodied and communal sense of identity through the in-body formulas associated with blackness. But this does not explain why girls (and later, women) take a backseat role in mass popular-music production. Girls' attraction to the opposite sex, the caretaking roles that many daughters assume, teenage pregnancy, and raising one's own children at a young age may be contributing factors. Yet, with few exceptions, girls tend to stop playing their musical games sometime between the onset of puberty and the end of adolescence. As they depart from these games, girls appear to become primarily consumers (listeners and dancers), rather than producers (primary agents as composers and performers) of commercial popular musical and cultural activity, even though the games they once played closely resemble aspects of contemporary hip-hop practice and other commercial forms of popular song.

When I first made a connection between girls' games and hip-hop, many assumed that this suggested that girls were simply learning—were teaching themselves—how to become good listeners. While this is plausible, I assert that girls' games are a primary resource for the construction of black popular taste, and that their practices are exploited because they exist in the public domain where the right to copyright and royalties are not assigned, and because girls' musical practices are experienced as children's culture. They are used and co-opted in an adult domain, which tends to be dominated by men searching for the perfect beat that appeals to mass audiences and, particularly in the black public sphere, that appeals to women.

Over a significant period of sharing stories from my interviews with colleagues and friends and listening to various songs mentioned in these interviews, I discovered a trail of mass-mediated popular dance songs performed by male artists that correspond to a trail of popular handclapping games and cheers featured in African American girls' play. In one case, the rhyme and performance of "Mary Mack" appears to precede a mass-mediated recording that usefully borrows material to engender social interaction around a provocative dance in the early 1960s, known as the Dog. In another case, a handclapping bridge and a cheer are apparently based on popular hits associated with Michael Jackson when he was an emerging teenage heartthrob.

There are other, more ambiguous cases where the direction of influence is not so apparent. Taken together, these instances are evidence of the various levels and directions of transmission that constitute a dialectic of the popular production, facilitated by kinetic orality, that exists between the games black girls play, and hit songs by male performers, from rhythm and blues in the late 1950s to rap and hip-hop in 2000 and beyond.

Down, down baby / Down your street in a Range Rover

The most recent connection between girls' games and hip-hop involves the game "Down, down baby," also known in some circles as "Hot dog," the title of which points to the suggestive hip rotation that accompanies the performance.

> Section A:
> *Down down baby, down down the roller coaster*
> *Sweet Sweet baby, I'll never let you go*

Section B:

> *Shimmmy shimmy ko-ko pop*
> *Shimmy shimmy pow [or bop]!*
> *Shimmmy shimmy ko-ko pop*
> *Shimmy shimmy pow!*

Section C:

> *Grandma, grandma sick in bed*
> *Called the doctor and the doctor said*

Section D:

> *Let's get the rhythm of the head, ding dong*
> *We got the rhythm of the head, ding dong*
> *Let's get the rhythm of the hands, [clap clap]*
> *We got the rhythm of the hands, [clap clap]*
> *Let's get the rhythm of the feet, [stomp stomp]*
> *We got the rhythm of the feet, [stomp stomp]*
> *Let's get the rhythm of the hot— dog [gyration overlaps with "hot*
> *   dog"]*
> *We got the rhythm of the hot— dog [gyration]*

Section E:

> *You put it all together and what do ya get:*
> *Ding dong, [clap clap], [stomp stomp], hot— dog [gyration]*
> *You put it all backwards and what do you get:*
> *Hot— dog [gyration], [stomp stomp], [clap clap], ding dong!*

Each section of "Down, down baby" is its own contained unit. These units are exchanged between other game-songs, analogous to the cut-and-mix culture of sampling. These units are also linked to vernacular discourse documented from the 1930s, and to popular songs over a fifty-year period (1950–2000).

The first connection to popular song is the most recent. Section A appeared as the chorus in a song called "Country Grammar," by the Grammy award–winning rap artist Nelly, who hails from St. Louis. Nelly credits himself as the writer of the lyrics, with music by Jason "Jay E" Epperson (Basement Beats/Universal Music Publishing/ASCAP, 2000), but on his website (www.nelly.net), he states that the chorus is based on a chant from a "children's game" (choosing not to specifically attribute it to the gendered sphere of "girls'" play).

While it is true that both girls and boys may perform "Down, down baby," it is clear in the everyday performance of such play that boys consider girls the primary agents and performers of such games. Girls "own" these games in much the same way that boys and men are seen as the primary agents in hip-hop performance, whether in the everyday, or in the music industry.

Nelly's song employs significant elements of "Down, down baby": the melodic or tonal approach, the rhythmic delivery, and key linguistic features of the lyrics, including "sweet sweet baby," revised and coded as "Street sweeper baby / cocked ready to let it go." These are the lyrics to Nelly's version:

> *I'm going down down baby / yo street in a Range Rover*
> *Street Sweeper baby / cocked ready to let it go*
> *Shimmy Shimmy cocoa, wha? / listen to it now*
> *Light it up and take a puff / pass it to me now.*
> (Repeat)

He has recontextualized the lyrics to meet the demands of hip-hop's masculine-coded identity politics, altering the "sweet, sweet" line to emphasize being "cocked ready to let it go" and signifying, in the last line, on the marijuana culture that can be linked to hip-hop and youth culture.

The entire title listed for this track on the compact disc reads, "Country Grammar (Hot . . .)." The ellipsis in the parenthetical title telegraphs the vulgar omission of language in the phrase, "hot shit," which predicts and boasts of the imminent popularity of the track. And Nelly's debut album quickly became "hot shit": it reached number 1 on the pop (rather than rap) charts within five weeks of its release.

The hook in this "hot shit" unwittingly drew in male *and* female fans of various ethnicities because many of them would have been familiar with the popular game-song, not only as it appeared in schoolyards and playgrounds, but as it was featured briefly in director Penny Marshall's film *Big*, starring Tom Hanks (1988).

In casual conversations with female listeners, I began to query them about the origins of the chorus, and it became clear that they immediately recognized Nelly was "sampling" their former play. But the male listeners were not so quick to see the connection. Only when I made the connection plain in our conversation did men realize—often expressing the relief of solving a puzzle—that they knew the tune all along. Guys were not expecting, and therefore were unable, to see the connection between a girls' musical practice and the masculine hype of the latest rap single.

Though they knew it was familiar, they simply couldn't retrieve it from their social memory, a memory that perhaps should be from a black and male time past.

This demonstrates a gender-divided consciousness regarding how we view (and what we expect of) the sources and resources of hip-hop sampling. It also suggests a gender-divided consciousness of black social memory that may be shaped by the distinctions made between childhood and adulthood, and the local popular versus the mass popular sphere. All of this is blurred by the context of orality itself, which does not allow one to readily trace and know the source of repetitions and revisions.

Shimmy Shimmy Ko-Ko Pop

The B section of "Down, down baby" (Shimmy shimmy ko-ko pop / Shimmy shimmy pow!) not only appears in Nelly's "Country Grammar," but it also connects to other sources. It can be linked to a book about girls' games called *Shimmy Shimmy Coke-Ca-Pop! A Collection of City Children's Street Games and Rhymes* (Langstaff and Langstaff 1973), but more notably to a refrain in a popular novelty song by the name of "Shimmy shimmy ko-ko bop," recorded by Little Anthony and the Imperials and released in 1956. The opening verse (now glaringly racialized) refers to "sittin' in a native hut," and frames a context of the then-popular dance known as *the Shimmy*. (One website indicated that Little Anthony omitted this song from their repertoire when they performed on the oldies circuit in 2003: despite the popular appeal of the song for his audiences, I've read that he hates the novelty of it.)

What I find interesting about the game-song "Down, down baby" is the oral-kinetic dynamic of the dancelike and suggestive rotation of the hips in time to the undulation and inherently rhythmic punctuations within the tonal expression "hot— dog" (the expression rises and builds up to a closed, or stopped—rather than explosive—"t" sound, eliding with the initial consonant and thereby punctuating the word "dog"). The word "shimmy" is itself a form of phonic manipulation (or stimulation) that also reflects the ideal of dramatically contrasting timbres in black musical aesthetics (Wilson 1992). "Shimmy" also points to an actual kinetic behavior, making the whole phrase/action aesthetically funky. This highlights the interplay between orality and kinetics. "Shimmy Shimmy ko-ko pop / Shimmy shimmy pow!" Here, words are set in motion that point to actual movement. There is no lexical meaning, which is why many people assume black girls' games (and some black musical speech) is "nonsense." But something *is* being said, being languaged, that is beyond immediate comprehension but makes sense aesthetically. It's music, movement, and meaning combined. Then, section B ends when the motion of the words stops on a dime at "pow," forcing a break in the flow of the "music" as well as a space for something new to come.

As mentioned in a previous chapter, a synergy of word and body—a somatic form of onomatopoeia—becomes apparent in the kinetic orality of girls' play. By "onomatopoeia," I mean the naming of a thing or action by a vocal imitation—not only the sound associated with, say, shaking one's hip in a beaded flapper dress—but also associated with the rhythmic accents internally associated and felt by embodying such movement. This gyrated gesture ("hot dog") appears to suggest the movements of sexual intercourse to an onlooker, but for girls it's merely play. The movement is also, however, a way of learning to move one's hips in a way that will become useful, on and off the dance floor, in their embodied relations with others.

This gesture is distinct from the rocking back-and-forth of the "head [ding dong]," or the actions of the "hands [clap clap]," and the "feet [stomp stomp]." The gyrating performance of the lower "feminine" torso, from the waist to the hips, is not alluded to in the verse as are all the other movements. Instead, "hot— dog" replaces and omits any reference to that part of the body, and the gesture is only felt and witnessed rather than spoken—a gesture that clearly recalls Shimmy, the dance.

When I discovered that the same material was present in a song performed by a well-known black, male doo-wop group in 1956, and in a black girls' handclapping game-song performed in 1995, it once again raised the chicken-or-egg question: which came first? I wondered if there might be something to say about girls' games influencing popular songs by male artists, particularly those involving popular dances like the Shimmy. The popular songs that included the title Shimmy were recorded —or more accurately covered—by black and white male groups during the period. Some kind of musical as well as oral and kinetic dialogue and exchange are at work. The question is what it might tell us about the interplay between race and gender in African American music.

Grandma, Grandma—sick in bed

I discovered an interesting connection to the "Grandma, Grandma—sick in bed" section of "Down, down baby" that speaks to the long and slow generation of folklore, as it is traditionally conceived. If you were to take the notion of the lyrics literally, the cure for what ails you is to apply rhythm to parts of your body (head, hands, toes, and pelvis), or perform rhythmic, and in some cases sonic actions, through embodied display (clapping, stomping, gyrating).

In my earlier work (1997) I indicate that girls are learning how to move their hips in unison, or synchrony, associating them with words or ideas. The undulation of the voice saying "hot— dog" is matched in time and space with the rotation of the hips. Girls (as well as boys) need to learn this to become proficient dancers who can socialize well within different contexts of a black community.

How are they preparing to learn a life-long repertoire of social dances that often involve pelvic thrusts, hip rotations, and torso contractions and releases (as percussive and visual punctuation)? Such danced gesture would play a role in discovering another connection between "Down, down baby" and mass popular culture.

In the 1930s, Lydia Parrish collected folklore in the Georgia Sea Islands among people of African descent residing there. The material was originally published in 1942 as *Slave Songs of the Georgia Sea Islands* and reprinted in 1965. This island is known as one of the richest regions of African retentions in the United States to this day. Since the islanders did not suffer under the watchful eye and penetrating rule of whites (because the whites were primarily absent from the island), Africanisms were allowed to thrive in forms of language and behavior that scholars have been able to observe throughout the twentieth century.

Among a variety of stories and games, Parrish documents a game called "Ball the Jack." In her transcription of the game, I stumbled upon a familiar lyric that bears a striking resemblance to "Down, down baby." Compare the two segments:

> *Hot dog*:
> Grandma, grandma / sick in bed
> Called the doctor / and the doctor said
>
> *Ball the jack*:

> Old Aunt Dinah / sick in bed
> Send for the doctor / The doctor said

This, alone, might not warrant making a clear association between a girls' game-song practiced in Ann Arbor, Michigan, in 1995, and a folk game-song from the Georgia Sea Islands in the 1930s. But a stronger connection between "Down, down baby" and "Ball the Jack" became apparent to me when Parrish described the movement of the players. In a chapter titled "Ring-Play, Dance, and Fiddle Songs," she describes the practice in possessive characterizations that reflected the power-laden discourse of an early-twentieth-century folklorist—one who also had certain privileges as a white woman:

> Several of our Negroes "Ball the Jack," as well as the African performer who did a similar serpentine wriggle [Parrish suggests "snake hip" as a far more appropriate nickname for the dance] . . .
>
> Some day, if I ask enough questions, I may discover the original name of the dance—if it had one. Just why it should have been called by a railroad term I can't figure out, unless its African name had somewhat the same sound.
>
> Susy's head and shoulders are stationary and so are her feet, but there is a flow of undulating rhythm from chest to heels, with a few rotations in the hip region, done to this rhythmic patter:

> *Ole Aunt Dinah*
> *Sick in bed*
> *Send for the doctor*
> *The doctor said:*
> *Get up Dinah*
> *You ain' sick*
> *All you need*
> *Is a hickory stick*
> *An' I ball the jack on the railroad track.*

And so on ad infinitum; the words are of no particular moment, only sounds for carrying the rhythm. A box and a stick would do as well.

"Ball the Jack" was brought to the St. Simon's [Island] about fifty years ago by an "up-country" Negro, and has been performed ever since

—to the accompaniment of shrieks of contagious laughter by the little Negroes. (Parrish 1965, 117)

The name of this ring play or dance, "Ball the Jack," reminded me of a song I had seen printed in my *Real Little Ultimate Jazz Fake Book* (Hal Leonard, 1992) called "Ballin' the Jack" (1913). When I read through the song, with words by Jim Burris and music by Chris Smith, I recognized the tune. I had heard it before:

> *First you put your two knees close up*
> *Then you sway 'em to the left, then you sway 'em to the right*
> *Step around the floor kind of nice and light*
> *Then you twis' around and twis' around with all your might*
> *Stretch your lovin' arms straight out in space*
> *Then you do the Eagle Rock with style and grace*
> *Swing your foot way 'round then bring it back*
> *Now that's what I call "Ballin' the jack"*
> (Words by Jim Burris and music by Chris Smith, Christie-Max Music and Jerry Vogel Music Co., Inc., 1913)

What connected "Ballin' the Jack," "Ball the jack," and "Hot dog" was a "twis' around," a "serpentine wiggle" that suggested a shimmy, whether as erotic display or dance, and a hip gyration. Dancing has been nongendered in African American history. By that I mean that both women and men do not see it as limited to one sex or the other. However, the roles within social dances and certain gestures can surely be read differently on the male and female body, depending upon the social mores and class values of the times or specific sacred or secular contexts.

What if we consider, for a moment, that the shimmy or serpentine wiggle signified an African retention, in opposition to the more Victorian-based and Protestant values found in dominant U.S. culture? Might it explain why this suggestive gesture remains and continues to be picked up again and again, across time and place, in black performance cultures?

With "Down, down baby" alone, we see the oral transmission of material that connects culture across time and place. We have Nelly's "Country Grammar" in 2000, "Shimmy Shimmy Ko Ko Pop" by Little Anthony and the Imperials in 1956, an allusion to a popular game in "Ball the

Jack" (1930s), and the "twis' around" movement in "Ballin' the Jack" (1913).

We must pay attention to the meanings of both oral and kinetic transmissions of culture. Girls' games are the vehicle for teaching the ideals of black music-making, but it also becomes a practice that teaches notions of gender. In each case, except for the Georgia Sea Island connection, there is a difference in the sex of the performer and the sex of the subject in the chant—a voiced separation of gender.

Lydia Parrish does not make any reference to sex or gender relations or differences between the sexes when she records details about "Old Aunt Dinah" or "Ball the Jack." But there is a suggestion about the kinetic behavior—a reaction to it—that Parrish records. There is something provocative and sexual about the serpentine wiggle she describes—the same gesture that becomes the centerpiece of a game-song practiced by girls through the latter part of the century. Young girls—girls who are not of childbearing age, practice it.

Girls are generating this oral-kinetic material, and I wonder if they are generating or if they are regenerating it (as in appropriating it from popular songs by male artists, or from the local popular culture). Both popular songs and the game-songs are tapping into the "real" popular, as Stuart Hall (1992) refers to it: the vernacular performance of songs and dances.

Might the use of girls' games be catapulting fans' interest in these male artists, and even generating popular taste and interest? These songs use girls' games to generate the popular taste, but because most of us do not assume that girls and women are *producing* music culture—that *children* are producing culture, in the industrial sense—no one is concerned with the borrowing of this music from the public domain. No authority or ownership is ascribed to the folks it came from. As in Nelly's case, it is simply considered "black" culture—it is not seen as gendered.

From these connections, we get a rich picture of a gendered musical blackness that circulates between the sexes as social dance. It allows one to consider that women and girls are playing a vital role in the production of popular taste—not just an appetite for black sounds but also black embodied performance and interaction.

Mary Mack and Walkin' the Dog

Next, I discovered another connection from an interview with Linda (b. 1948), who said she was kicked out of high school in 1963 for practicing a particular dance known as "the Dog." The dance accompanied a song by Rufus Thomas, which began with Mary Mack. This again suggested the chicken-and-egg relationship, or what I began to conclude was more accurately a form of oral-kinetic discourse shaped by a gendered dialectic between the sexes. That's when I began to look for it in other places.

The practice of "borrowing" from one setting to another is inevitable in music, where orality is still the dominant form of transmission. The lyrics and gestures found in game-songs and in various forms of recorded music suggest a dialectical relationship: between the culture of children and adults, between so-called folk music or music of the everyday and recorded songs, and between the popular music of local performances and mass-mediated music. Ultimately, this points to the uselessness of juxtaposing "folk" music (implying the past, communal transmission, generation, and the everyday) and "contemporary" or "popular" music (implying a break with the past, the present, youth culture, and commercial mass media).

In black cultures, dances are acquired as a kind of cultural capital: learned from parents or older siblings, borrowed from dance shows on television and cable, appropriated from distant relatives (young and old, on summer vacations), and even acquired during interactions between Northern and Southern relatives during funerals and family reunions.

Parallels exist between a black popular social dance and the song lyrics about it (for example, "the Twist," performed by Chubby Checker, "the Dog," associated with a song by Rufus Thomas, "The Tighten Up," sung by Archie Bell and the Drells, and "Rock Steady," by Aretha Franklin). These parallels are important because words that describe movement in conjunction with those gestures (i.e., an onomatopoeia of the body) demonstrate the critical synesthesia within kinetic orality.

Dances are often linked to specific songs or musical styles; certain dances are gesticulations of the sonic textures and timbres associated with funk, soul, or more minutely, a specific dance is linked to a particular song(s). For example, the dance the Dog was performed to "Walkin' the Dog," recorded by Rufus Thomas in 1963, and the Bounce was performed to a popular song of the same name by rapper Jay-Z (1998).

The top-ten hit song "Walkin' the Dog," written and performed by Memphis radio disk jockey and humorous R&B artist Rufus Thomas (1917–2001), which was later covered by the Rolling Stones on their first album, borrows several ideas from "Mary Mack." Thomas's fondness for recasting familiar tunes as party songs (which were later labeled "novelty songs") is reflected in other songs he recorded based on girls' game-songs, as well as other children's musical play, such as "Little Sally Walker" and "Old MacDonald Had a Farm." "Walkin' the Dog" helped to popularize a provocative dance known as the Dog in black communities across the nation; this dance involved rhythmically thrusting one's hips back and forth to the beat of the song.

The four-measure intro to "Walkin' the Dog," recorded on Stax Records, samples from the traditional recessional wedding march by Felix Mendelssohn—the same motive used two years later in 1965 for the opening theme of ABC's *The Dating Game,* written by Chuck Barris and David Monk. The music then settles into a soulful Memphis groove with an ascending bass line, beginning on the tonic and walking up the scale through degrees 2 and 3, 5, and 6, and then the octave (delineating a major pentatonic scale), before returning to the tonic on the downbeat of the next measure.

This bass line sounds distinctly like the bass line that would later accompany "My Girl," written by Smokey Robinson and recorded on Motown by the Temptations; the dance that my mother taught me to perform to this style of music was called the Stroll. All roads lead to the mating game between a boy and girl: strolling down the avenue with my girl, or walkin' the dog with Mary Mack:

> 1st verse (8 measures):
> *Ma-ry Mack dressed in black / Silver buttons all down her back*
> *How low, tip-see-toe / She broke a nee-dle and she can't sew*
> Chorus (8 measures):
> *Walkin' the dog / Just-a walkin' the dog*
> *If you don't know how to do-it / I'll show you how to walk the dog.*
> 2nd verse:
> *I asked my ma-ma for fifteen cents / See the elephant jump the fence*
> *He jump'd so high, he touch'd the sky / Never got back 'til the fourth o' July*
> Chorus:

Walkin the dog / Just-a walking the dog
If you don't know how to do-it / I'll show you how to walk the
dog.

Middle eight (rap over sax solo):

Come on! Come on, love! / Ba-by, ba-by / Quite con-tra-ry / Tell
me how your garden grows? / You got / Silver bells / An' you got /
Cockle shells / Pretty-maids all in-a row.

Chorus:

Walkin' the dog / Just-a walkin' the dog
If you don't know how to do-it / I'll show you how to walk the dog

Recorded on June 17, 1963, the use of a girls' handclapping game-song as a resource for making a popular hit probably went un-noticed, as did the exploitation of black artists for profit, which was a standard practice during the segregated politics of the era. Infringement on copyright wasn't a problem. This commercial song-version closely emulates the game-song "Mary Mack" in its verses, which are set to a different melody. The reference to the popular chant "Mary, Mary, quite contrary"—in the middle eight bars—suggests that the implicit subjects and explicit objects of the song are girls and childhood.

Then, as now, the game-song "Mary Mack" would have been considered public domain, the property of the public, assignable to anyone legally, except, perhaps, girls and children. Thomas would own exclusive rights to the song because children's music is folklore, part of the public domain. As "the property of the public," everyone except the girls, who are the primary agents of such music-making, can claim ownership to "Mary Mack" as intellectual property. In fact, Thomas borrows the lyrics from "Mary Mack" for "Walkin' the Dog," but he uses a newly composed melody, perhaps to claim authorship forthrightly, or he may have simply added the text to a previously composed melody.

References to the popular children's rhyme "Mary Mary, quite contrary" in the middle eight bars or the bridge, and the use of the verses from "Mary Mack," all suggest that gender plays an important role in the production of popular music. Male artists like Thomas serve the status quo of sexual orientation by appealing in one way or another to the Marys out there. The music and dance was luring girls and women to the dance floor at a time when social desegregation created a need to legitimize the social status of blacks. Thus, girls needed to be respectable and avoid lewd dancing and other incorrigible behavior with boys. But black popular dancing has always been about the ritual of romance, though it does not necessarily lead to sex. Leslie Segar (aka, Big Les), hip-hop choreographer and former host of BET's *Rap City* in the early 1990s, said it best: "They say dancing is the vertical expression of the horizontal fantasy. It's true, because dancing is extremely sexy to me" (Allah 1993, 50).

The practice of "borrowing" from one setting to another is a natural outcome of oral-kinetic communication and the relations between sexes; the performances between dance partners is the practice of call-and-response as kinetic orality. Children's music, like youth or popular music, is influenced not so much by schooled learning or the direct involvement of adults, but by an informal network of learning to be musical, which is found in everyday culture (Riddell 1990, ix). Analyzing the intertextuality between black girls' games and popular songs helps us discover overlooked and significant connections in the production of music and culture, as well as in the learning of black musical aesthetics.

The process of social memory at work in girls' games has a great deal to tell us about the production of black popular musical taste. We might want to seriously consider that girls are a primary influence on the production of popular taste by way of male artists borrowing from the female sphere of black musical activity. Male artists are mirroring the production aesthetic that exists in everyday culture.

Because of our definition of folklore, we don't talk about the oral culture's production of popular music. Gene Bluestein recognizes five essential qualities that characterize "true folklore," according to folklorists: "it must be oral, traditional, anonymous, 'formalized,' and present in different versions" (1994, 13). Quoting material representing the International Folk Music Council of 1954, he further defines that the term "folk music," as an orally transmitted practice, "evolved from rudimentary beginnings by a community *uninfluenced by popular and art music . . .* The term does not cover composed popular music that has been taken over ready-made by a community and remains unchanged, for it is the refashioning and recreation of the music by the community that gives it its folk character" (ibid., 14–15). Bluestein contends that this definition may be useful in European folk contexts, but does not do justice to the processes operating in the United States. He counters:

Almost from the beginning, [U.S.] popular culture has had a very close and symbiotic relationship with folk sources of our society. . . . At the same time that folk and popular styles continue their own development in both rural and urban regional settings, materials from folk tradition have strongly colored popular expression. . . . The relationship between the two is so intimate that it makes more sense to talk about poplore than folklore in the United States. (66)

This is a useful argument that explains part of what is going on between girls' games and black popular musical genres, such as hip-hop: there exists a symbiotic or dialogic relationship in which both spheres are creating and refashioning new musical ideas, based on pre-existing material from the other realm. The circulation of culture at work in girls' musical play is arguably a microcosm, or a mirror image, of what takes place in certain instances within the production of mass popular musics, such as Nelly's "Country Grammar." In other cases, the direction of the influence is not as clear, suggesting a constant musical interchange and a gendered interplay between the local popular sphere of girls' games and the mass popular production of musics from rhythm and blues to hip-hop.

If the everyday practice of girls composing and interchanging bits of familiar chants, and making beats out of popular approaches to body percussion, functions as one of the earliest popular music formations in African American communal culture, then the interrelationships between black girls' "popular" musical culture and similar musical expressions in male artists' mass popular music unveil ways that black actors become aware of their own gendered sociality. Yet this is disguised by the masculinist construction of mass popular music and the seemingly peripheral participation of women and girls.

In his 1981 essay "Notes on Deconstructing the 'Popular,'" Stuart Hall advanced a critical point about popular culture. Consider how forms of mass or commercial popular culture offer elements of "something approaching a recreation of recognizable experiences and attitudes to which people are responding" (1981, 233). The appeal of mass popular music is not necessarily a matter of a passive consumption of patriarchy in music, market manipulation, or the debasement of—in this case—African American music or culture. He asserts that popular culture plays on the contradictory domain of the "real vernacular," or the local popular culture—the ordinary musical experiences that males and females make in African American culture everyday, such as girls' musical play (ibid.).

Girls' games give us a musical insight into black girls' and women's participation in a contemporary style of music that, on the surface, seems misogynist, sexist, and hostile to females, while hip-hop co-opts feminine behavior and dress (i.e., black women's styles of hair [see Snoop Dogg], and long baggy pants that resemble dresses rather than conventions of men's clothing).

At best, hip-hop as a male-dominant practice figuratively and rhetorically excludes women ("Bitches ain't shit but hos and tricks," Snoop Dogg on Dr. Dre's *The Chronic*, 1987). At its worst, hip-hop excludes women from participation in the community-building role that music tends to play in the lives of black youth and in black popular culture.

Hip-hop is a contradictory space for women. On one hand, it offers young women the possibility of a "popular" or social identification with an African American group-consciousness through musical participation. On the other hand, hip-hop uses these same musical and cultural practices—making beats with technology, rhyming or rapping, and encoding ethnicity and gender (black and male)—in ways that deny the former agency and authority of women and girls, which deny things feminine, and co-opt behaviors associated with female gender roles and power. My research suggests that power works in both directions between males and females, but the popular (read: mass culture) context of hip-hop tends to eclipse our comprehension of the dialogic and interdependent social formation of a black musical identity and popular music.

What I find compelling is the fact that I have yet to discover any examples of female hip-hop artists "sampling" from the female realm of the popular: borrowing popular phrases or ideas from game-songs that articulate a feminist or womanist agenda and audience in hip-hop. If Nelly can use it for masculinist purposes, why can't Queen Latifah, MC Lyte, Queen Pen, or Lauryn Hill flip the script? Why haven't they used girls' games? Neither the "Name Game" by Shirley Ellis from the 1960s nor "Gossip Folk" by rapper/singer Missy "Misdemeanor" Elliot, which samples a 1981 hit called the "Double Dutch Bus" by Frankie Smith, are based on actual songs or chants borrowed from girls' musical play. They both allude to it but do not musically sample it. One wonders if that might be the ultimate upsetting of the ways in which gender signifies masculine dominance in performance and practice. Men can adopt and co-opt girls' games, and still be masculine, hard. Are female artists avoiding using their "girl" culture because it might be viewed as excluding men? The complaint that women's cultural performances exclude or denigrate men is often launched against black women in popular representations of culture, and was particularly evident during the controversy around the film adaptation of Alice Walker's *The Color Purple*. Men seem threatened by films, videos, or songs that suggest female dominance or the rejection of male dominance or patriarchy. When I asked several students to ponder why they thought women didn't sample from girls' games, they arrived at some interesting conclusions. Perhaps it appears weak or too easy. After all, the art of sampling is about finding rare grooves, and perhaps men and others would view it not only as easy but childlike and unsophisticated.

This omission is surely complicated by the fact that many female artists discarded such play at a young age for more "adult" activities. While rapping tends to be ageless and even somewhat universal, girls' games performed by women is feminine, easy, and fixed as a marker of the exclusion of males. This might even seem counterintuitive for many female rappers, who constantly struggle to fit into the masculinist economy of hip-hop's performers, songs, and audiences.

Stuart Hall states that "transformation is at the heart of popular culture studies because it involves the active re-working of traditions" (Hall 1981, 228). Popular culture is that something that appears to persist; yet new relations are developed. "What matters is *not* the intrinsic or historically fixed objects of culture, but the state of play in cultural relations: to put it bluntly and in oversimplified form—what counts is the class struggle in and over culture" (235). Females are also in a struggle in and over culture.

Girls' musical games are situated in relationship to historical and social moments in the lived experiences of African American "actors," whose practices point to the phenomenology of a distinctly gendered African American identity, community, and social memory, manifest through the kinetic orality of musical behavior.

As a realm of female practices and discourse over time, the repertoire of black girls' games reflects an ongoing "dialogue" with other musical realms that occupy the public sphere, such as jingles in advertising campaigns, or black popular songs and popular social dances mirroring those practiced in the black community past and present. A significant dimension of this dialogue takes place through the musical intertextuality that occurs between the gestures and dances, chants, and lyrics that operate in the realm of a larger world of popular music produced by males. This intertextuality gives body to both an individual and communal experience, because girls' game-songs and gestures, as well as mass-mediated popular music and dance, are primary among the "material and symbolic resources required to sustain" the notion of a black musical identity:

> In common sense language, identification is constructed on the back of a recognition of some common origin or shared characteristics with another person or group, or with an ideal, and with the natural closure of solidarity and allegiance established on this foundation. In contrast to the "naturalism" of this definition, the discursive approach sees identification as a construction, a process never completed—always "in process." It is not determined in the sense that it can always be "won" or "lost," sustained or abandoned. Though not without its determinate conditions of existence, including the material and symbolic resources required to sustain it, identification is in the end conditional, lodged in contingency. Once secured [identification with blackness for instance] does not obliterate difference. . . . Like all signifying practices, [identification] is subject to the "play" of *difference*. It obeys the logic of more-than-one. And since as a process it operates across difference, it entails discursive work [the process of making sense of things, making meaning of what's happening], the binding and marking of symbolic boundaries ... [Identification] requires what is left outside, its constitutive outside, to consolidate the process. (Hall 1996, 2–3)

Girls "play with" notions of race and gender relations, a "normative" sexual orientation, and musical behavior that will later be used in sexualized dancing. In the performance of these embodied musical formulas, players learn to inhabit metaphors of difference: the difference of blackness (vs. whiteness or even African-ness), musical blackness (vs. "white" identified music cultures), a musical black(female)ness (vs. musical expressions conceptually linked to black masculinity), and more. The collective discourse of musical embodiment may signify a racialized, or ethnic, musical difference, distinguished from "mainstream" culture. But it also functions as a communal agent, offering the power to make differences of gender, class, age, and nationality meaningful *within* the social economy of African American culture.

5

Who's Got Next Game?
Women, Hip-Hop, and the Power of Language

When it comes to gender and power, language plays a critical role in defining the context of the games girls play, whether in their youthful activities or in their participation in musics such as hip-hop. It shapes how we interpret who dominates and who is dominated: we use language, consciously and unconsciously, to evoke and reinforce certain differences between the sexes. We also use language to limit or encourage certain kinds of musical behavior or participation. This chapter focuses attention on the mediation of the term "game" that is a common iterance in hip-hop culture. Recently, I introduced the name of this book to a friend, who was certain I was writing a book about the "romantic" games girls and women play. The idea of the musical games we once privileged as youth never entered her mind, and when I revealed my actual subject she was amused that she hadn't thought of girls' musical games first. So let us explore language as a context for understanding the negotiation of gender for men and women from girls' games to hip-hop.

In discussions about performance that have nothing to do with sex or sexual differences, I have noticed that people often bring up something which implies that women are the "weaker sex" (e.g., *women can't rap*; *I can hang with the boys at the jam session*). These comments suggest who should or shouldn't be there, or that female presence is exceptional, as if one's sex has anything to do with one's ability. But there is nothing inherently "sexual" about rhyming words, improvising melodies and rhythms, or making beats.

Our perceptions of gender roles in the black community have been shaped by so much negative public and governmental discourse that it's often difficult to distinguish whether the influence came from the past, or from views about our past that we act out in the present and future. For example, a 1965 congressional Moynihan Report on poverty and the black family suggested that black women were too masculine and "matriarchal"—not letting their men strut—which rendered black men socially impotent and created dysfunctional families. In this chapter, I call attention to the multiple ways in which males and females talk about their participation in various "games" of music.

The title, "Who's Got Next Game?" has multiple connotations: who wants to join in, who has the next game of play, or who has the guts or courage to jump in when play gets serious or competitive? Hip-hop has been so commonly described as a "male thing" (by males of every age and adult females) that a lot of girls who "have game"—who have the skills to rhyme or beat-box—may find themselves confronted by a need to prove themselves every time they enter an all-male cipher.

Ciphers are three or more emcees that improvise or "freestyle" rhymes, one after the other, over a beat, usually within a tight circle. Many girls and women drop out of the game because of their fear that being sexually different may affect their ability to perform freely. In this context, who determines who leads the cipher, or who determines the "rules" (such as establishing sexual topics, whether cussing will be allowed, whether references to "niggers" or "your mama" are off-limits, or whether anything goes). "Whose game" can also refer to the contest over who's winning at a given moment of play (Q: Whose battle is it? A: It's his/hers to take.). It seems that men are always winning the social battle, but in the latter part of this chapter, I allow women's voices to make the musical playing field more complex.

> Players are "agents," skilled and intense strategizers who constantly stretch the game even as they enact it . . . players are defined and constructed (though never wholly contained) by the game. (Ortner 1997, 20)

In 1982, the first international debut of hip-hop culture toured Europe under the name of the New York City Rap Tour. It featured musical performances primarily from the street culture of the Bronx. And with one exception, males dominated the line-up:

> The bill included [founder of the nonviolent peace movement known as the Zulu Nation] Afrika Bambaataa, Fab 5 Freddy [who later hosted *Yo! MTV Raps*], Rammellzee, and Grandmixer D.ST and the Infinity Rap-

pers. Also aboard were the break-dancing Rock Steady Crew, the Double-Dutch Girls, and the graffiti artists. (Adler 1991, 17)

I would not expect them to have had top billing, but in hindsight, the inclusion of the Double-Dutch Girls on this tour is curious, surprising, and even paradoxical. How did they get included in this game, and why didn't double-dutch become the fifth element, complementing the four elements of hip-hop: rapping, graffiti-writing, breakdancing, and turntable-spinning. Why not rope-jumping?

In a telephone interview, DXT (formerly known as Grandmixer D.ST) recalled that he was about nineteen at the time of the New York City Tour. He vividly remembered how incredible the four members of the McDonald's-sponsored Double-Dutch Girls were, though their names were lost on him (personal interview, September 29, 2004).

DXT is an important figure in the history of hip-hop. In 1983, a year after the tour, he collaborated with Herbie Hancock and others to record "Rockit," which became a No. 1 hit single on the pop charts. And DXT's scratching, during a break in the track, became the first use of the turntable as a musical instrument outside of the context of hip-hop or rap music. In 2004, DXT continues to produce hip-hop and other music. With his own studio in New Jersey, he remains an active participant in the evolution of hip-hop culture. When asked why he thought the Double-Dutch Girls had been included in the tour, he said it was probably because the practice was seen as an authentic part of the street culture being marketed to audiences in Paris and London.

Was girls' performance of double-dutch chants and jump rope considered a vital part of the "music" of hip-hop culture, or were the Double-Dutch Girls, with their usual, embodied street performances, simply window-dressing? Double-dutch reflects the aesthetic principles of "flow, layering, and rupture" (Rose 1994, 21), emblematic of hip-hop as music then and now, the question remains: What shifted? Was there a shift to exclude double-dutch and females from the explosive street music of hip-hop after 1982? Or was there no shift at all? Perhaps the Double-Dutch Girls, with their bodies bouncing in the air, were simply eye candy, similar to what is witnessed in contemporary rap videos. In rap videos, women are merely one of the boys, or are shown from the waist down, shaking their backside for male consumption, and female imitation.

How do language and gendered discourse foster the notion of masculine dominance in hip-hop? First, I will introduce this topic, then show how women's voices offset the notion that they are merely peripheral in black music practices. Since games and notions of play are part-and-parcel of the discourse surrounding both hip-hop and the relationship to the opposite sex, I begin with a glimpse at the discursive language of "being in the game" of the rap business. This discourse is highly gendered, and structures men's and women's participation through heterosexual metaphors of power, which contributes to the view that women's participation in hip-hop is limited.

The chapter then shifts into the voices of women remembering their own musical lives, and their participation in black musical experience and social play. There is a saying that it's all in how you play the game. The discursive language represented in this chapter points to the negotiation of gender and power, and points to the reality that gender—or the relations between the sexes and the notion of patriarchal dominance—is constantly in play, rather than fixed or static, as we tend to perceive it.

Players: Masculinity as Hegemonic Power in Hip-Hop

Theorizing the intersection between race, gender, and music is essential to examining contemporary African American music studies, the ways that power gets played out through the concepts of the masculine and feminine, and through the musical performance and conversation of both males and females. Of these three intersecting areas, gender is the least theorized. While it has always played a role in what, and how, scholars write about music history (often at the expense of her-story), musical performance among African Americans remains a gendered, or intersex phenomenon, from juba-patting and corn shucking, to field hollering and gospel shouting, from griots and griottes, from (male) master drummers to (female) blues queens. All musical practice and discourse exists inside the structures of gender and sexuality that shape our interpretations of African American musical behavior, our language about black music and identity, and our notions of power in and out of musical contexts.

In contemporary black cultures from Harlem to London, the "untidy patterns of differentiation and sameness to which the diaspora" gives rise through music, are reduced to *black masculinity* as the primary, if not sole, signifier of *race* in mass popular culture. "Today's crisis of black social life is routinely represented as a crisis of masculinity alone. The integrity of the race is defined primarily as the integrity of its menfolk" (Gilroy 1993b, 7).

Being "in the game," or working in the music industry as a hip-hop player, reflects the same "serious" business about men, and the musical contributions of black girls and women are rarely entertained in conversations about that rap game. While handclapping games, cheers, and double-dutch share aesthetics that are similar to (if not the same as) sampling, rapping, breakdancing, crafting beats, and making popular hooks, the games girls play seem peripheral to the real game of power that male rappers and DJs play in the entertainment industry.

As it is colloquially described, "being in the rap game" is a cynical affair not to be engaged in for mere amusement or diversion, especially since hip-hop offers young entrepreneurs a serious alternative to an ordinary nine-to-five job working for someone else or hanging on the street corners of urban and suburban cities. Instead, they work overtime for themselves, but the discourse of such labor carries many of the same codes of masculine bread-winning found in traditional gender roles. In hip-hop, men still view themselves as the primary breadwinners of the black family and community (perhaps at the expense of being seen as anything but that), while female rappers are not necessarily at home in the rap game because of the politics of masculinity.

The early, party culture of hip-hop started out as amusement, but now it's about the business of balancing what you love to do (making music) with holding down a job—making a living. Male artists struggle to balance "pullin' in the Benjamins" (hundred dollar bills) to support the lifestyle of a performing artist, without selling out their artistic vision, or street credibility, to the highest bidder. There is always noise on the street about artists who are no longer "true to the game": true to whoever or whatever they claimed to be when they first entered the hip-hop game.

Language in the game of hip-hop is decidedly gendered, pointing to the complex negotiation of power between the genders. In a "how-to" DVD titled *Hip Hop 101: The Game* (independently released by Win Media in 2003), rapper, producer, and industry pro Ghostface Killah, of the hardcore group Wu-Tang Clan, expresses the emasculating pitfalls of working in the rap industry:

> When you come into this game it's like a whole 'nother world, you know what I mean? It's just like on the block, like on a bigger level. Now you got to be able to understand all that shit because if you don't, you're

gonna suck dick, you gonna get burned, and you gonna lose your ten Gs or whatever the fuck you gonna act like you was coming into or whatever, you know what I'm sayin'? (*Hip Hop 101* DVD 2003)

Gender defines the nature and meaning of social relationships based on perceived differences between the sexes. No longer solely constructed by kinship, gender is described as the "primary way" we signify relationships of power (Scott 1988, 42).

The *Hip Hop 101* DVD is marketed as a tool for surviving the hip-hop industry. "If you're serious about making music your career, then viewing *The Game* may keep you from being played," or played out of the game, says a review in *The Source,* a magazine on hip-hop culture and politics quoted in the press kit accompanying the DVD. Being "true to the game," or "keepin' it real," means knowing how to win the game of making beats and rhymes to sell records, so you won't have to "suck dick"—sell out on your own (heterosexual and patriarchal) credibility as a man. Negotiating a record deal, or running your own independent label in conjunction with the major distributors—Sony, BMG, Universal, AOL Time Warner, and Capitol Records—can no doubt be an affront to any man's, much less a black man's, self-esteem, agency, and sense of power and autonomy.

Ghostface Killah's words are more warning than advice. The business can reduce a man: treat him like a "woman" with limited power or control. He warns men not to let other men subject them to degrading acts— acts that are acceptable when men subject women to them. Social norms and expectations about one sex are, by omission, telling information about the other (Scott 1999, 32). Ghostface Killah exemplifies the internalized conflict of one's subjective identification with male gender as a source of exerting power and female gender when subjected to others' power.

To vindicate political power, the reference [to differences between the sexes] must seem sure and fixed, outside human construction, part of the natural or divine order. In that way, the binary opposition and the social process of gender relationships both become part of the meaning of power itself; to question or alter any aspect threatens the entire system. (ibid., 49)

In other words, if we question why it is normal that women "suck dick," or have to be subjected to a loss of power or a diminished position in hip-hop, the entire system of masculine and male dominance comes into question, and the conscious—or at least, complicit—exclusion of the "lesser" sex becomes apparent. If we treat the opposition between male and female as problematic rather than known, as something contextually defined, repeatedly constructed, then we must constantly ask not only what is at stake in proclamations or debates that invoke gender to explain or justify their positions, but also how implicit understandings of gender are being invoked and reinscribed (ibid., 49).

One old-school rapper claims that the rap game is losing its edge, businesswise. Scarface, on Ruthless Records, expresses the sense that something is missing:

The game is so [pause] shot and shook up. There ain't nobody out there jammin' hard no more like they used to back when. Well, there's a few exceptions with some of the artists today. But back when you picked up a Ruthless record . . . you already knew what it was. When you picked up a Death Row record you already knew what it was. When you picked up a Rap-a-lot record it was no question about it [the dependability and quality of the product], you know. But nowadays, man, people take the rap game for granted, man, [they think] the world is one big party.

Scarface, a former member of the Houston-based Geto Boys, and later a respected solo artist, seems to be calling attention to the lack of work ethic (as opposed to partying) he once knew in the game. Not surprisingly, women are rare on the *Hip Hop 101* DVD, but one nameless, twenty-something, female artist interviewed shares her point of view about being in the rap game. She could have just as easily been speaking of the stereotypes about the entertainment business as a whole, when she said, "I think what it takes to make it in the hip-hop industry is like you have to know a lot of people, sleep with a lot of people, suck a lot of dick, get a lot of pussy."

Though it takes two to tango, her brief, run-of-the-mill comments reflect sentiments associated with the gendered myth that women (but not men) sleep their way up the social ladder to become MCs or "video hos" in the world of commercial rap or underground hip-hop. Women's games involve sleeping with men, while men's games are more serious business.

The *101* DVD is emblematic of the kind of rhetoric that circles around the rap game, and one can begin to see how girls' musical play can get lost in the mix. Throughout the DVD, conversations about being in the game occasionally focus on making beats, more so than on making it in the business. When this happens—when the attention returns to making beats and the social interactions surrounding both production and circulation—the relevance of girls' musical play could be brought back into the conversation about hip-hop or other black popular musics.

Hip-hop discourse is highly gendered in a number of ways that are, and are not, about the subjugation of females and the feminine, whether such language emanates from the mouths of men or women.

> *Bitch I'ma kill you! You don't wanna fuck with me / Girls neither—you ain't nuttin but a slut to me . . . Hahaha, I'm just playin' ladies. You know I love you.* (From "Kill You," Marshall Mathers, aka Eminem, 2000)

> *I represent not only in the bedroom / But in the boardroom / So give me more room.* (From "Freedom [The Theme from Panther]," Queen Latifah, 1995)

> *Consciousness, consciousness!! / Balance your mentality / With masculinity and femininity / One represents your analytical nature / the other represents your creative nature.* (From an audio recording of a freestyle, by KRS-One with DJ Kid Capri, on air with Hot 97 FM radio's Angie Martinez in New York City, 1997)

Reading hip-hop as primarily hypermasculine and misogynist, as the rhetoric of the early 1990s asserted, has tended to inflect the gendered "pitch" of the beats, rhymes, and lives of hip-hop culture away from noticing how the musical games African American girls play shape black popular music and taste. What also inflects this misdirection is that we tend to hear about women and girls only as fans of hip-hop: as record-buyers, party-goers, club-dancers, promoters, producers, and hip-hop journalists and academics. Rarely are women taken seriously as creative and influential artists who contribute to the art form itself. Black women are no less important than the male fans of various ethnicities that the industry targets through album covers, video games, and commercials for products like Budweiser. But leaving females out of the picture causes hip-hop to be viewed as male.

According to Tricia Rose, "few popular analyses of rap's sexism seem willing to confront the fact that sexual and institutional control over and abuse of women is a crucial component of developing a heterosexual masculine identity. . . . [Rap music] has become a scapegoat that diverts attention away from the more entrenched problem of redefining the terms of heterosexual masculinity" (1994, 15–16).

The sphere of girls' play offers a unique window into the ways we discover and play with our identifications of ourselves as "black," as "black" and "female," as "American," and as "African." These games tell us not only about black girls and their musical socialization, but also about the ways that black *men and women* negotiate their subjectivity in a society where black popular culture and black musical identities have exceptional appeal and function as a kind of cultural currency.

Bringing Gender and Girls into the Picture

In 1993, Congresswoman C. Delores Tucker initiated congressional hearings against gangsta rap, and became a leader in a national moral movement against it (particularly the lyrics of Tupac Shakur). As a staunch defender of minorities and women, she took a moral stance against the misogyny and sexism of gangsta rap, which, she argued, was exemplified by its emphasis on violence, sex, drugs, and criminal behavior. She identified distributors of the music, and then targeted Time Warner, urging other major record labels to censor and ban rap videos. As a result, Time Warner dropped rapper Ice T, but gangsta rap topped the sales chart at the time. For example, from 1992 to 1996 Death Row Records sold approximately 25 million records and earned $170 million, according to one source (*Hip Hop 101* DVD).

The hearings generated a great deal of controversy, but the momentum of gangsta rap, with its misogyny and sexism in tow, barely skipped a beat.

> *America was violent before rap, FACT*
> *Warner, Elektra, Atlantic equals WEA*
> *Instead of fighting them why don't you go free Mumia.*
> (From "Free Mumia," KRS-One featuring Channel Live, 1999)

Mumia Abu-Jamal is an award-winning Pennsylvania journalist who exposed police violence against minority communities. On death row since 1982, he asserts that he was wrongfully sentenced for the shooting of a police officer. Instead of spending tax dollars to fight culture wars against rappers, hip-hop artists like KRS-One, as well as various public intellectuals, think our time would be better spent elsewhere. Mumia's case is but one to consider. Social historian Robin D. G. Kelley points to three factors, among others, that warrant attention: (1) the gendering of crime as black and male; (2) the social development of males, linking masculinity, power, aggression, and violence; and (3) patterns of "higher rates of unemployment and greater freedom from the restraints of the household . . . that makes earning power a measure of manhood" (Kelley 1996, 127–28). These are the major causes of criminal activity, and gangsta rap is not among them. Kelley adds that this may be why gangsta rappers were so reticent to renounce violence during the height of the controversy (ibid.).

Still, many find it difficult to understand why black girls and women tolerate, and even appreciate, hip-hop music with misogynist lyrics and sexist images. This controversy among women often appeared in popular rap magazines. In one case, women were interviewed about specific songs that featured misogynist lyrics. Malike was asked to comment on the popular "Bitches Ain't Shit (But Hoes and Tricks)" by West Coast rapper Dr. Dre, on his 1993 album *The Chronic*. She commented: "I don't admit to liking it because it is downing women in everything that the song says. I shouldn't like it, but I love the song 'cause it's the jam." Alisa responded to a query about DJ Quik, whose classic "Tonite," from his 1991 album *Quik is the Name*, was a popular hit: "It sounds like he's always talking bad about women [in his records], and I guess he is, but I just love DJ Quik. His beats are going on" (Posey 1993, 5).

From an observational standpoint, women appear to be disassociating themselves from the misogynistic lyrics, but their stance leaves them looking like they are afraid to criticize black men in public. It also leaves them looking like their participation is all about the body, not the lyrics. The lyrics, and lyrical study, are a major arena of male participation among fans; that's where males live when they are not watching videos with women's bootys bobbing up and down.

For females, the appeal of being able to move to the latest jam, and falling in love with the beats that drive one's body, is a learned desire. But without any insight into women's participation or contribution to the actual music-making, their participation is perceived as merely stereotypical: men are the producers, women are the consumers; men work the intellect, and women work the body. Oh, the games we play!

What is curious about examples of women defending their love of the beats, but not the rhymes, is that the women who do magazine or talk show interviews are not themselves performers. But emcee Toni Blackman is a perfect antidote to this phenomenon: she is the founder and executive director of the Freestyle Union (FSU), an organization of hip-hop artists working to create music that respects individual dignity and difference.

An accomplished freestyler, and an acclaimed musician/performer, she was appointed by the U.S. Department of State as the American Cultural Specialist and Hip-Hop Ambassador, and currently travels abroad in that capacity. Her latest venture is the Artist Development Institute in Harlem, which provides training and networking opportunities for emerging female hip-hop emcees to foster progressive community action and participation within their art. The five women currently in her program, who range in age from approximately eighteen to twenty-four, often ask how to fit in when they're dressed differently, or deemed different because of their sex. In response, one elder emcee from the West Coast named Medusa advised the young women to put on a sweatshirt with a hood and blend in until men "get" that you got skills.

Gender roles are a product of social conflict, rather than any consensus about what is masculine or feminine, or who is female or male (Scott 1988, 43). We rely on symbols and signs of gender in language to "structure perception," though we are often unaware of such interpretive moves (e.g., *man, woman, girl, boy, sister, brother, bitch, motherfucker*). Words structure aspects of our social reality—so much so that we think certain social relationships and meanings are concrete rather than negotiated.

My argument is that females are actually attracted to their own sphere of musical practice subverted within hip-hop practice. They are dancing to their own beats, the beats they learned to disseminate as part of the kinetic orality of girls' games that are so closely aligned with hip-hop musical aesthetics and sampling practices.

The rest of this chapter is about the voices of black women, and their interactions with music and musical games throughout their lives. I offer you their memories of learning to be musical—from girlhood to womanhood—and what it means to be female in African American culture, American culture, and the diaspora.

Games Females Play: Getting Their Word Out

To all the ladies in the house: lemme hear you say "Ho"! (Ho!)

In 1983, while countering the stereotypical hype about rap being a fad, rock critic Robert Christgau brought attention to the sexual politics of the lyrics these new recording artists were writing. He mentions the battle between the sexes that occurs in the form of an answer, or response record, where one text is substituted for another without substantial change to the music (of the original recording). It is a phenomenon in black popular music that can be traced back to the "battles" between the recording of Big Mama Thornton's performance of Leiber and Stoller's "Hound Dog" in 1953, and Rufus Thomas's lyrical rendition on Sun Records called "Bear Cat" recorded and released that same year. Blurred notions of playing games and sexual politics as a game of power surface from my reading of Christgau's account:

> Reports of rap's death have been arriving regularly since 1981, yet at the moment it seems stronger than ever. There are so many good 12-inches around that you can tune out [DJ] Grandmaster Flash's analysis of "women's lib" without doing irreparable harm to your butt. . . . I'm getting a rise out of [MC] Jimmy Spicer's "Money" [with its refrain, "Dollar, Dollar Bill, Y'all"] (Spring Records) . . . and the Disco Four's 1982 "We're at the Party" (Profile Records), the apparent source of the Roy Bittanism piano arpeggio that hooks the tenacious Sweet G song-rap-sermon "Games People Play" (Fever Records). [He adds:] (skip Gigolette's answer-rap "Games Females Play," which don't know women's lib exists). (Christgau 1983)

The gendered or sexual politics of play here involves a "call-and-response," or lyrical dialogue, in the battle between the sexes, from Sweet G (male) to Gigolette (female). These battles are common in black popular music, and differences are not only marked by sex, but also by differences in musical genre. For instance, the R&B #1 hit single of 1999, "No Scrubs," by the Atlanta-based female trio TLC, or "Bills, Bills, Bills" by the female quartet (and later trio) Destiny's Child, were met with biting male response singles that same year: respectively, "No Pigeons," by Bronx-bred male rap trio The Sporty Thievz and "Get The Hell On (Get Gone)" by Houston-bred male R&B quartet Ideal. The opponents in these sparring matches are R&B by black women and rap, and sometimes R&B, by black men. I have never seen white artists enter this boxing ring.

One scholar notes that themes of unemployment and poverty frequently shape the musical discourse between the sexes in these call-and-response records. Brian Ward writes:

> Male R&B always needs to be seen as part of an ongoing, often hilarious, sometimes vicious, and usually highly inventive dialogue with female R&B. It is a dialogue which has dramatized, sometimes caricatured, but in turn helped to shape a genuine debate over sex roles and domestic responsibilities within the black community. . . . [Black female artists] offered sharp and witty critiques of black male inadequacies—usually transposed into the sexual and economic spheres—and a measure of female assertiveness and genuine eroticism which had no equal in the white pop canon. (Ward 1998, 79)

Women's lyrical assertiveness allowed them to construct themselves as sexual subjects, rather than remaining trapped in the sexual objectification of songs by male artists across the twentieth century (starting with the blues in the 1920s, doo-wop and rhythm and blues in the 1950s, and rap music videos beginning in the 1990s).

I invited more than fifteen African American women to tell me their musical life stories, beginning with the earliest memories of their musical interactions with parents, siblings, and playmates. Although all of their voices are not presented here, the ones I share speak to playing musical games, participating in various kinds of music-making, and coming of age and living life as a black and female musical being. Their voices tell fascinating stories about music, race, gender, and the body.

Liese (b. 1962): A Kinship with Movement through Music

Hip-hop is one of the musical soundscapes in which Liese [pronounced Lisa] located herself as a Bronx teenager in the late 1970s. The youngest of four, with two older brothers and a sister, Liese was born in Manhattan, raised in Queens and then the Bronx, and spent summers with extended family in Cape May, New Jersey. At the time of our interview, she was thirty-two and pursuing her doctorate in social psychology at the University of Michigan. When I asked her about musical games, she said:

Whoever had jump ropes brought 'em out. And most people were out. [Girls] were out in the morning by nine o'clock you know, eight-thirty, nine o'clock. It's like most of the girls that I would have been hanging out with, we would all be there . . . and the games were all predicated on rhythm. [You] jump to patterns. You were cool and you had rhythm. (Personal interview, January 2, 1995)

Liese's words call attention to the way language about rhythm keys into the social consciousness surrounding youth and black popular music culture. Being cool—acting like you are an insider to the latest trends in music, style, and fashion—is essential to participating in black popular music, as demonstrated most often by embodied practices: dance, walking, talking, etc. Being able to dance to the beat is a critical cultural imperative in black circles.

It was dancing that allowed Liese to explore sexuality, while defining her blackness and femaleness in political ways in her youth. The dance music of her teenage years was social commentary, as well as entertainment. The "message" that rap broadcast at outdoor parties in the Bronx accompanied her "coming-of-age":

I loved rap when it first got started . . . you know, being in New York at that time [with] Grandmaster Flash and the Furious Five, [their song] "The Message," you know that kind of stuff, it always was political, a lot of it was extremely political. Even that song "Dollar-bill" [by Jimmy Spicer] was all about being seduced by money. I can't think of anybody in New York who listened to that who couldn't identify with the down hill progress of what was going on.

Her daily life was marked by music, in her own words:

You could walk through the entire neighborhood, and the neighborhood is like a huge six blocks, and never get away from music. What they used to do in my neighborhood was go to a baby park in a bigger park that we called River Park, that was right on the East River, and someone would bring a turntable down to this little baby park area. Most of this stuff happened after dark, and everybody would go down to this little area. See, ya had to be cool. You had to! [You'd] hang out and see who was down there, who was doing what, and we'd all go down and dance. That was when the [popular dance known as the] "Freak" was real hot.

You go down there and I mean, dance—the stuff your mama didn't wanna know about on the dance floor [she laughs in recognition]. And that was cool!

Like I said, it was political and around the time that rap was coming into fruition, I was probably in high school. So it was political and you're becoming sexually aware. So you could do a lot of stuff on the dance floor that you wouldn't have dared to do on your back with your boyfriend [pause]. You could do a lot and still people could get their needs met without going in the direction that could be overly dangerous.

As if afraid her mama might read this, Liese turned to me and said, "You're not going to write all that are you?" and then upon second thought gave me permission to leave it in.

Liese's thoughts on being musically black take us in another direction later, when she describes what it's like to embody music:

Kyra: When you say "get into the music," describe what you think you feel when you dance.

Liese: I feel my little body moving. I feel a sense of . . . I don't know what they call it. I feel in tune with it. It feels good, like James Brown. It does. It feels good. I feel good. I feel life. I feel connected, too. And I do believe that ancestrally we were connected to those beats. Paying homage to the beat. That beat being a big part of our heritage, so I think that's true, to be guided by that beat. To get into it and to let it move you is a certain kind of kinship with movement. I think that's still the reason why we [black folks] dance more frequently than others.

Now, Liese is a tall, milk-chocolate-skinned, "healthy" (or full-figured) woman. So her reference to moving her "little" body may be a play on words, or she might have used it as a diminutive, to express something dear. In any case, the somatic significance of the musical body, sensuality, and sexuality in black musical practice are clear, as she discursively shapes a sense of her own social identity and affiliation through dance, and what experiencing dance means to black people.

It is common to think that black music is guided by beats and rhythms, just as early writers about African and African American music have done. While some of Liese's thought might be viewed as "essentialist," avoiding such talk means losing insights into the uses and implications of movement within African American culture, and in gendered consciousness. Such thinking is not true or false; it is a valid way of "making the world" over to ourselves and to others (Jackson 1996, 11). "Truth . . . is what happens to a belief when it is invoked, activated, put to work, and realized in the lifeworld" (ibid.).

It is striking that Liese's comments about movement and music do not appear to express any explicit reference to, or identification with, females, femaleness, or femininity. There is only a subtle reference to James Brown, who is equally admired by both black women and men for the importance of his dance music (with names like "Mother Popcorn," referring to the musical action of women's bootys poppin' on the dance floor). Liese makes no distinction between men's and women's ability to be musical or to dance. Indeed, none of the women in the study makes such a claim, but many noted that black women seem to be more expressive and to populate the sphere of dance more readily than do black men.

Musical embodiment may allow black people to privilege a non–gender-specific, unified blackness, through the highly visual and kinetic medium of the body, dancing. The body then becomes a musical interpreter—the repository of various dance styles, and multiple bodies can be observed and analyzed as a set of somatic historiographies of black social life, or interpreted as nonrepresentational commentary about social identity and identity formation. We are dancing ourselves into our identities and our identifications with black and female communities.

Women, Music, and Other Things Besides Singing

"There are so many other things in black music besides singing," said Linda (b. 1948), who was born and raised in Detroit, and came of age with the rise of Motown (personal interview, October 3, 1994). She linked her memories of playing handclapping games and jumping rope to other musical experiences: growing up in the black church, watching *American Bandstand,* and the highly competitive trash-talking involved in playing a hand of Spades.

She reminisced about the good girls and the bad girls: the ones who didn't do it, and the ones who'd already had sex. The bad girls represented different cliques; they would show up at house parties dressed as the Supremes or Martha and the Vandellas, and lip sync the songs with elaborate choreographed numbers, competing for "Best of Show" among their peers. Linda had been one of the girls who didn't do it.

Her experience at parties speaks to the way that girls in her clique were learning to compete, and were learning competence in social musical behavior through role-playing at social gatherings like house parties. There is a long tradition of performance within social gatherings. The most obvious are the black fraternity and sorority step-shows that often take place in parties for the whole black student population at HBCUs (historically black colleges and universities), and at PWIs (predominantly white institutions).

I asked Linda where she learned to dance, and she quickly answered *American Bandstand*. This seemed curious to me, since I was aware that *Bandstand* was racially segregated when she was young. They occasionally have had an all-Negro ensemble of dancers, but then *American Bandstand* avoided any implications of miscegenation by having separate shows. What Linda and I explored was the possibility that she had extracted the black dance from what seemed like mediocre performances by most of the white dancers on the show.

Stuart Hall asserts that it is necessary and inevitable that mass popular culture makes black popular culture easily available for expropriation (1992, 26). While this is the contradictory nature of the popular, no matter how weak the performances, we continue to see the "experiences that stand behind them" (27).

Though the women I interviewed ranged in age and region of origin, and the conditions of black life have changed and evolved since Segregation, there was much resonance among their memories and experiences. The social conditions of race and gender, and dominant representations of African American experience through mass media, contributed to these similarities across regions and ages as much as did the natural interaction of traveling to funerals down South and visiting family for reunions.

"[Playing musical games] was something to do after the street lights came on," said Linda and a host of other women, whether from Chicago, Baltimore, or Philadelphia. It was a twilight zone of time that you didn't want to get caught in. If your Mama was calling out your name down the street (or, as we say, calling you *out* of your name), one of the girls you hung with would tell on you to your face, "Ooo, you in trouble!" After twilight, during summer evenings in segregated Detroit, Linda, her two brothers, and other kids from the block met to play games.

We always used to end up on the front porch. In the summertime we
didn't have to go to bed. But we still had to be on the porch. We called
them "porch games." We called them "rock school." Oh I remember
well. Everybody sat at the bottom of the step [and] we would do this for
hours. And we had all these other games we played on the sidewalk. We
jumped rope endlessly. (Linda)

Patricia (b. 1949), who was raised in Baltimore, recalled that musical play
was "just something to do after school" with her sister and their friends
on the stoop of their row house in a segregated neighborhood (personal
interview, November 21, 1994). Greta (b. 1971) remembered teaching
handclapping games (she had learned in her black neighborhood) to her
white friends at an integrated school in Highland Park, Michigan (personal interview, February 8, 1995). Ruqaiijah (b. 1974), an only child
who grew up in the Detroit metro area in the late 1970s and early '80s,
became really animated when she recalled the thrill of "going very fast"
—both when playing handclapping games and when "keeping the beat"
as a fast rope-turner in double-dutch. She said:

Most double-dutch had rhymes. But it's more what you do in the [in the
center of the ropes]. People play off what went before them [what moves
girls did in previous turns] and try to bring attention to the game. (interview, August 16, 1995)

Clearly, Ruqaiijah considered these games as a kind of performance,
where rhythm, rhymes, and social interaction take center stage.

One strong similarity between nearly all the women I interviewed was
the perception that playing games was merely a cure for boredom: a trivial practice to pass the time away. Their conversation resembles male conversations around rapping and DJ-ing: we didn't have anything else to do,
so we started *writin'* rhymes or *playin'* records for parties.

There has been so much talk in the past about black folks being lazy,
that these notions sometimes go unchecked; in my opinion, they are being
passed on without thinking. There is nothing wrong with girls passing
their time away, but because it is made to seem as if there was nothing else
to do, it sounds like it's about wasting time. Eventually, such leisure behavior is written out of the game of becoming an adult—the game that
leads to responsible and gainful employment, or a record contract.

Doris (b. 1940) had the most complex musical life I encountered. She was raised in Detroit and recalled playing handclapping games, but couldn't remember any specifics at first. Then, slowly, she remembered not being a "good jump-roper," and began to share various musical interests and memories that provided insight into the diversity of her musical world —a musical world, which is not unlike many others, including mine.

While pursuing a graduate degree in public health, she sang and played recorder in the Ann Arbor Recorder Society, and also played recorder with a group of senior citizens known as the Burns Park Pipers. Over the years, her listening tastes had run the gamut: Native American flute music, classical music (Gregorian chant); gospel (the Winans, the Clark Sisters, and James Cleveland); jazz; and what she called "traditional black artists" like Luther Vandross. As a young adult, she identified with Nancy Wilson, Roberta Flack, and Nina Simone. Of Wilson, she said: "I remember her as very elegant, very classy," and she very much wanted to be that. She added:

Nina had that deep, sultry voice. I wanted to sing like Nina. I perceived her as being an educated person that had some college experience. She was always performing at the Delta's functions [Delta Sigma Theta sorority at her college]. I think the types of songs she sings were kind of all bluesy. See, we had a lot of blues back then. But *now* I wish I could really sing gospel.

Although Doris was raised in the Catholic Church, she participated in music-making in local Baptist churches when she was young. This was, and remains, a common experience in many black cities and communities. As Doris said: "Music in the black church is such an important part of the service. You need some music to build up the sermon and it kind of keeps things going . . . the music is so moving."

In her childhood home, everyone but her mother played an instrument. She recalled the gendered roles that she learned early on from musical experiences in her immediate family:

As a child we always had music around. My father kind of played by ear. My older brother played the piano and he was playing for the neighborhood church when he was eleven years old. My other two older brothers, one played trumpet and one played saxophone. So we had a little family band. I would play the clarinet and I also played in a school band and eventually played in the district band.

There was pressure on me to play piano because I was a girl, more so than my [five] brothers. It was OK for them to play the saxophone, clarinet, trumpet, whatever. There was a lot of pressure on me to play the piano. That was something that girls shouldn't be doing, playing wind instruments like boys. And, of course, I resisted learning piano. They finally got tired of paying for lessons 'cause I wasn't learning anything (she laughed). Now, of course, I wish I had learned how to play. [Piano-playing] would be very valuable. That was one of the differences I noticed, that there were types of instruments that were perceived as being feminine or masculine.

Earlier in the interview, Doris had vividly recalled pattin' hambone better than her brothers:

Handclapping? Yeah I did that and we used to hambone [she begins to pat her thighs]. But they always told us girls aren't supposed to do that. I thought I was good at it, you know.

I wondered if she had observed similar differences among black females and males around dancing, which is akin to the musical embodiment of hamboning. She replied:

Doris: One of the things [people] always say is that black people have rhythm [naturally] which I found not to be true (she laughed). Lord, in my family no one is a very good dancer. It took a long time to learn how to do the little two-step. And when everyone was doing the Bop, it was like, somebody show me, please! I had lesson after lesson after lesson before I could finally learn how to bop.

Kyra: Where did you bop?

Doris: Oh, there were all these parties in the basement . . . somebody's basement. And, uh . . . oh! St. Charles Church [a Catholic church in Detroit] always used to have teenage parties on the weekends. That's where we bopped in the community center and sock hops. I guess dancing was like a big social event. To fit in you have to know how to bop (laughs).

I always felt that girls could just dance better than the boys. That was just my personal thing [opinion]. I don't know if it's about the looseness of [girls'] movement or if it's just more pleasing. I think the same thing [about] music. It's like joining a [church] choir. I sang in the Baptist choir, but I didn't want to belong to a Baptist church. I wanted to sing in the choir, you know. Because it was the thing to do: singing in the choir. It was more than just [singing], it was a social event. You got to know the people. You know they were friends and your neighbors.

This extensive passage from my interview with Doris demonstrates the complexity of an individual African American's musical experience. It highlights the significance of learning musical behavior (Doris begged for assistance to learn how to do the Bop), and it highlights the significance of gender in black musical subjectivity.

Tosha (b. 1972) recalled that she and her playmates in Memphis, Tennessee, referred to cheers as *scolds*. In other cases, cheers are also known as *steps*—linking them with the popular black, Greek-lettered, fraternity and sorority tradition known as "stepping." I invited Tosha to explain what she thought *scolds* meant, and she speculated that it probably had a lot to do with the competitive exchanges and put-downs—the call-and-response—that often took place between performers within the frame of specific cheers. She couldn't recall specific examples, but likened scolds to playing the Dozens. Scolding is one of the many names black folks have used for the linguistic practice and verbal art.

In African American vernacular English, these terms often refer to the oral and competitive verbal art of *signifyin'*—put-downs, loud-talkin', soundin', markin', talkin' shit, snappin', bustin', or scoldin' on somebody or something (cf. Gates 1988; Abrahams 1990; Mitchell-Kernan 1990). It usually involves overt or covert, direct and indirect "serious, clever conflict talk," "aggressive witty performance talk," and "nonserious contest talk" in everyday conversation, or in oral performance narrative traditions like playing the Dozens. These forms of expression have typically been associated with verbal competitions among males, including "your mama" jokes (Gates 1988, 78). Both African American linguist Claudia Mitchell-Kernan and black power poet H. Rap Brown have offered evidence that women partake in the verbal artistry of signifyin', and that is a common practice in both sexes.

Male folklorists and urban anthropologists have had a tendency to write about black verbal conflict, or dueling, as a male preoccupation. This is another example of how there is nothing inherent in sex, or sexual identity, in terms of being able to spar verbally—using metaphors, metonyms, synecdoches, or other codes of speech and speech play—to say one thing and mean another (double entendre, indirection, etc.). Girls share in this tradition regularly through their daily performances of hand-clapping games, cheers, and double-dutch.

In conclusion, comparing women's and men's conversations about gender, power, and sexual politics offers us an invaluable way to think about black musical experience that cannot be gleaned from simply studying song lyrics, musical styles and genres, or the great figures of black music history. The voices of ordinary people have much to say about the game of music, and I hope this gives readers a glimpse of what more can be done in the arena of black music studies concerning gender.

6

Double Forces Has Got the Beat

Reclaiming Girls' Music in the
Sport of Double-Dutch

One could divorce double-dutch from the stylistic innovations of black popular music, but if one understands mass popular music as a derivation of black vernacular expression and performance, the relationship is undeniable. This chapter introduces the musical performance of double-dutch and discusses its transition from public street play to the "privatized" institution of a sport where gender norms, musical performance, and the freedom of youthful expression are policed and scrutinized. The impact of this transition on double-dutch as music becomes apparent in the perceptions about, as well as the actual presence (or absence) of, music and musical behaviors within the sport. Despite this transition, black girls who compete in the American Double Dutch League (ADDL) find ways to re-insert musical elements that were often privileged in their street practices, thereby re-asserting their agency into a highly regulated and, to a certain degree, masculinized event.

What this suggests is that black girls' social practices are read differently in private and public spheres, depending on whose subjective position we are thinking from, transforming ideals of black musical play into taboos that demean female respectability. Freedoms in performance that would be "fair game" in the somewhat exclusively female rhythms and rhymes of double-dutch street play are often regulated—and thereby restricted in certain ways—by adults legislating *sportsmanlike* conduct in the mixed race and sex public competition of double-dutch.

Double-dutch and its accompanying game-songs are the culmination of something special in black girls' same-sex play. After junior high school it begins to fade into the background and be dropped off into the past with the onset of puberty and a stronger interest in dating boys. Double-dutch jump roping is a symbol of black female ingenuity. It requires a minimum of three players, and as many as eight or nine can rotate into the practice.

Performing Street Double-Dutch: Ropes, Bodies, and Beats

Imagine a jumper navigating an elliptical space above the pavement outlined by two turning ropes. The pedaling feet of a jumper dance in quick alternation, leaping above the turning ropes as they pass below. The two turners, facing one another, navigate each rope in towards the other. Their unusual rope play involves rhymes and chants, songs to dance to, as well as humor accompanying musical gestures, and the spectacular kinetic ability of specific individuals and their collective interplay.

The primary "rule," or aesthetic ideal, behind double-dutch play is to remain within the undulating ropes consistently while exploring one's kinetic potential and energy in a significant span of *musical* time and space. Time and space are linked by the pedaling of the feet, maintaining a steady pulse or beat, developing an inner pulse or so-called metronomic sense while completely in motion. This is an ideal found in black dance and music-making: keeping the rhythm, not interrupting the meter and the flow of the musical expression. It is a critical skill required for black social music-making, which facilitates the learning of new styles of dance, vogue gestures, and is often accompanied by vernacular oral expressions, all performed in highly stylized ways.

Double-dutch represents a way of experiencing "black-femaleness" as being connected to a *black* sense of musical time—to expressing stylized musical movement in ways that are "on time." What happens when you are not "on time"? In double-dutch, as in all other girls' games, you get eliminated from play momentarily: mistakes open up the elliptical stage to the next performance, the next jumper and/or turner.

If a jumper gets the ropes tangled around her feet, or one of the circulating ropes is clipped by an arm or a bobbing head, your time is up, but your participation does not end. The concept of "musicking"—defined by Christopher Small as the act of taking part in musical performance whether as composer, listener, dancer, or performer—is useful as we observe those "eliminated" from the circle of the double-dutch ropes. Non-jumpers act as both audience and singers to the ongoing street perfor-

Downbeats	1	2	3	4	1	2	3	4
Footfalls	*r-foot*	*l-foot*	*rf*	*lf*	*rf*	*lf*	*rf*	*lf*
	I *went*	down	town	( )	to *see*	James	Brown	( )
	He *gave*	me a	nick-el	( )	to *buy*	a	pick-le	( )
	The *pickle*	was	so-ur	( )	He *gave*	me a	flower	( )
	The *flower*	was	dead	so	*this*	is what	he said:	( )
	Hoppin'	on	one	foot	one	foot	one	foot
	Hoppin'	on	two	foot	two	foot	two	foot
	Hoppin'	on	three	foot	three	foot	three	foot
	Hoppin'	on	four	foot	four	foot	four	foot

Source: Representation of chant based on example found in Riddell 1990, 138.

"James Brown" double-dutch chant.

mance, and therefore all the participants are actively involved with the success of double-dutch as a musical performance.

"Red hot pepper," or the individual words "hot," "pepper," or "fire," signify the exciting footwork of double-dutch. Both the skipping of the ropes and the syncopated footfalls on the pavement, or "blacktop," act as a timeline against which gestures, tuneful melodies, and rhymes are performed in complex musical ways. In an example referring to *James Brown* (the "godfather" himself), the accents within the rhymed chant direct the coordination of synchronized movements (i.e., touching the ground or turning around within the undulating ropes).

In the figure above, I have highlighted the measured phrasing of this chant synchronized with the footwork. These words highlight the downbeats, while certain silent (but internally felt) beats are indicated by an empty set of parentheses.

From this chant, we get a glimpse of the rhythmic complexity involved with performing double-dutch—the syncopated coordination of oral and kinetic behavior. Girls must learn to maintain the steady articulation of the pulse, sounded jointly by the jumper's feet slapping the pavement and the sound of a clothesline or telephone cords skimming its surface.

The dare-devilish leaps and funky chants that accompany jumping and turning clotheslines in the streets continue to reflect, or at least serve, the expressivity of black-femaleness through their performance of vocal expressivity, gender, and the body. In street play, the expressive forms reflect both the *collaborative* music-making efforts and the skillful coordination of play stereotypically associated with girls, as well as the competitive athletic and acrobatic efforts of play stereotypically associated with boys.

After a girl finds her way into the center of the double-dutch ropes, pedaling her feet above the skipping ropes all the while, she will typically perform a few choreographed "tricks." A variety of tricks have developed over the decades of double-dutch play, which has New York City as its epicenter, and each trick highlights a specific choreography that is collectively learned by the girls. Tricks with names like "turnsies" (hopping 360 degrees on one foot after each clip of the rope on the ground) and "pop-ups" (popping high up into the air, allowing two skips of the rope to pass below one's feet, thus expanding the rhythmic feel of one's footwork) are among the most popular moves found in any locale. Girls are expected to master the choreography in order to conform to the social conventions of double-dutch play.

While there is room for improvisation, one needs to demonstrate the ability to conform to the social expectations about a trick, and consistently execute it to fulfill an impromptu challenge from girls watching your turn in the ropes (*"Do pop-ups!"*).

Around 1999, I watched two sisters (one nine and the other thirteen, assisted by a neighborhood friend) perform a series of double-dutch game-songs in their home in Philly. They had rolled back the living room carpet with their mother's permission, defying their father's rule: no jumping rope in the house.

As they performed their repertoire, Candace, the older sister, kept complaining to her younger sister, Bridgette, that she didn't really learn her "turnsies" right. Interestingly, the rap "Criminal Minded" by urban poet and recording artist KRS-One was the basis of their play. The opening lyric of the rap was more-or-less the same lyric that opened their game-song:

> *Criminal minded, you've been blinded*
> *Lookin for a style like mine you can't find it*
> (Boogie Down Productions, 1987)

When asked, it was clear that the girls could not claim any knowledge of the original recording from an album of the same name released in 1987 (around the time the oldest sister was born). Yet, the trio could claim the game-song as their own popular or everyday music-making—a product of girls' agency and play in the late 1990s.

As their performance continued, the complaint turned into a tit-for-tat squabble, where Bridgette unsuccessfully defended her case against the cool instigations of an older sister. Despite yelling and feigned tears the girls never skipped a beat of the double-dutch games they were demonstrating. They continued taking turns jumping rope while the younger sister tried to prove her case once and for all: she performed her turnsies again and again, providing evidence, ignored by her sister, that she had mastered the art of the skill.

To anyone who has failed at either the physical or social skills of performing double-dutch, myself included, the real art of play is learning how to get into the ropes and learning how to do a good "dismount": exiting the ropes without interrupting their constant flow, so the game can proceed seamlessly, non-stop, into the next turn. There is also the turners' skill and artistry in accommodating more than one jumper, usually two or three at the most. Despite the complexity of the skills needed to participate in double-dutch, there is an assumption that every player will learn how to turn the ropes, as well as jump.

The art of turning the ropes, however, does lead to a sort of specialization acquired by those who are not "double-handed." Being double-handed means you don't know how to turn the ropes evenly: double-handed turning sounds like a shuffle rhythm (long-short long-short), while a good turner creates a completely even pulse as the ropes skip across the floor.

Competition between double-dutch jumpers and turners (not unlike that between rappers/emcees) encourages innovation, improvisation, and individual expressivity. Double-dutch and hip-hop music may seem to reflect separate expressions because of the separation of males and females. However, these seemingly separate gender performances actually reflect a shared cultural and musical expressivity as mentioned in previous chapters.

While the choreographies found in double-dutch are more or less distinct from handclapping games and cheers, the same chants can be found as an accompaniment to them all. For example, the chant for the handclapping game-song "Down, down baby / Down, down the roller coaster / Sweet, sweet baby / I'll never let you go" was practiced by a group of adolescent girls (ages ten to fourteen) in Ann Arbor, Michigan in the summer of 1995. During the summer of 2002, I observed a girl employing this same chant for use in a double-dutch game in Charlottesville, Virginia. She had learned it in Atlanta, Georgia where she had formerly lived.

Double-Dutch, Double-Jewish, Double-Black: Children Performing Difference

Despite its presence in the south, double-dutch's origins seem to be based in the multi-ethnic streets of New York City. It was and is also prevalent in several other cities including Philadelphia (Abrahams 1969), New Haven, Detroit, Los Angeles (Merrill-Mirsky 1988, Riddell 1990), and Washington, D.C., among others.

The origin of its name alone highlights its curious association with ethnicity in New York City that does not seem to be limited to African American culture. Many of its local associations are defined by stereotypical views of immigrants and their language as "foreign" or "alien." According to ethnographers Amanda Dargan and Steven Zeitlin, the successive waves of immigration in New York heightened concerns about ethnicity and American-ness, and the alienation of new immigrants was often apparent in the form of ridicule of the sounds of "foreign" languages. Children, as well as adults, passed on such prejudices and attitudes about non-English speech and community. "Girls jumped in an American style but called it 'double Dutch' or 'double Jewish.' . . . Prejudice insinuated itself into the games of the smallest children" (Dargan and Zeitlin 1990, 24).

Racial and/or ethnic prejudice is at the heart of the matter, whether one is castigating Jewish, Irish, or African American children. Contrary to the racial insinuations of outsiders, double-dutch play among black girls created an arena where race and gender identity moved from the periphery to the center, sometimes embracing and reinterpreting the very epithets that others used to signify inferiority of their race and sex.

Double-dutch is an unusual name for a girls' game and it is probably impossible to determine where African American girls or the Jewish girls who also performed this practice in neighborhoods throughout New York City got the idea of the practice itself. It may stem from colloquial meanings already present in the metropolitan migrant communities.

References to the elliptical uses of the adjective "Dutch" in the *OED Online* (2005) suggest three arguable, but likely, sources: (1) "double Dutch" ("a language that one does not understand; gibberish" dating back to a translation of Moliere in 1876); (2) "to beat the Dutch" ("to do something extraordinary or startling"); and (3) "that beats the Dutch" ("that beats the Dutch, that beats everything"), all of which could apply to the everyday practice generally attributed to African American culture.

"The hang": Regional differences and rivalries disappear in the summer heat as sport returns to street play behind the scenes at the American Double Dutch League International Competition, 1995.

From my reading of the *OED Online,* the term does not appear to have any direct connection to the adverbial phrase "going Dutch" or to the use of the noun "the Old Dutch" to refer colloquially to "a wife," though the gendered connotations might be of interest here. It is most likely attributable to the three definitions above, for the game of double-dutch lies beyond the realm of verbal language or explanation. Many observers identify it as something extraordinary in sight that looks impossible to achieve, even magical. It is, I believe, a game that beats all other games girls of any ethnicity play, hands down.

The Double-Dutch Cops' Beat: Policing Girls' Play

In 1973, New York City police detectives David Walker and Ulysses Williams organized a local competition of double-dutch that took place at the mall area in front of Lincoln Center. June Goodwin chronicles the emergence of the sport in a *Christian Science Monitor* article, and quotes former detective Williams as he recalled his thoughts about inner-city girls and sports. He articulated that double-dutch does not have an image of being a "butch" sport. The detectives' idea was to produce a sport that was not a hand-me-down from *men,* so *girls* wouldn't feel like second-class citizens. "[Because] when I watch *women's* basketball I get ghost vision: I see *men superimposed over the women*" (emphasis added; Goodwin 1980, B8). Williams thought a girls' sport shouldn't be too "masculine," implying that sports are a boys' thing. Double-dutch *is* a girls' game —fun enough for a man, but made for a woman.

The genetic or biological differences assumed between the sexes continue to inform the structuring of behavior and performance in public and/or institutionalized competition. Though there are certain biological differences, we tend to confuse sex difference with assumptions about gender behavior. Such interpretations privilege the "naturalness" of gender roles in society and culture: males are "naturally" competitive and aggressive, while females are "naturally" cooperative and nurturing. If, as Williams insinuates, women basketball players are butch, too masculine, and, thus, "out of bounds," women can only be viewed as less than boys and men. Their lack of "penetration" means women are not able to assert power in male spaces. Such spaces are, arguably, homo-social realms of serious patriarchal play.

Basketball is not inherently "masculine" and "male." Nor is double-dutch an inherently female social activity. Yet we make choices based on our hegemonic interpretations of history and culture which imply assumptions about authority in the present. Detective Williams' comments ultimately say more about what kind of vision informed his choices in formulating rules for girls' performance in double-dutch competition.

Back in 1973, Walker and Williams had been looking for a new sport for girls for a long time. Once they found double-dutch, they spent months making up rules, and began to dream of creating a tournament. They recruited several Columbia students to teach the new contestants the rules of a practice that, like street ball, had its own existing "rules." It wasn't long before girls were jumping to the new rules in order to win, and the two policemen eventually became known as "The Double-Dutch Cops" (ADDL Souvenir Program, 1995, under "Double Dutch Background").

Walker and Williams were themselves African American and Walker actually remembered that his sister had played double-dutch during his youth, so it was by no means new to him, nor was it new for police officers to serve children's play. The double-dutch competition the officers founded was part of a mission affiliated with the Police Athletic League. The PAL was founded in 1914 by New York City Police Commissioner Arthur Woods, on the premise that police captains would seek out vacant lots to function as supervised play spaces and try to keep children off city streets (Dargan and Zeitlin 1990, 158). It was the continuation of a movement to reform children's play that began in the late nineteenth century:

[The police] saw in organized play and sport ways to ameliorate social ills associated with the effects of new immigration (which crowded New York streets with children), and industrialization. . . . One of the reformers' strategies was to take children off the street and supervise their play in controlled spaces, including parks, playgrounds, and designated "play streets." (Ibid., 155)

An early mission of the community-based PAL was the protection and/or control of the locus and nature of children's play. Street play became a nuisance as cars, buses, and trolleys began to occupy urban streets. Thus, the increased mobility of the adult world led to adult intervention of public space, where children had once ruled the day. Children "fought back by incorporating cars into their games and continuing to play amid traffic, but eventually they lost" (ibid.).

In the early 1970s, amid urban blight and mismanaged infrastructures, the PAL undoubtedly was fraught with concerns about the idle minds and bodies of inner-city boys and girls. Their continuing efforts surely confronted newer demands: juvenile delinquency among both boys and girls was becoming an alarming issue in inner cities (although public attention was undoubtedly focused on male delinquency in the streets).

In a 1995 telephone conversation, David Walker recalled that his interest in founding the ADDL was piqued while he was working in a Harlem bicycle program. During that time, he observed that girls were not attending the programmed events, and he eventually noticed how black girls in the city liked to "show off their routines" while playing double-dutch, and how they taught each other rhymes. Double-dutch "was a neighborhood challenge on the streets. Like breakdancing" (telephone interview with David Walker, May 14, 1995; also see Walker and Haskins 1986, 7–8).

Gender continues to play a pivotal role, and associations with hip-hop culture continue to surface, in my interpretation of black girls' musical games. Researchers have documented breakdancing and several other street practices in the city as if they are exclusively male and masculine expressions of black urban culture. The most remarkable example involves the folklore and performance of the Dozens, signifying toasts or raps. "The toasts are a male's genre, not only in performance, but in content: in only a few does one find women included in any purpose other than exercise of male options, male power, and male anger. . . . There is little *romance* here" (emphasis added; B. Jackson 1976). (For other sources that suggest the exclusivity of males performing urban verbal art, see Sorenson 1959; Hannerz 1969; Jackson 1976; Dance 1978.)

Romance symbolized a female or feminine sphere that was not evident in the streets among black males. Therefore, we might assume that female occupation of the street posed a "sexual" risk, posing the "real" possibility of females becoming socially rather than sexually "butch": acting or performing in masculine ways in male spaces.

Moving double-dutch off the streets allowed Walker and Williams the ability to provide an outlet for young inner-city girls, because "women are loners, going from toys to boys at an early age" (Goodwin, 1980). Walker's rhymed explanation—"from toys to boys"—implies that girls are limited to certain kinds of "games" and that the objects of their play cause a certain kind of dependence on boys. Actually, boys go from "toys to boys" as well, given their involvement in exclusively male sports activities.

Though Williams and Walker were likely acting in good faith, they were "policing" female behavior and social sensibilities in an increasingly gendered and taboo-conscious public sphere. But their efforts soon precipitated a national organization.

In 1975, Walker and others founded the American Double Dutch League (ADDL), which gained support from the New York City Board of Education, the New York City Police Department, and Mobil Corporation (Walker and Haskins 1986, 17). The ADDL, a not-for-profit organization, is currently headquartered in Washington, D.C., and now conducts local, national, and international competitions year-round. Because of its early affiliation with the police department and the Police Athletic League, police or juvenile justice officers as well as social and youth advocacy groups including the 4-H Club, Girl Scouts, and the Salvation Army, have often administered and sponsored local double-dutch competitions throughout the League's twenty-year history.

The sport of double-dutch is considered a lighting-quick team sport, testing speed, strength, agility, and creativity. The promoters of the sport would like to see double-dutch rope play become an Olympic sport one day. According to the program for the 1995 competition of the ADDL, the sport of rope jumping originated with ancient Egyptian, Phoenician, and Chinese rope-makers. Clearly, the organizers of this competition needed to legitimize double-dutch as a serious sport, masking its recent incorporation and its absence from older, more conventional and legitimized, "male" activities. History, it would seem, lends itself towards legitimacy. As folklorist Henry Glassie once eloquently wrote about tradition, "History is not the past. It is the artful assembly of things from the past for usefulness in the future" (Glassie 1995, 295).

Learning the Ropes of Competition: Disciplining Gender, Sports, and Freestyle

The theme of the ADDL's 1995 international championship, held in North Charleston, South Carolina, was "Rope Not Dope," highlighting the improvement of the quality of health, education, and recreation (ADDL Souvenir Booklet, June 17, 1995) and signaling the significance and tenor of the adult intervention behind the sport. The "policing" of the competition links concerns of delinquency to race as well as female and male gender, given the overwhelming participation of black girls and boys at the competition. In creating an "authentic" sport for girls, the verbal expressivity of double-dutch was *arrested* by the official rules and adult concerns for monitoring the free speech of young children in a public contest.

One of the initial goals in formulating the ADDL was the creation of a uniform set of rules for the sport. These rules and guidelines, initially written by Williams, formalized girls' performance in order to define a means for judging the competition (Goodwin, ibid.).

The result was an *official* rulebook (which cost thirty dollars in 1995). Its size and cost clearly privileges adult intervention in an arena that was formerly ruled by the performers themselves, whose play was never aided by literacy; adult participation, judging, and numerous amendments to the rules are now as much a part of the maintenance of the sport as turning and jumping in the ropes.

Formal competition requires qualifying in three distinct rounds: compulsory, speed, and freestyle. This segmented competition resembles the structure of other sports that either feature women or highlight the performance of the voiceless female body, such as ice skating or gymnastics. Competition is divided into age groups from grades four through twelve, and teams advance through preliminary rounds through a process of elimination—points may be deducted for transgressions of certain rules. There is also an open division for competition among teenagers who have completed high school.

Inside this competition, double-roped sidewalk play had evolved into a spotlight for athletic performance in places not conventionally associated with the flair of urban play, such as South Carolina, and the sport included practitioners from beyond the borders of the United States including Canada, France, and Japan.

The teams competing at the 1995 World Invitational Championship included Pepper Steppers, Pepper Steppers, Jr., and Hot Steppers. Teams whose names included "hot" and/or "pepper" generally hailed from New York City and its boroughs. Among the few international representatives were the white Canadian teams the Lincoln Leapers (including one male) and their extraordinarily gymnastic counterparts, Jump Energy, and the Oriental Peppers from Japan (including one male). This demonstrates the exportation of American popular practices steeped in black cultural contexts of play and performance. Not unlike hip-hop, double-dutch has found great appeal in international settings, particularly becuase the traces of musical experience and style are being transmitted primarily by the black female and male participants from urban centers like New York and D.C. While double-dutch has far less market appeal than commercial popular music, it still represents the kind of border crossing youth culture can achieve across race and nation.

Once, culturally defined gender roles forbade boys' participation, or at least kept boys from admitting their participation. As of 1980, however, the athletic competition allowed the limited inclusion of boys (one boy allowed per singles team of three, two boys per doubles team of four). The rules of competition limit boys' participation, assuming boys might "overpower" or overwhelm the athletics performed by the girls. Double-dutch continues to be considered and perceived as a girl's game (Walker and Haskins 1986, 26).

So, boys are in, but the game-songs, the chants that once accompanied double-dutch as play, are out. This brings up a question: What do we make of the absence of girls' rhymes and singing practices in the competition? There is little to clearly explain its disappearance. Obviously, words (or verbal expression) bring a different kind of attention to the sport—one that may not have been desired. Many of the game-songs that black girls played contain articulations about the racial female body and allusions to sexuality and vulgarity as a source of musical energy and linguistic play. For example:

> Mailman, mailman, do your du-ty,
> Here come the lady with da African boo-ty.
> She can do da wah-wah, she can do da splits,
> She can do anything to make you split, so split!
> (Merrill-Mirsky 1988, 179, 213)

Of all the musical games that black girls play, double-dutch requires the most complex physical ability. It also draws attention to female bodies that are in the throws of puberty, adolescence, and often menstruation—setting the development of female sexuality, subjectivity and difference all in motion. Perhaps this breast-bouncing locomotion within the ropes and the negotiation of both mind and body explains the absence of the verbal dimension recognized as game-songs. Girls, their bodies and their agency would be prominently figured and openly articulated through such irrepressible musical expression as found in their game-songs.

When asked, David Walker was unable to offer a sufficient explanation during our conversation. He simply claimed the rhymes "died out." When I arrived at the 1995 competition, my first interaction was with Janice Melvin, the president of the ADDL. I asked several questions that linked double-dutch to hip-hop in an attempt to inspire her to allow me behind the scenes. I had made no previous arrangements and was desperate to be involved after making the extensive journey, my first to Charleston, by train.

Melvin was a short, stocky, African American woman, who appeared to be in her fifties or early sixties. As I shared my thoughts from my research, I sensed that she was anything but fond of, or indifferent to, hip-hop. The responses she shared led me to speculate about the rationale for excluding the verbal dimensions of street play, or at least the justification for continuing to exclude them. She seemed to direct her responses away from any relationship between double-dutch and hip-hop culture stressing that (1) "music is not allowed" in the competition (i.e., boomboxes);

(2) double-dutch "is *not* dance, it's a sport"; and (an apparent contradiction) (3) double-dutch is akin to street "ballet": a respectable art form often associating the female body and its movement with "beauty" and "high" aesthetic ideals and also accompanied by anorexic dieting.

Melvin's responses appeared to elevate double-dutch from its "low" beginnings in the streets of popular music to the heights of a balletic "art." She seemed to be dissociating the sport from its everyday orality and kinetics, as well as from the "offensive" boomboxes that serve as the musical accompaniment to dance and double-dutch in the streets.

From her comments, I garnered a sense of concern about "appropriate" female behavior (and appearance) among young black girls, in particular. Melvin, herself a black female past her youthful days and girlish figure, worked among many female and male justice officers who desire to model high morals rather than sexy street smarts and innovation (given the problems in inner cities in the mid- to late twentieth century). Obviously, hip-hop music and the popular styles of behavior that accompany it, including girls' gyrating hips and pelvic thrusts, are not the kinds of expressive behavior that reflect ideals sanctioned within the competition (where adults and children compete to define space, gender, and acceptable public performance). The "sexualized" dance of popular street play is a form of double "Dutch" or "body-English" that parents and justice officers generally wish to ban or censor from sports, the arts, and the street. It is the inherent double-ness of performance within the competition—the public *and* private, the musical *and* athletic, the formal *and* informal, the playful *and* the competitive—that allows girls to remember the street as they compete.

Next, I'd like to focus on the one segment of the competition that is most reminiscent of the street aesthetics and flow of double-dutch: the freestyle rounds. Freestyle would seem to imply the invention or composition of movements within the ropes—improvisation of style within socially circumscribed expectations. However, the "freestyle" component of the competition is anything but "free" in its style. There were a few moments of the 1995 competition in South Carolina that approached the kind of freestyling I had anticipated.

The freestyle rounds were limited by the rules, causing most of the performances to seem routine—to look exactly the same, with few exceptions. Each presentation must not exceed sixty seconds and must include three to five "tricks" (Walker and Haskins 1986, 54).

Walker and Williams instituted the term "tricks" as a means of identi-fying and framing the "judged" elements of the competition. Ironically, the use of the term "tricks" for freestyle moves, a term meant to denote the expressive acts performed by females formerly occupying street space, seems peculiar. The unintentional association of "tricks" in the street with the "tricks" of prostitution seems directly relevant to my concerns about the policing of female expression in private and public spheres.

In the 1995 World Championship, the "tricks" appear to be the same turns and jumps required during the "compulsory tricks test":

1. Two right-turn jumps on right foot
2. Two left-turn jumps on left foot
3. Two right-foot crisscross jumps (right foot in front of left)
4. Two left-foot crisscross jumps (left in front of right)
5. Ten high steps (alternating jumps in which you lift each knee up to your waist)

    Executed by a singles team (two turners + one jumper) in thirty seconds, and by a doubles team (two turners + two jumpers) in forty seconds (The Compulsory Tricks Test; ibid., 52).

The rulebook encourages freestyle "tricks" that use props, including balls, batons, and short, three- to four-foot ropes usually employed in squatting leaps (ibid., 54). In the freestyle presentation, as always, the ropes must keep turning without interruption during the entire sixty sec-onds or deductions will occur.

The control of the body appears to be critical to judging performance in the competition, even in the freestyle rounds. One of the first gen-erations of double-dutch teams in the public competition of New York City was the 1977 championship team known as the Fantastic Four. Since their performance was still closely tied to street play, a particular incident involving their public performance in the competition exem-plifies my concern about the reinterpretation of black-female partici-pation.

The team included African Americans Robin Oakes, Nicki Adams, De'Shone Adams, and Delores Brown. In the book *Double Dutch* (1986), David Walker recalls that a male member of the New York City Board of Education thought that Robin Oakes was "too fat" to compete. In re-sponse to his criticisms, Robin invented as many "tricks" as she could the

"Rockin' the blacktop": A singles team rehearses at the American Double Dutch League between rounds.

following year and became one of the most innovative performers in the freestyle competition. It was her expressive skill that year which ironically earned the Fantastic Four a television spot in a McDonald's commercial (Walker and Haskins 1986, 25; also see Goodwin 1980).

The comments from the member of the Board of Education implied the assumption that the ideals of fitness found in other athletic sports required a certain female body type. The board member was monitoring black girls' bodies, rather than the unique skills that double-dutch performance inspired, particularly in the freestyle competition. In addition, the board member's comments suggest a lack of awareness and understanding about one of the more liberating aspects of street double-dutch: any able-bodied girl of any shape or age can "fit" into the ropes of double-dutch play; double-dutch is unconditionally a "one-size-fits-all" activity.

As Christopher Small has noted in discussing the ideals of music-making in African and African American performance, "it is assumed that everyone is musical," everyone can participate in music-making, and specialization is not privileged or sacrificed as a result (Small 1987, 25).

Girls Will Be Girls: Re-Remembering within Choreographed Endings

> Those who construct masculine notions of blackness and race progress
> . . . are remembering a particular history. . . . [W]e have some *powerful*
> *lot of re-remembering to do.* (emphasis added; Brown 1994, 145–46)

Although the institutional arms of the ADDL may legislate specific oral and kinetic behaviors from girls' street performance out of the competition, the expressive interventions of the girls themselves demonstrate the "re-remembering" of everyday play, musical expression, and a true sense of freestyle. Black girls find ways to reclaim their hidden double-dutch voices, reinserting the rhyming and body-music-making aspects of their street game-songs into the marginal spaces of the institutionalized competition, as well as the free time between the judged rounds of competition.

At the 1995 international competition, one could distinctly observe that retention of street elements among the black U.S. teams, who commonly bear names such as the Hot Peppers, Hot Steppers, and Red Hot Peppers—names reminiscent of the lyrics and codes of play in street double-dutch (ADDL Souvenir Booklet, June 17, 1995).

The "speed" round of competition was probably formulated from the "hot pepper" element of jumping double-dutch. Yet the idea of absolute speed (speed for speed's sake) was not in and of itself an aesthetic ideal in playing street double-dutch. Rather, the adventure and challenge of pushing the collaborative effort and creative ideas to new limits seemed to be a goal, which precipitated faster tempos.

If one were to guess, the "freestyle" component of the competition would be the obvious place for reinserting the use of rhymes, music, cheers, and dancelike expression when the competition was first formulated. As with any arena of publicly displayed freedom, attempts to control the limits of that freedom are never far away.

The inclusion of a freestyle round could have served an educative role, nurturing both oral and kinetic literacy, and creativity based on ideals prominent in black performance contexts. Had participants been required to develop rhymes, as well as the mute and limited "tricks" described earlier, the ability to improvise rhythms, rhymes, and melodies may have become an interesting feature of the sport. But, not unlike the improvised social music-making of rhythm 'n' blues or jazz scatting—of partners "cutting a rug" with *the Lindy*, breakdancing, or rapping in the public sphere—so little of black vernacular performance is recreated in its full complexity as musical expression in multi-ethnic settings. Hand-clapping games, cheers, and double-dutch are no exception.

Among the exceptions to rules legislated in the sport of double-dutch came certain amendments that reflected what I believe to be the ongoing agency found in girls' street play that reappear in the marginal spaces of the competition. In October 1995, the required choreographed ending was amended to read: "The Freestyle team must demonstrate *Turning, Acrobatic, Dance and a choreographed Ending* in the routine (T.A.D.E.). Omitting any one of the four elements will result in point deductions from the team's Execution Score. The judge in charge of scoring T.A.D.E. will deduct 1 point (not 5 points as noted [earlier]) for omission of a choreographed ending" ("ADDL Rule Book Changes," October 6, 1995. Chapter VI—page 13, Article 3, c: First Sentence).

During the summer competition in North Charleston, there were moments of expression that were clearly emblematic of girls' original chants and play. In idle moments, it was not uncommon to find black girls breaking out into handclapping games and cheers. I never observed any of the nonblack girls engaged in such play. Similar moments of chants, hand-claps, and foot-stomps were apparent in the choreographed endings of almost every black team, whether from the United States or France, the only non-U.S. team of African descent. These black girls were reclaiming and recontextualizing their own gendered ways of sporting street double-dutch. Their stylish handclapping and body-patting, their "old-school" ways of addressing gender, race, and authority through play, were remembered through the social interactions that they maintained and continued to play in their everyday performances.

Some of the choreographed endings re-presented flashes of contemporary black dances, such as the up-and-back hip-swinging bowed-legged movements of a dance called the Tootsie Roll. This dance was incorporated into the freestyle performances of the fourth-grade team Twice as Nice from Ohio, and was also featured in the ending of a high school division team from Washington, D.C. The Tootsie Roll borrows its namesake from the popular chocolate candy and received national recognition by way of a 1994 party song called "Tootsie Roll" based on the style known as "bass music," performed by the southern rap and bass artists the 69 Boyz (see 69 Boyz, "Tootsie Roll," *Tootsie Roll: Hip-Hop Mix,* 1994).

The song and dance gained popularity in the Washington, D.C., area for its title resonated with African Americans' local knowledge of D.C. as the "Chocolate City." A singles team from D.C. performed the Tootsie Roll, the dance and the accompanying chant from the chorus of the song: "up / back / side-to-side / 'n' this is how we tootsie roll."

In another special moment (this time not simply a choreographed ending), the all-black French team, Generation Ébène, generated quite a reaction from the primarily black audience of kids, parents, and adult sponsors during the preliminary rounds of the freestyle competition. This team of young-spirited black teenagers looked like they had leaped right out of a West coast rap video with their red bandanas, braided hair extensions, baggy athletic gym clothing, and all the latest athletic footgear. Ébène elicited the most spectacular moment of the entire competition when they incorporated the "street ballet" of breakdancing into the middle of their routine (i.e., a back-spin, known as a "windmill" in hip-hop) was executed between the twirling ropes, which were slowed momentarily to make room for the jumper's spectacular gesture.

The crowd was momentarily dumbfounded, and then erupted into a bevy of screams and applause. Generation Ébène had surpassed any expectations of what was possible between the twirling ropes. They didn't even speak English, nor did they interact much with the U.S. counterparts from the diaspora because of the language barrier.

They wrapped up the routine, which was penalized for exceeding the freestyle time limit, with a cheer. *Stomp-clap-clap / stomp-stomp-clap-clap / stomp-stomp-stomp.* The singles team of three young women concluded with their fists punctuating the air exclaiming "Ébène!" (Blackness!) The trans-Atlantic conversation among black girls from the United States to France had registered its trademark on the competition—embodied musical expression.

Many other teams simply employed a choreographed ending that incorporated body percussion, often accompanied by a newly composed, rhymed chant, signifying the unique identity of their team, while also showing the diasporic unity among black girls' play from New York to Ohio to South Carolina. The white and biracial teams rarely used chants in their performances. Their athletic skill said it all. The exception was the Japanese who seemed to intelligently mimic black style in body and verbal expression. Here is an excellent example of a chant accompanying a choreographed ending from Double Forces, an Ohioan high school division team who demonstrated remarkable flair. Musically speaking, the first two lines of their chant end on an *off-beat*, a syncopated articulation against the regular ticking of the ropes; the last line concludes emphatically *on* the beat:

> Double Forces has got the beat.
> 'Cuz we do it with our feet.
> 'Cuz we . . . . . are . . . . BAD!

With the final utterance of the word "bad," the team flings the two double-dutch ropes off into the air and defiantly walk off stage without waiting for the judges, as if to say "So there!" or "Forget about this competition. We won!" (See transcription, p. 153.)

This is the dramaturgy of oral and kinetic expression in black musical performance at its best. It is achieved and amplified by the polyrhythmic anticipation and syncopation enacted when the girls stretched out the silences between the words in the phrase "we are bad!" This also allows their synchronized footwork and turning actions to be visually foregrounded by the absence of sound broken open by a disruption in the expected musical texture. It also highlights their bodies performing percussion. Listeners/viewers might anticipate an ending with the group's name, rather than an assertion of their bravado, making it all the more exciting. All the elements of hip-hop and African American performance aesthetics, from signifying to boasting, to the use of the body to accentuate musical and verbal expression, are here.

What is most fascinating in tracing double-dutch from street to sport is how black girls struggle for agency and power within the sport in ways that could be overlooked, especially if one was unaware of the significance of rhymes and music-making in local play. Ironically, music is finally being recognized by one of the "founding fathers" of the sport. Under the auspices of the International Federation of Double Dutch, David Walker has been touring the globe with one of the championship double-dutch teams from the ADDL, the Dynamic Diplomats of Double Dutch. With this group, he participated in an international dance festival in 1991 that was held in southern France, entitled "African Dance Rhythms and Music." During the event, an relationship between music and dance led to a revelation on his part: double-dutch was missing a critical relationship with music. He said "music was not there," though he acknowledged that the sound of the rope provided a timeline for the possibility of music. Out of this insight he invented "fusion double-dutch."

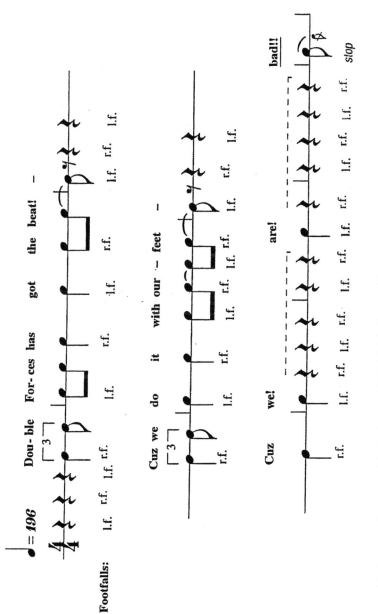

Double Forces' Choreographic Ending at 1995 ADDL Competition.

He told me, "I asked the girls to listen to the drum. The drum is the rope. The rope is the sound of the drum" (telephone interview, May 14, 1995). The rest is showtime at the Apollo.

Double-dutch was removed from Harlem street play, traveled the nation as a sport, and finally returned to Harlem's Apollo Theatre. The first Saturday of December at the Apollo hosts international teams from as close as East Flatbush, Brooklyn and as far away as Tokyo, Japan. These teams compete for "Best of Show" in the "freestyle" competition, which is dominated by the sounds and sights of hip-hop expression as an outgrowth of the sport known as "fusion" double-dutch. In 2000, at the ninth annual Double Dutch Holiday Classic at the Apollo, the Japanese won best of show for the fifth year in a row.

A *New York Times* article reported that Walker viewed double-dutch as a way of helping girls stay in shape and develop teamwork:

> "It's harmony, like the Supremes." . . . For those who compete—still nearly all girls, on the American teams—it is harmony plus style. . . . The Jumpers [with Style] wore black tops, red vinyl pants and black sneakers with prickly rubber bath-mat soles. While the Jumpers piked and flipped and did handstands between the moving ropes, a pint-sized boy in an Abercrombie & Fitch–style plaid shirt strolled across the stage, talking on a cell phone and strewing dollar bills like confetti, to the loud approval of the audience. . . . The Japanese teams had no such costumes. They wore baggy sweats and T-shirts. . . . [The] Japanese visitors said, through an interpreter, that they viewed Double Dutch as part of hip-hop culture, and they incorporated break dance moves into their routines. The Japanese fascination with American culture, down to the finer points of vintage Levi's, is well noted, as is their penchant for black American contributions like jazz, blues and hip-hop. (Dewan 2000, B3)

This extended quote is consistent with the perception promoted by the first international rap tour in 1982 mentioned in a previous chapter (see Adler 1991).

Walker sent me a videotape of "fusion" performances by the Dynamic Diplomats of Double Dutch, an open division team of two females and two males, that Walker has groomed since they were young teens. "Fusion" double-dutch involves performing the freestyle round of the competition to popular black dance music, such as "Real Love" by popular hip-hop/R&B artist Mary J. Blige or the latest R&B or rap hits. The fusion here supposedly is between double-dutch (the sport) and prerecorded hit songs (the music). Music, Walker asserted, allows the audience to be more involved in the exhibition of double-dutch, and yet he completely overlooked the music-making already present in the street performances of girls performing double-dutch. Might this have something to do with his definition of music? Is it that double-dutch, like rap, is not "real" music because it does not involve out and out singing or a literate approach to composition/improvisation?

Walker was unable to appreciate double-dutch as musical performance largely due to what's been at stake for him in establishing a sport. What sport legitimately involves music in its most competition? The games black girls play were omitted from the sport. No music allowed, said the rule book and ADDL officials. How convenient and, arguably, paternal of this Double Dutch Cop to invent "fusion double-dutch" within a diasporic meeting of the minds.

Conclusion

This case study of double-dutch, in which I have tracked its movement from street to sport to fusion double-dutch, should provide a unique model for analyzing the ways in which both "blackness" and "femaleness" are interpreted in public music performance, and may also dispel certain assumptions about gender roles in black music. Ellen Koskoff has suggested that both self- and other-defined sexuality (and interpretations of gender in general) affect music performance in perceivable ways. Cultural beliefs about women's inherent sexuality may limit or negate their participation in musical performance (Koskoff 1989, 6). Just as many aspects of music-making in the everyday culture among blacks are overlooked, misinterpreted, or "ruled out" as musical and/or respectable, so has female participation—whether in institutionalized double-dutch, basketball, or hip-hop performance.

The suave, percussive rhymes of rapper/singer Lauryn Hill, aka "L-Boogie," of the hip-hop group The Fugees, reminds listeners that women do counter masculinist interpretations of power in hip-hop, often represented by the images of gangsters. Lauryn's rhymes, and the polysemic meanings they create, evoke ties to the group's identifications with Haiti:

> *Who—do?* [double entendre: hoodoo] *I can do what you do, ea-zy.*
> *Belie-ve me, frontin' niggaz give me heebie jee-bies*
> *So while you imita'in' Al Capone*
> *I be Nina Simone*
> *And defaca'in' on your microphone*
> (Lauryn Hill from "Ready or Not," *The Score,* 1996)

Girls and women can do what men do, and easy, is Lauryn's claim. It's also my claim with regards to the connections between double-dutch and hip-hop. Girls have been dancing and singing, from ring games to double-dutch. Their tuneful rhymes and expressive gestures, from hand to hip, help them claim a black *and* female identity starting with performances about "Little Sally Walker" and "Mary Mack." The freedom of pre-adolescence allows black girls to "shake it to the east / shake it to the west," divining gender identity and black expressivity with gyrating hips and snarelike handclaps. Their performance of a social/musical identity is *punctuated* by idioms of sexuality and somatic expressivity that are misread or limited in many public settings like the ADDL event, leading to the regulation of such activity by many adult black females. When we allow a fuller understanding of the musical behaviors operating in girls' play from street to sport, black women's presence in secular music-making and public performance whether in sport, popular music, or ordinary play, can be viewed in more complex and authoritative ways, and women's agency as performers and artists becomes visible as well as audible beyond children's musical play.

This chapter was about the effects of institutionalizing double-dutch rope play on the music of black girls' play. I discussed how double-dutch moved from street performance to a "nonmusical" competitive sport to something called "fusion double-dutch." Between the masculinization of black nationalist impulses and the whiteness of feminist interventions, this black feminist or womanist critique of an economy of black vernacular and musical expression has implications, not only for thinking about the socialization of racial and gender inequality among black girls, but also may have implications for the institutionalization (rather than the commercialization) of African American musical practices in genres like hip-hop (this is a subject for future study).

> I am not one piece of myself. I cannot simply be a black person and not be a woman, too. (Lorde 1983, 262)

An examination of double-dutch shows how blackness and femaleness share similar geographies of race/nation consciousness that are conventionally attributed to black male experience.

7

Let a Woman Jump
Dancing with the Double Dutch Divas

Though she was long past the age of playing double-dutch, an African American student in the School of Music at Michigan whose voice reminded me of Jessye Norman's, once shared with me a nostalgic lament she had about the game. I had told Kim a few stories about my trip to the double-dutch competitions in Charleston, South Carolina, and she (in her mid-twenties at the time) admitted that she had never learned how to jump. "Nobody did it where I come from in North Carolina. I feel like I won't truly be a black girl until I learn to double-dutch."

Her confession was not unusual, and it testified to the power of double-dutch in the imagination of many African American girls; our longing for it is perhaps most expressed by those who were never exposed to it because of geography or other reasons like never getting the hang of jumping double-dutch because they perceived themselves to be too plump or not athletic.

Straight, or single rope-jumping, has been prevalent among girls of various ethnicities from North to South. But double-dutch has been primarily a Northern, and *urban,* form of street play, in which black girls have shined.

Though it has figured prominently in the lives and imaginations of African American girls across the nation for at least fifty years, grown women don't ordinarily play double-dutch. It continues to be viewed by adults of both sexes as a "girls'" game as the rap "Jump Sister Jump" composed by a member of the Double Dutch Divas suggests in its poetry:

> My daugh-ter said:
> "Hey, Ma-ma! What's the matter with you?
> Isn't jumpin' rope on-ly some-thin' kids should do?"

Chorus:
JUMP, JUMP—, Sister, JUMP! / JUMP!
(Ya) JUMP, JUMP—, Sister, JUMP!
One, two, three

I met the Divas at their weekly rehearsal in Midtown. I hadn't done the "after-school thing" since high school, but on a chilly evening in October 1999, at the age of thirty-seven, I was introduced to several African American *girls* ranging in age from twenty-seven to forty-nine who were still jumping double-dutch. On Monday nights, whenever the school system was in session, the Double Dutch Divas held court in the auditorium of Park West High.

We are the hard-core— jumpers and we / never fail
We jump on— through— the snow, sleet, rain-and— hail

Twenty years ago, Vy Higginson, a New York radio personality and producer of the Broadway hit *Mama, I Want to Sing,* founded a women's double-dutch group that performed in Central Park. She named it Jump Sister Jump to reclaim the games girls once played. Boys, Higginson recalled, continue to play the games they played in childhood, like basketball, football, and baseball. Girls, however, tend to abandon their games, as well as the athleticism and social bonding that develops through play (Franklin 2000). So she formed Jump Sister Jump with several adult women and what remains of the group lives on as the Double Dutch Divas (with other new members). From July through September on Sunday evenings, they can be found jumping ropes at 72nd Street in Central Park, next to the roller-skaters cruising around a makeshift rink dancing to house music, while a cavalry of drummers improvise on African rhythms nearby.

The eldest member of the Divas, Spirit, is the woman who authored the Jump Sister Jump poem, and she has a book full of poetry written for the group. She surprised me when she told me that Jump Sister Jump were the Double-Dutch Girls that accompanied Afrika Bambaataa, Fab Five Freddy, Rammellzee, Grandmixer DST and the Infinity Rappers, the Rock Steady Crew (and various graffiti artists), on the first European tour of rap from New York City, in 1982 (see Adler 1991).

There are many expressive dimensions to the Divas: music-making, poetry, dramaturgy, everyday play, and the collective memories (or somatic historiography) of black dances. All of this is carried on in the name of black female cultural traditions and double-dutch. Whether it's appearing on ABC's talk show *The View* (led by Barbara Walters) or traveling to introduce double-dutch to Japan through televised appearances and workshops, their performance is locked into a broad range of black music and culture that originates in everyday musical experiences.

I spent almost a year attending rehearsals and socializing with the Divas every Monday night from September 2000 to July 2001. The group's rehearsals were a feminist practice, oriented toward the mind, body, and spirit of black women (as well as anyone who joined them). Their practice reinforces and reflects my theories about the musical socialization of black girls' games and their importance in conditioning race and gender identity among black females. The Divas add force—not only to my thesis, but also to my own sense of what a black and female musical sensibility is—every time I am in the midst of their magical ropes of love.

Introducing the Hardcore Jumpers

I became acquainted with the Divas through Nicole Franklin, an African American video editor working for NBC's *Later Today,* who was spending her spare time producing an independent video documentary about double-dutch. The project followed the development of double-dutch from its origins as a street game through its evolution into "one of the earliest team sports for women" (quoted from a draft of Nicole's grant proposal).

In 1998, before moving to New York, I had published a piece on double-dutch, and Nicole learned of it from a graduate student at New York University. She subsequently asked to interview me for the documentary if I happened to be in New York City before she finished production in December 1999.

Two months before her deadline, I was flown to the city for one day only, to consult for the WGBH-Boston (children's television) series I mentioned earlier. I was to spend most of the day collaborating with a video crew on the shoot. Nicole set up an interview for first thing in the morning. During our conversation, I shared with her how impressed I was with the women who appeared in the rough cut of the documentary she had sent me a month earlier. She alerted me to the fact that the Divas were rehearsing that night, and said her video crew would be taping it. I jumped at the opportunity to meet these sistas and to see if I might spend the next summer doing fieldwork with them. So Nicole gave me the phone numbers of Wilhelmina Sandford, one of the main contacts for the group, and I phoned her at the last minute to get permission to attend.

During our conversation, Willie, as she preferred to be called, invited me to join them. She warned me more than once that the Divas wouldn't be jumping that evening; she obviously didn't want to disappoint me. The group was planning, instead, to talk about "going pro": they were deciding whether they should continue to function as an amateur group or move into a more professional mode of performance. "We're *just* talking tomorrow," Willie emphasized, "but you're welcome to come."

Despite feeling a bit disappointed, I knew it would be worth adding the trip to my tight schedule. So I welcomed the chance to do a little fieldwork, even if it was just meeting with the Divas.

Wrapping up our phone call, Willie gave me directions to the school, which was located in midtown, and I thought I detected more warmth in her voice than I had heard at the beginning of our conversation. She came off as very businesslike, but was a sweetheart in person. "We usually start at 7:00 P.M., which means things won't really get started until 7:30," she said, adding with a chuckle, "C.P. *time* [colored people's time]. Just tell the security guard you're with the double-dutchers."

Practice usually consisted of developing musical and social relations by jumping rope to popular songs, choreographing "doubles," "triples," or "quads" (routines with two or more women in the ropes), and using the exercise to stay in shape. The rehearsals provided a weekly opportunity for members to catch up on joyful and troubling events in their lives and the lives of their family members: engagements were announced, a relative's wedding pictures were shared, the report on a mother's struggle with diabetes was met with comfort. And after all was said and done, there was always the possibility of visiting one of their favorite restaurants: Ollie's Noodle Shop and Grille.

Throughout the year, the Divas appeared at schools in the city, camps in the Catskills, theme parks in Darien, Connecticut, and various festivals —including the Pittsburgh International Children's Theater Festival, the Milk International Children's Festival in Toronto, a festival in Sioux City, Iowa, and the Smithsonian Folk Festival—to name some of their activities in 2001. Before leaving each Monday night, they received updates on upcoming travel, or checks from their recent gigs.

I had been blown away by the videotaped performances and testimonies Nicole sent me. She called the vignette featuring the Divas her "money shot": it gave life to her visual narrative, and made the piece more marketable. In fact, I often showed excerpts of this footage at conference presentations, and my audience always got a kick out of watching these grown women do their thing. As everyday women, their athletic and musical display defied our expectations and triggered delight. For me, however, the real pleasure came from the fact that the Divas exhibited a mature and innovative approach to double-dutching that both children and adults had rarely, if ever, seen before: they were the first organized group to perform double-dutch to music long before fusion double-dutch became an idea in David Walker's mind.

Lydia, who was one of the senior members and was of Caribbean descent, generally brought the boombox. They played compact discs, which anyone was free to bring and share, or cassette mix tapes that Lydia had selected and prepared over the years. The tapes featured popular hip-hop, R&B, reggae, merengue, salsa, and house, as well as occasional rock 'n' roll, country and western, and Broadway tunes.

Each week, the group casually discussed the latest recordings by artists, from Luther Vandross and Janet Jackson, to hip-hop head Michael Franti and his group Spearhead. Anything with a good beat for jumping was fair game.

In the ropes, the Divas transformed the rigmarole moves of young girls' play by adding new individual and social choreography. The ticking ropes, turned in eggbeater fashion just ahead of the beat of the music, served as a steady timeline for improvised movement, singing, chanting, and all kinds of playful drama that marked the pulses and the playfulness of the groove. All the moves were mastered with the same lighthearted, communal interaction found in young girls' play.

Young girls may *play* double-dutch, but they don't *perform* it as music like these women did. Nicole's "money shot" culminated with the following chant, recorded during a street performance in Harlem. Though the Divas usually sang this chant, young girls might have considered it a post-exhibition cheer or even a choreographic ending.

> *We are the hard—core— jumpers and we / never fail*
> *We jump on— through— the snow, sleet, rain-and— hail*
> *And we can jump when we are tired, we can jump when we're blue*
> *We jump-on when we can think of OTHER things to do*

We jump-on (HEY) no matter what mood— we're in
Cuz—, you know you get OUT what you put IN
We are the hard—core— jumpers and we / never fail
We jump ON, we jump ON, we jump ON, we jump ON, THANK
you!

While the collective is clearly a significant dimension of the Divas' performance, individuality is also prized within the group. As a member, each Diva acquired a special nickname, and just before they sang the closing chant in the video, the individuals of the group introduced themselves by their nickname and age—beginning with the youngest, Smooth, at twenty-seven, and ending with Spirit, at forty-nine. Most of the women introduced themselves rather simply. But Willie, who at forty-seven was one of the oldest members, and, by day, worked as the assistant to the president of Godiva Chocolatier, said, "My name is Heart." And with actions that spoke louder than words, turned her booty to the crowd, adding, "because I have a *BIG one.*" Her hips unpacked her adjectives as she punctuated "big" and "one" with two equally robust hip gestures.

In most places, except on the dance floor, many African American women resist associating their public persona with their backside. Since the art of the Divas was about music and dance, Willie's intro deliciously transgressed all kinds of boundaries. Her gestures flew in the face of stereotypes about African American and African female sexuality, countering hegemonic interpretations of the Venus Hottentot, like the early 1990s rap song "Baby Got Back," by Sir Mix-a-lot. Willie's embodied delivery expressed her comfort with her curvaceous body, and, she added, "and I can *really* jump fast," contesting any notion that only small bodies can move. The dance floor in black contexts is one of the few places where women's "black" bodies—with their "African" bootys—represent a norm, and are not constrained by the images of "white" femininity (which also hamper white women's everyday bodies in the public sphere).

The Divas' nicknames—Faith, Spirit, Heart, Lady Di, Smooth, Spice, and Joy—were clearly symbolic. Initially, I assumed that they had named themselves to symbolize some aspect of their personality. After some issues that had arisen a few years earlier about the loss of individuality among group members, the Divas began a tradition whereby existing members named the newcomers: existing members began to characterize a neophyte's style of moving in the ropes. They combined this information with the new woman's approach to the group, or her relationship to performing double-dutch. For example, Faith, a fairly recent member, had been named on the basis of her determination to join the group. She had never jumped before, but she kept coming back. I was eventually dubbed "Dr. Diva" for my role as a researcher and talking head in the documentary about the group.

The Meeting

As my cab pulled up to the curb in front of Park West High, I was nervous and excited. I stepped onto the sidewalk fumbling with my wallet, while the unusually chilly fall weather transformed my breath into smoky clouds of air. My mind was racing, so I tried to slow down. I told myself: *Don't forget to give a tip. Check the time. It's just after seven. And don't leave the video camera, or your brown leather backpack, in the back seat.*

As I crossed the threshold into the high school, a Puerto Rican–looking security guard stopped me with the question, "Are you looking for double-dutch?" I nodded—hoping I resembled a jumper or a turner—as he pointed down a long corridor with metal lockers lifelessly lining the walls. "Turn right after the double doors at the end of the hall and look for the auditorium. That's where the Divas usually practice."

A bit of brotherly love was tucked under the smile in his voice at the mention of the Divas. It turned out that this guy had "a thing" for one of them, and often came down to say hello during rehearsals. The brothers guarding the building had a certain attraction, I'd say, to the spirit of what these women did, as much as they felt for specific members. Double-dutch is, after all, part of the black public sphere of social performance and romantic play.

Once through the double doors, I turned right as instructed, but found myself in a maze of unmarked doors. After greeting one locked door after another, a guard sitting nearby pointed to the one right behind me. Offering him my thanks, I pulled the metal clasp of the door's handle, and the sound ricocheted into the empty space of a sizeable auditorium, whose only guests were four women milling around onstage quite a distance from where I stood. Not one took note of my entrance. As I traversed the gulf, drawing closer, I knew I was in the right place. Their faces were familiar, although I only remembered one of their nicknames from Nicole's video.

Here they were in the flesh—dressed in Danskin leggings, New Balance and Nike athletic shoes, and extra large, yellow T-shirts that had the group's name across the chest and their nicknames on the back. Here were Lady Di, Spirit, Faith, and another *sista* whose name eluded me because her T-shirt was on inside-out. I didn't learn it that night, so I called her Diva X in my initial notes.

I didn't see Willie, but I did see ropes lying across the stage. Talking was no longer the business at hand. Nicole had told me the Divas encourage visitors to join their rehearsals, and though I might have been twenty-five years late for my lesson, I was ready to take my turn and learn double-dutch that night.

The Divas jockeyed to seat themselves in a ring on the hardwood floor, and began their warm-up, stretching their muscles before they jumped. Lady Di popped a cassette of house music into the boombox, setting the vibe for an evening of jumping. As she joined the ladies on the floor, they spread their legs wide and reached up and over their torsos. The flow of their breath and the flow of their movements began to synchronize. Lady Di, an elementary school principal with an obsession for exercise, assumed the role of the instructor or mistress of ceremonies. (She told me she had a completely separate closet just for her Diva and other athletic gear.) In addition to a rigorous daily routine at school, she trained for the New York Marathon every year and took an invigorating single jump-rope class at Skate Key skating rink in the Bronx before heading to Midtown for Monday night rehearsals. She directed our every move in a funky style of aerobics.

"In-HALE——." The hissing sound of air drawn through pursed lips and teeth followed her rising tone. "EX-hale——." A *whoosh* escaped every mouth. Breath and tone quickly evaporated as each Diva melted into a deep prostrate position. Tranquility surfaced as the small talk disappeared and soft laughter emerged, suggesting a warm circle of girl-friends.

I was afraid to interrupt them, but was still hoping to get the chance to jump, despite my appearance. I was dressed casually in a white v-neck T-shirt with blue jeans that were snug after gaining several unwanted pounds.

Just then, Nicole's video crew arrived to record the event. Marcia (*mar-SEE-ah*), a Brazilian woman who was the director of photography for Nicole's production, unloaded her camera. I recognized her from the morning interview, and she introduced me to Sheria, Nicole's production coordinator. Then I waited for an invitation to join the Divas. I did what I thought I should do as an ethnomusicologist: wait for permission—wait to be invited to join *others'* cultures—even though I thought it was mine.

Just then, Lady Di strutted by, heading toward the boombox to slip a different cassette into its drawer. She didn't like the vibe she had chosen earlier. As she passed, I introduced myself: "Willie said it was OK for me be here." Without missing a beat, Lady Di gave me direct eye contact and asked, "Are you going to jump?" I nodded enthusiastically with relief. I was *in*—any "barricade" I created melted away.

The next thing I knew, I was down on the floor, stretching against the constraints of my jeans. Next to me, Lady Di (actually Diahann), who was forty-two, calmly urged us all to "Take it NICE!—. . . and EA-zy . . . Breathe IN!—. . . AND out . . ." As we continued, I checked out each brown girl in the ring.

First, there was Spirit (Shirley), a tall, gold-colored sista to the right of Lady Di, who was a designer for the McCall Pattern Company. She was forty-nine, with an intensity lurking beneath her quiet facade. Then there was Faith (Dee), to my left—a slender, long-limbed, and sturdy, medium-brown sista—who, at thirty-seven, complained about the inflexibility of her back as we tried to touch our toes. Diva X sat across from me with a jumbo water bottle next to her shapely thighs. She mentioned that she was trying to lose weight, and as we returned to a prostrate position, I noticed that her gaze was in some other world, far beyond our chatter.

What came next—which eventually became a game of embodied memory and improvisational choreography—transformed mundane aerobics into music and dance. Lady Di wound up the "nice-and-easy" routine: "OK! Let's stand up and move a little bit." Heel-toes, grapevines, and shuffling side-steps were the vehicles that transported our soon-to-be-glistening bodies to the popular sounds emanating from the boombox. A *deep house* re-mix was playing. The four-on-the-floor bass kick-drum, and ecstatic soprano riffing (à la Martha Wash, of disco's *Two Tons of Fun*) enveloped us with its atmosphere of late-night club dancing in wide, open spaces.

Alternating our feet as we moved left then right every four beats (*step step step tap)*, the momentum of our bodies made our hands come together, and we began to clap perfectly in phase. Nobody missed the first beat. Lady Di then gave us the go-ahead—as if we were playing a game of *Red light, green light*—directing each of us to take turns choreographing and leading the others in steps to the groove. One by one, we played follow the leader with different leaders.

There was no hesitation to take on the leadership, and everyone followed with glee. Unlike what happened during a soul train line I had organized in my mixed-race and mixed-gender hip-hop course, no one resisted the play of the moment (Gaunt 2002). But then again, we had all been in musical scenarios like this before—they are common in black communal settings.

As the shuffle of our feet kept the time between us, gestures spontaneously emerged, and our voices responded like fireworks on display. Joy, Lady Di's sister in real life, joined us. And Sheria, Nicole's production assistant, was encouraged to join in, too, while Marcia captured everything on camera. We tossed gestures around the circle in a *counterclockwise direction* as if they were objects of *soul,* relaying messages of unity and difference. Our gestures evoked a popular black social dance, suggesting the erotic shared among women, and praising the circle of life with outstretched arms.

Our enactments are not exclusive to women. They are found among black women and men in various public and informal gatherings, from the club to the sanctuary, from a house party to a concert venue, and from a community picnic to a family reunion. They reflect the past and the present—the continuum of black bodies swinging to Duke Ellington's big band, Aretha Franklin's soul, or Hezekiah Walker's contemporary gospel crusade.

Pieces of these worlds were embodied as a kind of discourse we passed around like it was a *phat* joint. We were getting high off each playful pass of embodied information around the circle, reminding me of the Harlem Globetrotters at center court.

With our steps traveling from left to right serving as a timeline, someone set up a soulful shrug syncopated away from the downbeat, known as the Bounce—a dance from the late 1990s—and we passed it around the circle in a wave. Somebody else threw out a sinewy shoulder-roll resembling the Snake from the 1980s. Our bodies knew these dances as we fit their different rhythms atop the four-four rhythm of our steps. And our claps, their snarelike flam on beats two and four, occasionally broke into an eight-beat, double-time pattern that commonly announces exciting moments in the club or at house parties. According to my mother this was common in the 1970s during her party days.

We hung our percussive and syncopated gestures on musical hooks marked by our feet and our hands, as we anticipated the next message passed around the circle. We were loose now—had let go—and were feeling close to the musical sensibilities that make us feel at one with being black, being black women.

The choreographies that the seven of us articulated were part and parcel of the kinetic orality that black people have shared intergenerationally throughout the twentieth century. Key among them are hip gyrations signaling different eras of blackness, such as the side-to-side rotation of the hips punctuating beats two and four of a four-beat pattern in a 1970s dance called the Four Corners. Funky, syncopated isolations habitually mark the torso, and sly, loose undulations of the neck are used not only in the service of dancing, but also recall the emphatic discourse of neck-popping in everyday nonverbal discourse (especially by women as an articulation of blackness). Our playful embodiment reflected all this, as well as the well-timed hops and kicks that are remembered and revived in the black dances of the 1920s, 1960s, '70s, and '90s.

This was a kinetic and nonverbal version of the game of oral transmission that children play known as *Telephone*. Instead of finding humor in the distortions a message suffers after it is transmitted through several people, we experience laughter from the recognition of the "changing same"-ness (Le Roi Jones, aka Amiri Baraka) of dances and social spaces re-remembered through play. Despite a lack of familiarity between some of us, despite the inevitable changes and losses that cultural messages might naturally suffer from body to body—through time and space—and despite the differences that surely existed among us as musical beings, we reveled in the unbroken chain that connects different generations of men and women who have called themselves Blacks, Coloreds, Negroes, Afro-Americans, and African Americans.

HEY!!! Shouts out of nowhere keyed our attention toward the latest message: the grapevine of someone's imaginative feet, arms, or torso. Our game of improvisation allowed us to choreograph history, time, and social memory out of our black consciousness and *black-female* social practice. As anyone who's been to a black club knows, at some point or another, there will be a group of black women dancing by themselves throughout the night—resisting the "meat-market" mentality of a single's night out.

"AW—yeah!!!" Di interjected, as I extracted a dance from the 1980s: the Cabbage Patch. No matter what age, we all recognized the dance and hopped on board the next train of motion. The dance looked nothing like the dolls chosen by the U.S. Postal Service to mark the decade, in its "Celebrating the Century" series. It did not appear to signify the love–hate relationship that black girls, and their black parents, had had with these dolls, which initially appeared only with blonde hair and white skin. There are several black dances named after popular commodities or stars —the Smurf, the Pee Wee Herman, the Jerry Lewis—all cartoonish figures. I have never really questioned why these figures were immortalized in black dances, or what these dances say about black folks' relationship to popular culture icons, American culture, and blacks' relationships with commodity culture. But there is obviously some embodied connection going on that I have yet to fully explore.

As one extended house re-mix faded out and another radiated in from the boombox, our voices wove in and out with exhilarating whoops and hollers, interjections ("Work it, y'all!"), and other exclamations, which were sometimes joined by a chorus ("Come on!" "Get down!"). Paul Gilroy suggests that the power of black music lives in the "anti- and pre-discursive constituents of black metacommunication," namely "dramaturgy, enunciation, and gesture" (Gilroy 1993a, 75). Since slavery, he contends, the power and significance of music among blacks dispersed by the economies of the trans-Atlantic slave trade "have grown in inverse proportion to the limited expressive power of [privileged conceptions of] language [including writing]" (ibid., 74).

Interjections, exclamations, and codes of embodied performance can, and do, intuitively produce meaning. We can, and do, infer the discursive meanings of a *range* of social and cultural expressions signifying blackness and black(female)ness. In other words, *DO your THANG, GIRL!; OO!; OH yeah, THAT's a GOOD one!;* and *HEEYY!* convey more than mere musical exuberance for the spirited circles of choreography we create in the moment. Such expressions call attention to black culture through collective memories and embodied musical histories.

Taking Turns in the Ropes

We hadn't even begun to double-dutch, and I was already *feelin' it*, as the expression goes. Whether warming up physically, shuffling back and forth to *house* music, or improvising with familiar repertoires of street dance, our musical interactions were about play. The vibe said, *we are to-*

gether, parts of a whole, of like minds . . . and bodies. What a meaningful by-product of participating in any musical experience! In black culture, it's like developing a sense of who you are through other people's movement.

Jesse Jackson always invited everyday folk to remember *I am somebody*—part of a body of people raising their voices in call-and-response as one. Following his lead, we shared various sense-abilities about languaging the body, tongue, and voice. We voiced, felt, and experienced being connected beyond any immediate touch. The Divas' warmup reflected a similar exchange. Vibing together, being in sync with one another musically, in spite of the differences we bear—wide hips (like Willie/Heart) or small ones (like Faith/Dee), a healthy "chest" or small breasts, skinny legs with a high butt or thunder thighs and gams, nappy hair bleached blonde (Lydia), or dreads (like mine)—is important business used to constitute social connections among diverse black women.

With our bodies warm and ready to move, individually and collectively, Lady Di and Diva X began to untangle the candy-striped plastic ropes that were lying on the stage. Diva X was actually Spice, aka Pandora—the only married member. She, Willie, Lydia, and Shirley have one daughter each; Pandora's daughter, at eight years old, occasionally performed with us that summer.

Finally, Willie arrived. A *healthy,* brown-skinned sista with a serious look in her eyes that said *I don't play and don't mess with me.* On the short side and full-bodied, Willie's gait reminded me of an old expression: *sure must be jelly cuz jam don't shake like that.* Her attire suggested that she had come straight from her "day" job: she was sporting a maroon knit top and skirt perfect for the fall weather, black stockings, and a pair of black-and-white saddle shoes.

Her saddle shoes seemed odd—out of place and time. While they disrupted my notion of business attire, they fit the notion of girls' games, reminding me of being a football cheerleader back in the day. Saddle shoes also signify the 1950s: sock hops, Sadie Hawkins, Pat Boone's dirty bucks, and the black and white of segregation.

"I thought we weren't jumping tonight," Willie said, seeking an explanation about the meeting. She sounded confused and perturbed. "I didn't bring my [athletic] shoes." Following familiar greetings, her concern went unnoticed as the others got set to jump, to get their groove on. Willie came partially prepared, as she rummaged through one plastic bag and then another, located a T-shirt, and headed to the bathroom. When she returned, her diva name, Heart, blazed across her back, and she took the ropes from Lady Di to turn them.

As we waited for Di to enter the ropes, Spirit—who is the epitome of lanky—asked me, "Do you double-dutch?"

"No, I can't, but . . ." and before I could explain, she interjected.

"*Never* say can't! You can DO it!"

In that split second, the rewind button in my mind triggered, and I played back Nicole's video in my head. There was Spirit, sharing intimate memories of older folks telling her, "*you can't.*" After meeting the women in the video who possessed the ability to defy the odds, to turn life's dramas into poetry, I was inspired. I spontaneously began to write poems about a few of the Divas who impressed me that first night, and they serve as brief character sketches here. For example, I wrote this about Spirit:

Maybe it was the years of interacting with the local media. Maybe something deeper, harder allowed her to powerfully divulge her strength through tears for the camera, to Nicole. With her short black twists outlining the margins of her face, Spirit gazes deep into the eye of the camera, back to people from her past, almost as if talking back to the little girl she was back then. "Never (she struggles to fight the tears welling up inside her, her voice barely letting it out) . . . say can't!"

While others jump in the background, she stands alone gathering her memories for an interview in a dark corner just off center stage. Physical play had been discouraged. A curved spine, a defect causing fear in adults who wish to prevent her from further harm. But in doing so, they nearly kill her spirit.

High cheekbones tense with feeling. Pursed lips trap the pain as a range of hard emotions and memories flash across her face. Tears. Sadness. A fought-for-smile. Frustration. Self-determination. Spirit possessing the camera's eye. To be viewed in other times and places by those whom she may never view, who'll only know her immediate and intimate interview. Once scarred by the power of words, she seeks only to nurture others.

"*Never* say can't! You can DO it!"

"Oh, *I'm ready*!" I shot back, to quell any doubt. "I just wasn't good at it when I was young. But I'm ready [to learn] now!" The only thought of "I can't" remaining pertained to getting out of my tight jeans.

Lady Di jumped first, showing off a deep devotion for *house* music. She danced, skipping across the ropes to the "hi-nrg" (high energy) beats of homegrown house music probably from New York or New Jersey where there is a hotbed of clubs featuring the genre. She "jacked" her body in a familiar style of house dancing that is light on the toes, nearly aerial. Enveloped in the feeling of the motion, she closed her eyes, and her body finessed the turning ropes passing under her toes.

Lady Di knew the ropes from years of jumping. The rapture and endurance of her turn in the ropes captivated not only me, but everyone else waiting in line for their opportunity to shine. Even the turners—Spice and Heart—were into the moment, smiling and maintaining ample room with the ropes so Di could do her thing without thinking about the ropes. The turners' bodies braced and straddled the earth with their feet turned out to keep the perpetual motion of the ropes split seconds ahead of the pulse of the music. That way, Lady Di's steps landed firmly on the beats.

One thing I've always disliked about predominantly white, middle-class, or mainstream staged performances (of any kind), is the lack of support the audience gives, or can sustain, when someone is singing or performing. Even when invited, they don't seem to understand that clapping encourages a better performance—it gives life to the moment—which gives positive feedback to the performers *during* the performance. All those in the room who were not turning ropes or jumping have their eyes tuned to the center action, while their bodies are vibing to the beat. Our mouths generously shout *alrights, umphs,* and *yeahs* though not to distract her focus or detract from her moment.

After what always seemed like hours, Lady Di exited the ropes, and we gave her *high-five* slaps that slipped into a grip of fingertips we pulled apart to create the sound of a shared snap. This is what some African Americans call giving *dap,* a congratulatory gesture symbolizing admiration, love, and transnationalism among people of African descent, from New York to Accra. The Divas' style of dancing in the ropes was not your daughter's double-dutch, where you alternate your feet and sing rhymes about *James Brown / went downtown* or *Teddy bear / teddy bear / touch the ground.* The dancing that the Divas do is a mix of jumping to keep time to the tick of the ropes and dancing to fill the beats in between the ropes to control and embellish one's bobbing body and limbs. It might be called *double-dutch dancing.*

Lady Di's dancing reminded me of the riffs and sonic-informed gyrations of a jazz saxophonist improvising on the bandstand—improvising not only the melody, but also the style of enunciation, the rhythm, and the timing—as if dabbling in a gospel shout, R&B phrasings, hip-hop sampling, and the riff-filled groove of house music.

The Divas take the tradition of jumping rope to another level, blending street double-dutch with learned vernacular or street dances. At once rejuvenating girls' games and reinvigorating grown folks' primary experience of play on the dance floor, like the spirit of havin' a *partay* (we love to elongate or nasalize vowels and change up the rhythmic emphasis of expressions that signify social values or prized social experiences).

After Lady Di leapt out of the cradle of the ropes, Spirit prepared to enter the ropes. She was supposed to be next, but she didn't care for the style of house music coming from the boombox, and chose to wait for the next song, which blended in from the mix tape Lady Di had brought. Usually, Lydia was in charge of the music, but she hadn't arrived yet.

The next song sounded like a gospel shout, but it was still house music. Gospel has become a common element in house music, which is a blend of styles to begin with. Now you can hear the voices of the most well-known traditional and contemporary gospel recording artists—from Tremaine Hawkins to Kirk Franklin—in club re-mixes. The spirit in gospel-house serves the elated and sometimes artificially induced states of euphoria found in nightclubs. This particular gospel-inflected house song featured a chorus of handclappers on beats two and four, and vocalized shouts reflecting religious ecstasy, which clearly moved Spirit's soul.

She entered the inner sanctum of the ropes with drumsticks in hand, exhibiting a whole different flavor than Lady Di. Gliding in between the ropes and establishing her pedaling feet, she began to pop up into the air between her steps ("pop-ups") and then bent down to strike the floor and the sticks alternately between and on two and four. This required a great deal of coordination, but it was second nature to her—a trick she developed that no one else did.

Often, when someone comes up with a special move or trick, others tend not to copy it. This one was referred to as "Shirley's move" (rarely did the women refer to each other by their *Diva* names; I do it here as a narrative device). There are *some* things you can't do; it's not a matter of improvisation and play at all costs.

She moves space with her moves (signaling the turners to move out of their static positions to travel with her in all four directions). She purposefully defies time, age, and the gravity of "I can't." "My diva name is

Spirit, and this is my motto: Just because you're getting older, don't sit aroun' 'n' whine—! Because I'm out here jumping rope, at the age of forty-nine!"

At last, it was my turn. I was thirty-seven years old and there was no question that I was a black girl, with or without knowing how to double-dutch. Since I knew I would be entering the ropes sooner or later, I had been watching how Lady Di, Faith, and Spirit entered them. When I was a kid, entering the ropes was always my stumbling block. I simply couldn't understand how to get in. This reminds me of the difficulty I had with basketball in junior high school. Though I loved to use my body in dance back then, I thought I was no good at sports. Sports were serious. They were not playful, like handclapping games or dancing. In my mind, back then, double-dutch was more sport than music. But I never really got far enough into the practice to really know what it was all about.

Lady Di got into the ropes effortlessly. It seemed she and the others didn't even think about it. But there had to be a "rhythm method" that protected them from getting hit by the oscillating ropes. I watched Di put her hand out in front of her body as she moved up to the perimeter of the ropes and felt the gaps between them. Her whole body moved with the action—reminding me of the young girls rocking back and forth toward the ropes before they entered.

Seeing my efforts to imitate the others, Lady Di offered to guide me through. All eyes were on me now. Willie and Spice tried to comfort me verbally. Spirit smiled at me. Lady Di began to carefully instruct me where to stand. As a school principal with advanced degrees, she was the best teacher for me. She even said to me that she understood how academics think. "I'm gonna break it down for you, and it's really simple. But you gotta do it the same way every time." After nailing down all the moves, I readied myself to take the plunge. "Remember! Plant both feet before you start to alternate [them]."

On my first try, the ropes tangled around my ankles. I teased the others and myself with the words from the story about determination, "I THINK I can, I THINK I can," while I circled back around to enter the ropes again from the same side. Usually a jumper has a particular side they prefer to enter on, and Lady Di suggested that I stay with the same side until I felt much more comfortable. It took me a few times to get it right.

"Jump right into the center of the ropes!" Di coached as she stood back to give me room. I spotted the floor, followed her directions, and, amazingly, found myself inside the ropes without much effort. I was so amazed at myself that I lost my focus on alternating my feet. But everyone was excited for me—giving me *dap* and encouraging me to try again. If we had been young girls playing in the street, I would have lost my turn and had to wait till everyone else went again before I got another turn. But we were grown, and the Divas treated me with care, coaching me with the compassion that childhood often lacks.

I tried once more, and though I was concentrating, I could hear several voices talking me through the ropes in the background. Then I was in! And once inside, I had a little difficulty finding the beat of the music coming from the boombox, but I knew I was home: I already knew how to dance. Lady Di was excited about my maiden voyage, but she remained calm and called out for me to move toward Willie, to get to the center of the elliptical dance floor. I hadn't settled into the beat of the next song, so she guided me through the eight-beat pulse of a Whitney Houston re-mix, calmly calling out "R'lax (two three four) R'lax (two three four) R'lax (two three four)," over-articulating the "l" and slurring the "x" sound into a syncopated off-beat.

Recently released recordings of black popular music, like this song by Whitney that was a favorite of mine, are regularly available as professional re-mixes produced by local and national DJ figures. I hadn't heard this re-mix before. I loved the percussive lyrics of the song: *It's— Not— Right / But It's O- kay— / I'm Gonna Make— It— An- y- way.*

It was Whitney's first single with any significant R&B (rather than pop) appeal in years—a funky, highly percussive track, opening her compact disc *My Love Is Your Love* (Arista Records, 1999). The coincidence had me hyped. I had finally gotten into the ropes on my own, and was getting the feel of this innovative, dancing-in-the-ropes thing, and one of my favorite new songs was playing. It was an exciting moment, and hanging in the ropes for a while was easy because I knew the music. I had sung it each morning for weeks after I bought it.

Finally I grew weary. This was work. But I got a lot of *dap* from the girls. Spirit and Lady Di literally hollered. Glistening with perspiration, I tried to catch my breath between smiles. Lady Di asked rhetorically, "Did you have a good time?" I experienced an exhilarating sense of timelessness—as if you are just *in* it, in there—but not by yourself. I had reached the limits of my physical endurance; my legs told me I had to quit. During the evening, I enjoyed many more turns. I even impressed myself a few times—or at least felt competent about getting into the ropes.

During one of my turns, Lydia arrived. I recognized her immediately, because I loved the style she sported in the video. Her essence was captured by her pseudonym: *"My name is Sassy and I'm forty-four."* I thought she was aptly named, and as I continued to dance through my turn, I heard Sassy's voice as she readied herself to warm up in the ropes.

Over the course of the year I spent with the Divas, I noticed that comments made to someone in the ropes are usually made in a musical way, to the beat, or even chanted as if they were lyrics to the song. In a rhythmic and slightly undulating voice, Sassy intoned, "Nice!!" holding the vowel out over the "bar line" and dropping the final "s" sound on the next beat. Willie nodded in agreement and in time with the tempo, and continued to turn the ropes for me. Their reactions felt good.

As I left the ropes again on the verge of a delirious exhaustion, Spirit yelled out, "I thought you said you couldn't jump." I snapped back wryly, "I said I couldn't JUMP—not *dance*!"

Each Diva has her own style, her own way of entering, grooving, playing with gestures and ideas, and stopping. But Sassy's turn in the ropes fascinated me the most. She seemed to be deeply aware not only of the art of footwork in dancing double-dutch, but the art of performance—of staging events shared and experienced with others. Like me, Sassy Lydia had asthma, and she had learned to know when to call it quits before any sign of fatigue showed.

Sassy! Swift and uninhibited in her fullness. Her short, natural hair—curly blonde—is a statement in itself about what is natural, who is black. Possessing the audacity to wear blonde nappy hair in an Afro. No perm. No (temporary) process to go through. A natural blonde in black? That's Sassy. Robust. Full of health and strength. Marked by richness. "Full-bodied," the dictionary says.

Even full-bodied, she's light on her toes. Even in the fastest ropes, she can double-time her feet or gallop between the ropes. Her intricate footwork makes her breasts heave and jerk, but her brown-oak face is solid, showing no sign of effort. Suddenly, she strikes a pose. Rooted in a stance that says, "This is my world!" everything stops and everyone erupts with joy. Sassy knows her stuff is tight! She's music divine and, like the funk group Cameo sang, "(I like— it) Yes, I like it! The way she wears her hair—! (I like— it) Ooo-!"

My mind was fixed on Sassy's finishing pose, à la John Travolta in *Saturday Night Fever*. In her next turn, she showed off even more. Although endurance is not eternal, I discovered from Sassy that one should develop a keen self-consciousness about the limits and strengths of one's body, and learn to create a polished performance; a choreographic ending can punctuate and wrap up a turn in the ropes.

There is a certain kind of liberty in the Double Dutch Divas' expressive and mature performance, in having minds of their own, in creating and reclaiming a mode of black female performance and community expressed through a marriage of music, gender, body, and play. Learning the ropes with them confirmed something for me about girls' musical play. Music, dance, and other expressive formations are vital to the worldviews of many black females—who they are, how they interact, and how they feel about their bodies as they grow older. Reclaiming this musical play is a reminder—a way of re-remembering who they were and can continue to be—as mothers, wives, girlfriends, lovers, and respectable adults. It was quite unusual, but it was a welcome change of pace to be with sistagirls who were not negatively concerned about having full hips or getting older, at least within the ropes. In this context, my hips and butt were OK —tight jeans and all. I felt free to be *more* of me.

The simultaneous process of renaming themselves and revisiting girlhood play signaled a symbolic and performative moment of freedom. The Divas reclaimed *being girls* playing double-dutch, and performing in ways that are often restricted to pre-adolescent female activity—before boys become the focus of our play, and having babies possibly ends it. They also reclaimed being *part of a collective of girls* (one of the *sistas*).

At the end of the evening, I was feeling free and part of the group, so I sang a few notes for the camera, since Marcia was still taping for Nicole's video. I hoped they wouldn't use my novice jumping to undermine my academic authority, as well as my street credibility! (I'd published about double-dutch, but now they'd know I didn't know how to do it.) Next, while Spirit looked on, I recited a poem I had written about girls' games and hip-hop.

> *Black can be me*
> *A black girl*
> *Stepping on the cracks of my mama's back*
> *Breakin'!*
> *Black and me, here, in hip-hop time?*

How can that be?
Me, not funkin' up a groove and makin' b-boy moves
 to make James Brown holler "Ow!"
Could God be cruel, and leave us out of our history?
Let me write a rhyme so I can rap myself in it.

Inspired by my performance, Shirley came forward with her own thing.

"I have a poem, since I can't sing," she said to the camera in a child-like voice, "It's called 'Jump Sister Jump.'"

My daugh-ter said:
"Hey, Ma-ma! What's the matter with you?
Isn't jumpin' rope on-ly some-thin' kids should do?"

Chorus:
JUMP, JUMP—, Sister, JUMP! / JUMP!
(Ya) JUMP, JUMP—, Sister, JUMP!
One, two, three

Well, who said twen— ty-one
Was over the hump
You wanna turn the rope, la-dies
Let a . . . woman jump?

JUMP, JUMP—, Sister, JUMP! / JUMP!
(Ya) JUMP, JUMP—, Sister, JUMP!
One, two, three

[Rap:]
You see, all— my— life— I have cherished the right— to do all of
the things I hold dear
JUMP!
I've had ob-stacles, yes.
I've had my share of strife.
But the goals all remained— crystal clear—
JUMP! JUMP!
Now the forces that be don't make life that easy [straight eighth
notes]
But from all situations you learn
JUMP!

And when problems do come, as you overcome some, [straight
eighth notes]
it's respect— for yourself— that you earn.
JUMP! JUMP!
So when you hear: "Hey, la-dies! Did you say it was true
That there is . . . no limit to the things you can do?"

JUMP, JUMP—, Sister, JUMP! / JUMP!
(Ya) JUMP, JUMP—, Sister, JUMP!
One, two, three
We say, Dare to dream
Shoot your shot
Put in this world for a reason
Go-and show-it what you got!

JUMP, JUMP—, Sister, JUMP! / JUMP!
(Ya) JUMP, JUMP—, Sister, JUMP!
One, two, three

The Double Dutch Divas and their musical play remind me that girls
need not give up their games as they once did. They can also return to
games like double-dutch, and bring a mature spirit to the playfulness that
shapes black social and musical aesthetics in the ropes and beyond. The
point of highlighting their performance was to demonstrate how their
musical interactions fit into a context of popular culture and communication that is evident in younger girls' musical play. The Double Dutch
Divas are a testament to the power of the social practices learned during
childhood, which are refined and taken to another level by adults. Their
interactions demonstrate the ongoing connectedness between older generations and contemporary popular musics. They demonstrate an ongoing process of rhythmic consciousness and improvisational social interaction; they demonstrate many of the ideals of black musical style: individuality within collectivity, rhythmic and metrical complexity, the
significance of the body, and more. Furthermore, the Divas drive home
my thesis about the need for a gendered analysis of black music studies
that considers the racial as well as gendered significance of embodied interactions in everyday musical life. Their rehearsals exhibit the interdependent relationships between everyday "popular" culture and mass-mediated "popular" culture, between the music of children and adults, be-

tween the gendered realms of masculinity and femininity that men and women share, more or less.

The Double Dutch Divas exemplify how black(female)ness is socially learned and constructed: through musical interactions including dance, dramaturgy, and gesture. No matter what age, girls are learning and working the ropes of black musical style. They are learning to embody the communal psyche of black musical identity and, in the process, they are maneuvering the ideological ropes of a race, gender, and the body in a musical context. Jump, sister, jump!

Conclusion

There is never only one game (race or gender). (Ortner 1997, 12–13)

In the spring of 2003, I was invited to present a chapter of this work at the Institute for Research in African American Studies at Columbia University. One of the most distinguished and renowned African American historians and political scientists Manning Marable was present, as were a host of graduate students and scholars—many of them women—ranging in age from about twenty-five to sixty. Marable recognized the popular songs from rhythm and blues in the 1950s and '60s that had been embedded within contemporary girls' game-songs performed during the last twenty years, while the young women in the room remembered references in game-songs of their youth as the popular songs of a more recent past, whether they had grown up in Chicago or Philadelphia.

My presentation rekindled the memory of several games once forgotten by a beautiful sister with locks who grew up in suburban Chicago. A jazz vocalist and a Ph.D. student wrapping up the final chapter of her dissertation on the spiritual voicings of Nina Simone, Abbey Lincoln, and Cassandra Wilson. LaShonda waited after the talk to perform for me. The cheer began with a triplet rhythm into the downbeat sung to a refrain that was remarkably familiar to my hip-hop ears:

> *Rock, Rock to the Planet Rock / BAM! / Don't stop! /*
> *Rock, Rock to the Planet Rock / BAM! / Don't stop!*

I immediately hit the "record" button on my hand-held computer and captured the popular music from her school days. I played it back to LaShonda on the spot to marvel at discovering another connection between girls' games and hip-hop.

181

"Do you know what that is?" I asked.

"No," she replied matter-of-factly. Now in her early thirties, LaShonda was into jazz not hip-hop. "Do you know 'Planet Rock' by Afrika Bambaataa?"

"No." She was not up on the beats of hip-hop and this is one of the classics from early recorded rap.

In 1982, "Planet Rock" humanized electronic technology in hip-hop for the body rockers on the dance floor. A former member of the infamous Black Spades gang in the South Bronx, Bambaataa (born Kevin Donovan, 1960–) founded the antiracist and nonviolent Zulu Nation, the first hip-hop organization. Its purpose was to transform the deadly battles of young gang members into friendly battles competing to become the grandmaster of DJ-ing or the king or queen of breakdancing or Brooklyn uprocking.

"Planet Rock" kicked off the electronic funk/electro-rap movement featuring the innovation of employing a TR-808 drum machine. "Planet Rock" was a wholly synthesized, twelve-inch single released in 1981 on Tommy Boy Records based on the techno-pop futurism of "Trans-Europe Express," an underground discotheque hit by the German "robot pop" group Kraftwerk. LaShonda's chant evolved from the hook of "Planet Rock" accompanied by a triplet pattern of foot-stomps mimicking the pulsating, planetary funk, kick-drum effects produced from the TR-808 drum machine. This particular kick-drum bass timbre became synonymous with hip-hop production throughout the 1980s. The end of LaShonda's introduction was mirrored in the four hard kicks that serve as a mini-break or a percussive fill throughout "Planet Rock."

LaShonda was clueless about the significance of the song outside her realm of memory of performing it with her sister. She may not remember it, but "Planet Rock" was surely the hot track circulating around the subculture of her adolescence as a teenager in the late seventies and early eighties. The oral-kinetic transmission of black girls' play was her direct feed.

A few weeks later, I invited LaShonda to visit my hip-hop course to teach her version of "Planet Rock" and several other cheers she grew up performing. They were all based on funk hits from the early 1980s, including Kool and the Gang's "Hollywood Swinging" and the S.O.S. Band's "Take Your Time." Upon hearing Afrika Bambaataa's original for the first time, she had no recollection of ever hearing it before.

This is kinetic orality at work. The link between black girls and adult popular music suggests that black girls' games represent a somatic historiography of black musical experience, and that tracing the interchange between girls' games and popular songs clearly points to a gendered, translocal, and intergenerational culture of black musical expression.

What was also fascinating, which I was unable to research and include in this book, was how many of LaShonda's versions of cheers (she remembered cheers and not handclapping games or double-dutch rhymes) involved a great deal of individual improvisation within the collective expressions of many chants. It was the first time I observed this phenomenon, the invention of vocal expression in the context of a social performance of a girls' game. Does this suggest a change in the transmission or performance practice of girls' games? It certainly suggests that research comparing a more comprehensive collection of games across region *and* time may reveal some exciting conclusions about how black musical expression is and has changed. Was Chicago in the early 1980s somehow a different locale of expression than outside Detroit, where I collected games in 1994–95? This can only be left for further study.

What this study calls attention to is the study of gender as the relations expressed between the sexes in African American popular music-making. It used to be that we only talked about women when we talked about gender. It used to be that we primarily talked about the sexual politics of men when we talked about hip-hop. This ethnographic study talked about girls and women so we could talk about the socialization of music, race, and gender in African American culture. The critical methods I used involved (1) examining the musical and social implications of learning the kinetic orality in black girls' games; and (2) interpreting their impact on popular music-making, the formation of black popular taste, and the social construction of female and male black musical identities.

From my analysis, I assert that black girls' sphere of musical activity represents one of the earliest formations of a black popular music culture. Girls are its primary agents: they are the leaders in composing the beats, rhymes, and multi-limbed choreographies of handclapping games, cheers, and double-dutch, as well as their accompanying chants. Then something happens. Girls abandon this agency, and their position of musical leadership, as they grow up. One reason seems to be that they, and others, never considered the games to be actual music. By eighteen, with the exception of the remarkable stylings of the Double Dutch Divas, most black women have left behind the musical labors of their games.

Oddly enough, black female rappers do not borrow from the potentially hot, "hit-making" hooks available in black girls' games. Why? Perhaps because borrowing from their own youth—from a female sphere of play—isn't as sonically alluring, or as provocative to women, as when male rappers like Nelly, borrow "Down, down baby" from the public domain of girls' former play. His sales blew up as a result. It was familiar to black listeners. It covertly flipped the gender script without jeopardizing his sexuality or stance as a "hard" rapper, and it sold millions of records, contributing greatly to Nelly's earning a Grammy award. What female emcee would follow that lead? Wouldn't it look like she was "biting" on Nelly's success? Or is this simply a case of women internalizing the misogyny ordinarily directed against them by men?

For older girls and women, musical games are merely a thing of the past. I have yet to find an example in any performance, before or after Nelly, where a female artist samples from a black girls' musical chant or beat. It seems strange because their games would be perfect hooks, but something keeps women from borrowing the material. Despite all this, the values and behaviors that girls learned and inhabited do not disappear. They are transformed into social dancing practices at co-ed parties and clubs, taken up into spiritual practices in sacred contexts, or transposed into the advanced choreography and kinetic orality of a sorority step show.

If I had not limited my examination to girls and women, the significance of their voices and musical experiences would not have emerged as powerfully nor drawn as much attention to how race and gender intersect musically. I found music to be central to the social construction of ethnicity and gender in African American culture. My analysis of girls' musical play, alongside the male-voiced songs of a fifty-year period, shed light on the musical and sexual politics that are still played out in other African American arenas (besides double-dutch and hip-hop).

Although black music often pops up as a topic in other scholarship, the study of black musical experience from an ethnomusicological standpoint, including ethnography and transcription, is rare. It is also rare that African Americans doing ethnographic work, in general, represent black musical culture. One notable exception is *Race Music: Black Cultures from Be-bop to Hip-hop,* by Guthrie Ramsey (2003). African Americans may be innovators in American popular music, but we are a fraction of its cultural ethnographers. Ultimately, my musical objective was to challenge essentialist and anti-essentialist notions of race, gender, and music, from a complex, black musical perspective.

> The ethnomusicologist is often engaged in a dance of midwifery. She can coach or nurse the traditions she studies into public perceptions, but she may not exercise its limbs because they do not move to the rhythm of the scholarly world. She is not the parent of the tradition; she is merely a facilitator. Yet how she brings tradition into the light may determine its survival and its acceptance. This is an awesome responsibility. Here, the birthing technique of the midwife is negotiated through her own cultural politics and through her willingness to address central cultural issues that have been rendered invisible (Robertson 1991, 362).

I hope I have responsibly, and with a sense of play, rendered visible the learned musical blackness and the embodied social phenomenology of black female practices.

Black music isn't usually danced in the classroom, as I ask my students to do. And the interactions between male and female bodies are often excluded from academic methods of musical learning, knowing, comprehending, analyzing, and synthesizing. What stops us is the fear that we don't know how to test such a subjective embodied experience. Might some of its teachers fail the test? We wouldn't allow a tone-deaf musician to teach Beethoven to music majors, so why do we allow nondancers to teach African American music? This is particularly relevant when the young and multicultural bodies in our popular music classrooms are appropriating black music and dance, with little or no critical and historical understanding of the representations of black bodies from minstrelsy to hip-hop.

New modes of inquiry (embodiment, sexuality, etc.) require new modes of measuring learning and success. Literate tests alone are not sufficient. Other kinds of "tests" (auto-ethnography, interviewing, descriptive transcription, prose, etc.) need to be returned to or introduced. Instead of expecting music majors to master sight-singing (translating visual notation immediately into melodic sound), we might expect them to master having rhythm, or have them learn at least six black dances including the Lindy-hop and breakdancing.

If I could leave readers with one concept I introduced, it would be the idea that girls' games are *oral-kinetic lessons* in black musical style, behavior, and social identity formation. This was a concept that evolved from the internal dialogue/conflict between my classically trained and europeanized self, and my trained-on-the-dance-floor, African American self.

A whole world of analysis and interpretation awaits subsequent musical ethnographies that explore the paradigmatic shift that comes from embracing the body in musical and social ethnography. From oral-kinetic "etudes" or lessons, I developed the notion of a *somatic historiography* of black music and dance. Interviews, video, film, and writing are, in this case, the essential tools for capturing ethnography. The stories that the body can tell are not the same conversations that we speak or sing. They are visual and kinesthetic. We feel them polyphonically and polyrhythmically. We resist letting these "stories" be analyzed, for fear of dissecting the whole so much that the spirit of the music and people are lost.

Performance studies scholar Barbara Browning asserts that "the body says what cannot be spoken" (1995, 9). Perhaps this is due to a certain hegemonic resistance to speaking about "vulgar" bodily functions, and the sexual expressions and acts of gendered bodies. If "the body is capable of understanding more things at once than can be articulated in language" (ibid., 13), and if the body's expressions *are* language, *are* linguistic (Birdwhistell 1952), then there is work to be done in the ethnomusicological studies of black music. There exists a need for more scholars and students of both sexes who are daring, courageous and, moreover, fun and playful, to pursue the simultaneities, and unpack the languaging, of a gendered musical blackness.

These game-songs are embodied scripts of music, inscribed into space, experience, and memory. We all witness this "music notation" and sightread it with some proficiency. But mastery is what I call for. We have yet to fully understand the social affiliations and disaffiliations of race, gender, and embodiment in music.

As movers to music, we are not *thinking* with or through the body as much as we are *writing* or inscribing memories into the world. This embodied literacy is taken for granted. It is why the concept of oral-kinetic etudes is valuable. Stemming from the literate exercises of my classical training, etudes have me "think" pedantically about my body. I was never encouraged to embrace classical music-making holistically, as I did the everyday experience of participating in girls' musical play.

The embodied scripts of play, the social narratives of street dance, and the "chapters" of somatic history, all require skillful ethnographers to interpret them. In many cases, we may need to recruit and train new scholars. But this is a beginning. Further studies are encouraged concerning the social, sexual, and phenomenological interactions between African American women *and* men in musical settings, in improvisation, and in and around the performance of popular and vernacular music, as well as jazz and classical music.

Women and men use romance and sex to get places in the business, or to get away from places (heartbreak), through the music itself. The discourse around black musical practices and performance needs to be examined to see how it sustains and disrupts gender and race norms. This is essential to the study of black popular music where the discourse of musical identity has played a pivotal role in sustaining stereotypical views of a rich and complex group of people.

Ultimately, I set out to question and critique my own, as well as others', assumptions about race, gender, and the body in African American musical contexts, and in black music studies. I urge others to pursue this kind of investigation into music culture because of the persistence of race and racism, sex and sexism, and more. These things shape the way people think about rhythm, syncopation, call-and-response, improvisation, and musical play, as well as the people who perform black styles of music.

In short, this book is a clarion call for expanding black musical studies to include gender and embodiment in its historical and cultural analyses of musical sounds, behaviors, and concepts.

Appendix

Musical Transcriptions of
Game-Songs Studied

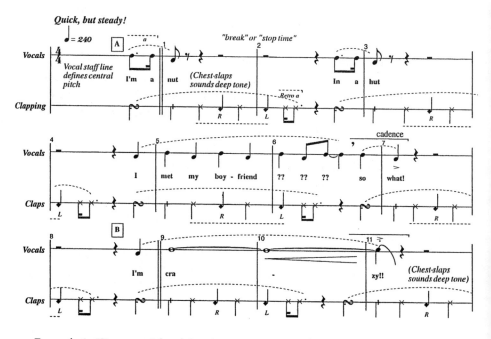

Example 1. "I'm a nut," handclapping game-song, performed by Jasmine and Stephanie (twins, age 9), recorded in Ypsilanti, Michigan

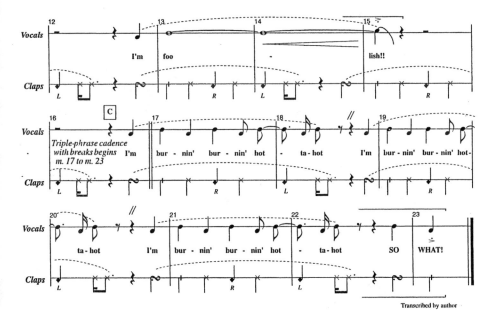

Example 1 *(Continued)*

Example 2. "Jig-a-low," cheer, by Jasmine and Stephanie

Example 2 *(Continued)*

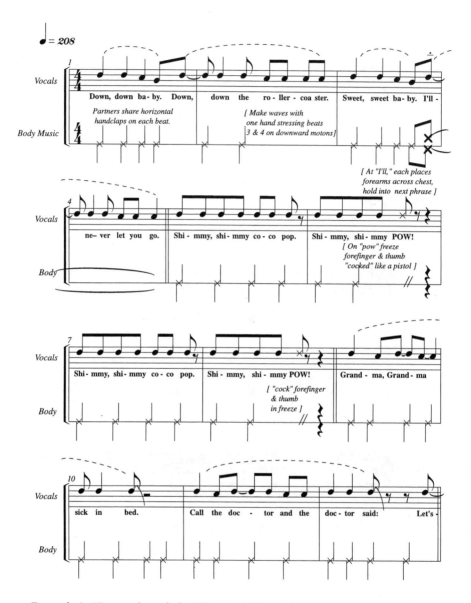

Example 3. "Down, down baby (Hot Dog)," handclapping game-song, performed by Karmetta and Olivia (each age 13), recorded in Ann Arbor, Michigan

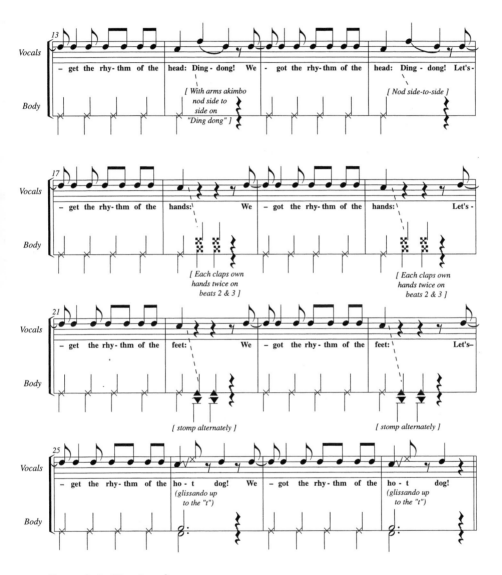

Example 3 *(Continued)*

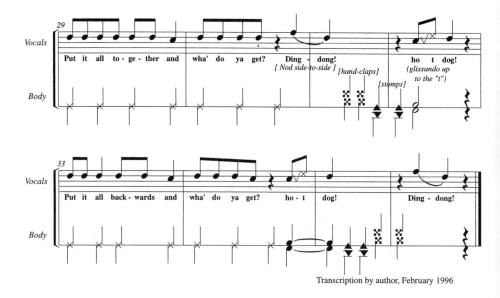

Transcription by author, February 1996

Example 3 *(Continued)*

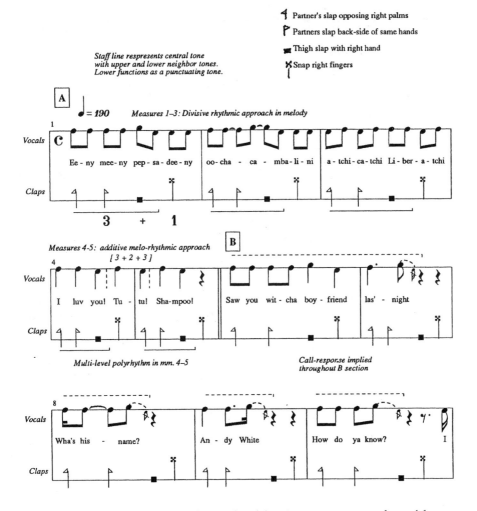

Example 4. "Eeny meeny pepsadeeny," handclapping game-song, performed from memory by Nancy Hopkins (age 32) raised in Philadelphia, recorded in Ann Arbor, Michigan

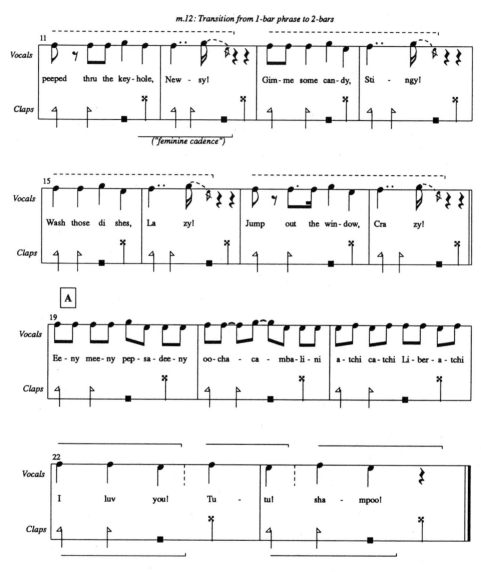

Transcribed by K.D. Gaunt, Oct. 1995

Example 4 *(Continued)*

Bibliography

BOOKS AND ARTICLES

Abrahams, Roger D. 1969. *Jump Rope Rhymes: A Dictionary.* Austin and London: University of Texas Press.

———. 1990. "Playing the Dozens." In *Mother Wit from the Laughing Barrel: Readings in the Interpretation of Afro-American Folklore,* ed. Alan Dundes, 295–309. Jackson: University of Mississippi Press.

———. 1992. *Singing the Master: The Emergence of African-American Culture in the Plantation South.* New York: Pantheon Books.

Adler, Bill. 1991. *Rap! Portraits and Lyrics of a Generation of Black Rockers.* New York: St. Martin's Press.

Agawu, Kofi V. 1995a. "The Invention of 'African Rhythm.'" *JAMS: Journal of the American Musicological Society* 48: 380–95.

———. 1995b. *African Rhythm: A Northern Ewe Perspective.* Cambridge and New York: Cambridge University Press.

Ake, David. 2002. *Jazz Cultures.* Berkeley: University of California Press.

Allah, Bilal. 1993. "Can't Stop the Body Rock, Part Two: Hip-hop's Fly Choreographers." *Rap Pages* (August): 48–51.

Aparicio, Frances R. 2000. "Ethnifying Rhythms, Feminizing Cultures." In *Music and the Racial Imagination,* eds. Ronald Radano and Philip V. Bohlman, 95–112. Chicago: University of Chicago Press.

Appiah, Kwamé Anthony. 1995. "African Identities." In *Social Postmodernism: Beyond Identity Politics,* eds. Linda Nicholson and Steven Seidman Nicholson. Cambridge: Cambridge University Press.

Birdwhistell, Ray L. 1952. *Introduction to Kinesics.* Louisville: University of Louisville.

Blacking, John. 1967. *Venda Children's Songs: A Study in Ethnomusicological Analysis.* Chicago: University of Chicago Press.

———. 1977. *Toward an Anthropology of the Body.* New York: Academic Press.

Bluestein, Gene. 1994. *Poplore: Folk and Pop in American Culture.* Amherst: University of Massachusetts Press.

Bourdieu, Pierre. 1977. *Outline of a Theory of Practice.* Cambridge: Cambridge University Press.

197

Bowers, Jane. 2000. "Writing the Biography of a Black Woman Blues Singer." In *Music and Gender,* eds. Pirrko Moisala and Beverley Diamond, 140–65. Urbana and Chicago: University of Illinois Press.

Brady, Margaret K., and Rosalind Eckhardt. 1975. "'This Little Lady's Gonna Boogaloo': Elements of Socialization in the Play of Black Girls." In *Black Girls at Play: Folkloristic Perspectives on Child Development,* eds. Margaret K. Brady and Rosalind Eckhardt, 1–56. Austin: Early Elementary Program Southwest Educational Development Laboratory.

Brown, Elsa Barkley. 1994. "Negotiating and Transforming the Public Sphere: African American Political Life in the Transition From Slavery to Freedom." *Public Culture* 7(1): 107–46.

Browning, Barbara. 1995. *Samba: Resistance in Motion.* Bloomington: Indiana University Press.

Butler, Judith. 1990. *Gender Trouble: Feminism and the Subversion of Identity.* New York: Routledge, Chapman & Hall.

Butler, Melvin. 2005. "Songs of the Pentecost: Experiencing Music, Transcendence, and Indentity in Jamaica and Haiti." Ph.D. diss., New York University.

Campbell, Patricia Shehan. 1998. *Songs in Their Heads: Music and its Meaning in Children's Lives.* Oxford and New York: Oxford University Press.

Caponi, Gena Dagel, ed. 1999. *Signifyin(g), Sanctifyin', and Slam Dunking: A Reader in African American Expressive Culture.* Amherst: University of Massachusetts Press.

Carby, Hazel V. 1990. "'It Jus' Be's Dat Way Sometime': The Sexual Politics of Women's Blues." In *Unequal Sisters: A Multicultural Reader in United States Women's History,* eds. Ellen DuBois and Vicky Ruiz, 330–41. New York: Routledge.

———. 1991. "In Body and Spirit: Representing Black Women Musicians." *Black Music Research Journal* 11(2): 177–92.

———. 1992. "Policing the Black Woman's Body in an Urban Context." *Critical Inquiry* 18/4: 735–55.

———. 1998. "Playin' the Changes." *Race Men: The W. E. B. DuBois Lectures,* 135–68. Cambridge, MA: Harvard University Press.

———. 1999. "Black Women's Blues, Motown and Rock and Roll." In *Cultures in Babylon: Black Britain and African America,* 40–50. New York: Verso.

Chambers, Veronica. 1996. *Mama's Girl.* New York: Riverhead Books.

Chernoff, John Miller. 1979. *African Rhythm and African Sensibility: Aesthetics and Social Action in African Musical Idioms.* Chicago: University of Chicago Press.

Christgau, Robert. 1983. "Christgau's Consumer Guide." *Village Voice* (June 28). Accessed online at http://www.robertchristgau.com/xg/cg/cgv6-83.php, 9/01/2004.

Citron, Marcia J. 1993. *Gender and the Musical Canon.* Cambridge: Cambridge University Press.

Cole, Johnnetta Betsch, and Beverly Guy-Sheftall. 2003. "No Respect: Gender Politics and Hip Hop." In *Gender Talk: The Struggle for Women's Equality in African American Communities,* 182–215. New York: One World Ballantine Books.

Cook, Susan C. 1996. "Music and Image: Domesticity, Ideology, and Socio-Cultural Formation in Eighteenth-Century England (Review)." *Signs* 21/3 (Spring): 769–74.

Cooper, B. Lee. 1986. *A Resource Guide to Themes.* New York: Greenwood Press.

Coplan, David. 1994. *In the Time of the Cannibals: The Word Music of South Africa's Basotho Migrants.* Chicago: University of Chicago Press.

Courlander, Harold. 1963. *Negro Folk Music, U.S.A.* New York: Columbia University Press.

Crenshaw, Kimberlé Williams. 1991. "Beyond Racism and Misogyny: Black Feminism and 2 Live Crew." *Boston Review* 16/6: 6–23. Reprinted 1997 in *Women Transforming Politics: An Alternative Reader,* eds. Cathy J. Cohen, Kathleen B. Jones, and Joan C. Tronto, 549–68. New York: New York University Press.

Cusick, Suzanne. 1994. "Feminist Theory, Music Theory, and the Mind/Body Problem." *Perspectives of New Music* 32(1): 8–27.

Dance, Daryl Cumber. 1978. *Shuckin' and Jivin': Folklore from Contemporary Black Americans.* Bloomington: Indiana University Press.

Dargan, Amanda, and Steven Zeitlin. 1990. *City Play.* New Brunswick: Rutgers University Press.

Davies, Charlotte Aull. 1999. *Reflexive Ethnography: A Guide To Researching Selves and Others.* London and New York: Routledge.

Davis, Angela. 1990. "Black Women and Music: A Historical Legacy of Struggle." In *Wild Women in the Whirlwind: Afra-American Culture and the Contemporary Literary Renaissance,* eds. Joanne M. Braxton and Andree Nicola McLaughlin, 3–21. New Brunswick: Rutgers University Press.

———. 1998. *Blues Legacies and Black Feminism: Gertrude Ma Rainey, Bessie Smith and Billie Holiday.* New York: Pantheon Books.

Dewan, Shaila K. 2000. "Local Talent Winds Up on the (Double Dutch) Ropes." *New York Times* (December 4): B3 (Metro section).

DjeDje, Jacqueline Cogdell. 1989. *Women and Music in Cross-Cultural Perspective* by Ellen Koskoff (Review). *Ethnomusicology* 33/3 (Autumn): 514–20.

DjeDje, Jacqueline Cogdell, and Eddie S. Meadows, eds. 1998. *California Soul: Music of African Americans in the West.* Berkeley: University of California Press.

Drewal, Margaret Thompson. 1992. *Yoruba Ritual: Performers, Play, Agency.* Bloomington: Indiana University Press.

Ehrenfeld, Temma. 1988. "The History of a Little Girls' Game." *Hudson Review* 40/4 (Winter): 584–602.

Epstein, Dena J. 1977. *Sinful Tunes and Spirituals: Black Folk Music to the Civil War.* Urbana: University of Illinois Press.

Eure, Joseph D., and James G. Spady. 1991. *Nation Conscious Rap.* Philadelphia: PC International Press.

Fabian, Johannes. 1998. *Moments of Freedom: Anthropology and Popular Culture.* Charlottesville: University of Virginia Press.

Fikentscher, Kai. 2000. *"You Better Work!": Underground Dance Music in New York City.* Hanover, NH: Wesleyan University Press.

Fine, Elizabeth C. 2002. *Soulstepping: African American Step Shows.* Urbana and Chicago: University of Illinois Press.

Fiske, John. 1989. *Understanding Popular Culture.* London and New York: Routledge.

Floyd, Samuel A., Jr. 1983. "On Black Music Research." *Black Music Research Journal* 3: 46–57.

———. 1991. "Ring Shout! Literary Studies, Historical Studies, and Black Music Inquiry." *Black Music Research Journal* 11/2 (Fall): 265–87.

———. 1995. *The Power of Black Music: Interpreting Its History from Africa to the United States.* New York: Oxford University Press.

Fox, Robert Elliot. 1997. "Becoming Post-White." In *Multi-America: Essays on Cultural Wars and Cultural Peace,* ed. Ishmael Reed, 6–17. New York: Viking.

Franco, Jean. 1999. *Critical Passions: Selected Essays.* Durham: Duke University Press.

Frith, Simon. 1996. "Music and Identity." In *Questions of Cultural Identity,* eds. Stuart Hall and Paul du Gay, 108–27. London: Sage Publications.

Gardner, Howard. 1999. *Intelligence Reframed: Multiple Intelligences for the 21st Century.* New York: Basic Books.

———. n.d. *Teaching Guide for MI: Intelligence, Understanding, and the Mind* (no publisher info).

Gates, Henry Louis, Jr. 1988. *Signifying Monkey: A Theory of Afro-American Literary Criticism.* New York: Oxford University Press.

Gaunt, Kyra D. 1997. "The Games Black Girls Play: Music, Body and 'Soul.'" Ph.D. diss., University of Michigan, Ann Arbor.

———. 2002. "The Two O'Clock Vibe: Embodying the Jam of Musical Blackness In and Out of Its Everyday Context (American Musics)." *Musical Quarterly* 86(3) (Spring): 372–97.

George, Nelson, and Sally Banes. 1985. *Fresh: Hip Hop Don't Stop.* New York: Random House.

Gilroy, Paul. 1993a. *Small Acts: Thoughts on the Politics of Black Cultures.* New York: Serpent's Tail.

———. 1993b. *The Black Atlantic: Modernity and Double Consciousness.* Cambridge: Harvard University Press.

Glassie, Henry. 1995. "Tradition." *Journal of American Folklore* 108(430): 395–412.

Gomme, Lady Alice Bertha. 1894. *The Traditional Games of England, Scotland and Ireland.* London: David Nutt.

Goodwin, June. 1980. "Double Dutch, Double Dutch: All You Need is a Clothesline and Jet-Propelled Feet." *Christian Science Monitor,* B ed. (October 7): 8+.

Gribin, Anthony, and Matthew Schiff. 1992. *Doo-Wop: The Forgotten Third of Rock and Roll.* Iola, WI: Krause Publications.

Griffin, Farah Jasmine. 2001. *If You Can't Be Free, Be a Mystery: In Search of Billie Holiday.* New York: Free Press.

Hall, Edward T. 1981. *Beyond Culture.* New York: Anchor Books.

Hall, Stuart. 1981. "Notes on Deconstructing 'the Popular.'" In *People's History and Socialist Theory,* ed. Raphael Samuel, 227–40. Boston: Routledge & Kegan Paul.

———. 1992. "What Is the 'Black' in Black Popular Culture?" In *Black Popular Culture,* ed. Gina Dent, 21–33. Seattle: Bay Press.

———. 1996. "Who Needs 'Identity'?" In *Questions of Cultural Identity,* eds. Stuart Hall and Paul du Gay, 1–17. London: Sage Publications.

Hampton, Barbara. 1992. "Music and Gender in Ga Society: Adaawe Song Poetry" in *African Musicology: Current Trends, vol. II,* eds. William Carter and Jacqueline Cogdell Djedje. Los Angeles: University of California Press.

Hannerz, Ulf. 1969. *Soulside: Inquiries into Ghetto Culture and Community.* New York: Columbia University Press.

Harwood, Eve. 1992. "Girls' Handclapping Games: A Study in Oral Transmission." *Bulletin of the International Kodaly Society* 17(1) (Spring): 19–25.

———. 1993. "A Study in Apprenticeship Learning in Music." *General Music Today* (Spring): 4–8.

Herndon, Marcia, Suzanne Ziegler, and Max Peter Baumann. 1990. *Music, Gender, and Culture.* Wilhelmshaven: Noetzel Florian Verlag.

hooks, bell. 1990. *Yearning: Race, Gender and Cultural Politics.* Boston: South End Press.

Hungerford, James. 1859. *The Old Plantation and What I Gathered There in an Autumn Month.* New York: Harper & Bros.

Hunter, Tera W. 2000. "'Sexual Pantomimes,' the Blues Aesthetic, and Black Women in the New South." In *Music and the Racial Imagination,* eds. Ronald Radano and Philip V. Bohlman, 145–64. Chicago: University of Chicago Press.

Jackson, Irene V. 1985. *More than Dancing: Essays on Afro-American Music and Musicians* (John W. Blassingame and Henry Louis Gates Jr. Contributions in Afro-American and African Studies; Number 83). Westport, CT: Greenwood Press.

Jackson, Michael, ed. 1996. *Things as They Are: New Directions in Phenomenological Anthropology.* Bloomington: Indiana University Press.

John, Mary. 1989. "Postcolonial Feminists in the Western Intellectual Field: Anthropologists and Native Informants?" *Inscriptions* 5: 55.

Jones, A. M. 1959. *Studies in African Music,* vols. 1 & 2. Oxford: Oxford University Press.

Jones, LeRoi. 1980. *Blues People: Negro Music in White America.* Westport, CT: Greenwood Press.

Kartomi, Margaret J. 1991. "Musical Improvisations by Children at Play." *World of Music* 33/3: 53–65.

Kelley, Robin D. G. 1996. "Kickin' Reality, Kickin' Ballistics: Gangsta Rap and Postindustrial Los Angeles." In *Droppin' Science: Critical Essays on Rap Music,* ed. William Eric Perkins, 117–58. Philadelphia: Temple University Press.

Kernodle, Tammy L. 2004. *Soul on Soul: The Life and Music of Mary Lou Williams.* Boston: Northeastern University Press.

Keyes, Cheryl. 1993. "We're More than a Novelty, Boys: Strategies of Female Rappers in the Rap Music Tradition." In *Feminist Messages: Coding in Women's Folk Culture,* ed. Joan Newlon Radner, 203–20. Urbana: University of Illinois Press.

———. 2002. *Rap Music and Street Consciousness.* Urbana: University of Illinois Press.

Kirk-Duggan, Cheryl A. 1997. "Justified, Sanctified, and Redeemed: Blessed Expectation in Black Women's Blues and Gospels." In *Embracing the Spirit: Womanist Perspectives on Hope, Salvation, and Transformation,* ed. Emilie Maureen Townes, 140–66. Maryknoll, NY: Orbis Books.

Kondo, Dorinne. 1990. *Crafted Selves: Power, Gender, and Discourses of Identity in a Japanese Workplace.* Chicago: University of Chicago Press.

Koskoff, Ellen, ed. 1987. *Women and Music in Cross-Cultural Perspective* (Contributions in Women's Studies. No. 79). Westport, CT: Greenwood Press.

Koskoff, Ellen. 1989. "An Introduction to Women, Music, and Culture." In *Women and Music in Cross-Cultural Perspective,* ed. Ellen Koskoff, 1–24. Urbana: University of Illinois Press.

Kubik, Gerhard. 1998. "Analogies and Differences in African-American Musical Cultures Across the Hemisphere: Interpretive Models and Research Strategies." *Black Music Research Journal* 18(1/2): 203–27.

Langstaff, John, and Carol Langstaff. 1973. *Shimmy, Shimmy Coke-Ca-Pop! A*

Collection of City Children's Street Games and Rhymes. Garden City, NY: Doubleday.

"Lee Andrews." *All Music Guide.* http://www.allmusic.com. Accessed May 5, 2003.

Leppert, Richard. 1993. *The Sight of Sound: Music, Representation, and the History of the Body.* Berkeley: University of California Press.

Limon, José. 1991. "Representation, Ethnicity, and the Precursory Ethnography: Notes of a Native Anthropologist." In *Recapturing Anthropology: Working in the Present,* ed. Richard Fox, 115–36. Sante Fe, NM: School of American Research Press.

Lipsitz, George. 1990. *Time Passages: Collective Memory and American Popular Culture.* Minneapolis: University of Minnesota Press.

Lorde, Audre. 1983. "My Words Will Be There." In *Black Women Writers (1950–1980): A Critical Evaluation,* ed. Mari Evans, 45–56. Garden City, NY: Anchor Press/Doubleday.

Lott, Tommy. 2000. "Kara Walker Speaks: A Public Conversation on Racism, Art, and Politics." *Black Renaissance/Renaissance Noire* 3(1): 66–91.

"Luther Campbell." *All Music Guide.* http://allmusic.com. Accessed May 7, 2003.

Magrini, Tulia. 2003. *Music and Gender: Perspectives from the Mediterranean.* Chicago: University of Chicago Press.

Magubane, Zine. 2001. "Which Bodies Matter? Feminism, Poststructuralism, Race, and the Curious Theoretical Odyssey of the 'Hottentot Venus.'" *Gender and Society* 15/6 (December): 816–34.

Mahon, Maureen. 2004. *Right to Rock: The Black Rock Coalition and the Cultural Politics of Race.* Durham: Duke University Press.

Malone, Jacqui. 1996. *Steppin' on the Blues: The Visible Rhythms of African American Dance.* Urbana: University of Illinois Press.

Marcus, George E. 1998. *Ethnography through Thick and Thin.* Princeton, NJ: Princeton University Press.

Maultsby, Portia K. 1990. "Africanisms in African-American Music." In *Africanisms in American Culture,* ed. Joseph E. Holloway, 185–210. Bloomington: Indiana University Press.

———. 1991. *Feminine Endings: Music, Gender, and Sexuality.* Minneapolis: University of Minnesota Press.

———. 2000. "Women and Music on the Verge of the New Millennium (Special Issue: Feminisms at a Millennium)." *Signs* 25/4 (Summer): 1283–86.

McClary, Susan. 1991. *Feminine Endings: Music, Gender, and Sexuality.* Minneapolis: University of Minnesota.

———. 2000. "Women and Music on the Verge of the New Millennium (Special Issue: Feminisms at a Millennium)." *Signs* 25/4 (Summer): 1283–1286.

McClary, Susan, and Robert Walser. 1994. "Theorizing the Body in African-American Music." *Black Music Research Journal* 14(1): 75–84.

Merrill-Mirsky, Carol. 1988. "Eeny Meeny Pepsadeeny." Ph.D. diss., University of California.

Miller, Dan. 1991. "Absolute Freedom in Trinidad." *Man* 26 (June): 323–41.

Mitchell-Kernan, Claudia. 1990. "Signifying." In *Mother Wit from the Laughing Barrel: Readings in the Interpretation of Afro-American Folklore*, ed. Alan Dundes, 310–28. Jackson: University of Mississippi Press.

Moisala, Pirrko, and Beverly Diamond, eds. 2000. *Music and Gender.* Champaign-Urbana: University of Illinois Press.

Monson, Ingrid. 1997. "Music and the Anthropology of Gender and Cultural Identity." *Women and Music* 1: 24–32.

Morgan, Joan. 1999. *When Chickenheads Come Home to Roost: My Life as a Hip-Hop Feminist.* New York: Simon & Schuster.

Morrison, Toni. 1997. "Home." In *The House That Race Built*, ed. Wahneema Lubiano, 3–12. New York: Vintage Books.

Neal, Mark Anthony. 2002. *Soul Babies: Black Popular Culture and the Post-Soul Aesthetic.* New York and London: Routledge.

Nzewi, Meki. 1991. *Musical Practice and Creativity: An African Traditional Perspective.* Bayreuth: IWALEWA-Haus, University of Bayreuth.

Olaniyan, Tejumola. 1995. *Scars of Conquest/Masks of Resistance: The Invention of Cultural Identities in African, African-American, and Caribbean Drama.* New York: Oxford University Press.

Oliver, Paul. 1986. s.v. "Bo Diddley." In *The New Grove Dictionary of American Music*, eds. Wiley H. Hitchcock and Stanley Sadie. New York: Macmillan.

Ortner, Sherry. 1997. *Making Gender: The Politics and Erotics of Culture.* New York: Beacon Press.

Parrish, Lydia. 1965 [1942]. *Slave Songs of the Georgia Sea Islands.* Hatboro, PA: Folklore Associates; reprinted from Farrar, Straus.

Pelligrinelli, Lara. 2000. "Dig Boy Dig: Jazz at Lincoln Center Breaks New Ground, But Where Are the Women?" *Village Voice* (November 8–14).

Perry, Imani. 1995. "Who(se) Am I? The Identity and Image of Women in Hip-Hop." In *Gender, Race and Class in Media: A Text-Reader*, eds. Gail Dines, and Jean M. Humez, 136–48. Thousand Oaks, CA: Sage Publications.

Porter, Eric. 2002. *What Is This Thing Called Jazz? African American Musicians as Artists, Critics, and Activists.* Berkeley: University of California Press.

Posey, Carl, comp. 1993. "On the Street." *Rap Pages* (August): 5.

Pough, Gwendolyn D. 2004. *Check It While I Wreck It: Black Womanhood, Hip-Hop Culture, and the Public Sphere.* Boston: Northeastern University Press.

Radano, Ronald. 2000. "Hot Fantasies: American Modernism and the Idea of Black Rhythm." In *Music and the Racial Imagination*, eds. Ronald Radano and Philip V. Bohlman, 459–80. Chicago: University of Chicago Press.

———. 2003. *Lying Up a Nation: Race and Black Music.* Chicago: University of Chicago Press.

Radano, Ronald, and Philip Bohlman, eds. 2000. *Music and the Racial Imagination.* Chicago: University of Chicago Press.

Ramsey, Guthrie P. 2003. *Race Music: Black Cultures from Bebop to Hip-hop.* Berkeley: University of California Press.

Ransby, Barbara, and Tracye Matthews. 1993. "Black Popular Culture and the Transcendence of Patriarchal Illusions." *Race & Class: A Journal for Black and Third World Liberation* 35/1 (July–September): 57–68.

Reed, Ishmael. 1998. "Introduction: Black Pleasure—An Oxymoron." In *Soul: Black Power, Politics, and Pleasure,* eds. Monique Guillory and Richard C. Green, 169–71. New York: New York University Press.

Riddell, Cecelia. 1990. "Traditional Singing Games of Elementary School Children in Los Angeles." Ph.D. diss., UCLA.

Ridgeway, Cecilia L., and Lynn Smith-Lovin. 1999. "The Gender System and Interaction." *Annual Review of Sociology* 25: 191–216.

Rivera, Raquel Z. 2003. *New York Ricans From the Hip Hop Zone.* New York: Palgrave Macmillan.

Robertson, Carol E. 1991. "The Ethnomusicologist as Midwife." In *Music in the Dialogue of Cultures: Traditional Music and Cultural Policy* (Intercultural Music Studies No. 2), ed. Max Peter Baumann, 347–56. Westport, CT: Greenwood Press.

Rosaldo, Renato. 1993. *Culture & Truth: The Remaking of Social Analysis.* Boston: Beacon Press.

Rose, Tricia. 1991. "Never Trust a Big Butt and a Smile." *Camera Obscura* 23: 109–31.

———. 1994. *Black Noise: Rap Music and Black Culture in Contemporary America.* Hanover, NH: Wesleyan University Press.

———. 1996. "Hidden Politics: Discursive and Institutional Policing of Rap Music." In *Droppin' Science: Critical Essays on Rap Music and Hip Hop Culture,* ed. William Eric Perkins, 236–57. Philadelphia: Temple University Press.

Rudinow, Joel. 1994. "Race, Ethnicity, Expressive Authenticity: Can White People Sing the Blues?" *Journal of Aesthetics and Art Criticism* 52/1 (Winter): 127–37.

Schechner, Richard. 1992. "Drama Performance." In *Folklore, Cultural Performances, and Popular Entertainments,* ed. Richard Bauman, 272–81. New York: Oxford University Press.

Scott, Joan Wallach. 1999. "Gender: A Useful Category of Historical Analysis." In *Gender and the Politics of History,* rev. ed., 128–52. New York: Columbia University Press.

Shange, Ntozake. 1977. *for colored girls who have considered suicide/when the rainbow was enuf.* New York: Macmillan.

Slobin, Mark. 1993. *Subculture Sounds: Micromusic of the West*. Hanover, NH: Wesleyan University Press.

Small, Christopher. 1987. *Music of the Common Tongue: Survival and Celebration in Afro-American Music*. New York: Riverrun Press.

Solie, Ruth A., ed. 1993. *Musicology and Difference: Gender and Sexuality in Music Scholarship*. Berkeley: University of California Press.

Southern, Eileen. 1997. *The Music of Black Americans: A History*, 3rd ed. New York: Norton.

Stallybrass, Peter, and Allon White. 1986. *The Politics and Poetics of Transgression*. Ithaca, NY: Cornell University Press.

Stein, Danica L. 1998. "Clora Bryant: Gender Issues in the Career of a West Coast Jazz Musician." In *California Soul: Music of African Americans in the West*, eds. Jacqueline Cogdell Djedje and Eddie S. Meadows, 277–93. Berkeley: University of California Press.

Stuckey, Sterling. 1995. "Christian Conversion and the Challenge of Dance." *Choreographing History*, ed. Susan Leigh Foster, 54–65. Bloomington: University of Indiana Press.

Tagg, Philip. 1989. "Open Letter about 'Black Music,' 'Afro-American Music' and 'European Music.'" *Popular Music* 8(3): 285–98.

Toop, David. 1991. *Rap Attack 2: African Rap to Global Hip Hop*, 2nd ed. New York: Serpent's Tail.

Tucker, Sherrie. 2000. *Swing Shift: "All-Girl" Bands in the 1940s*. Durham: Duke University Press.

"Uncle Luke's World." Luther Campbell. Available online at http://unclelukes world.com/about.htm. Accessed May 7, 2003.

Visweswaren, Kamala. 1994. "Identifying Ethnography." In *Fictions of Feminist Ethnography*. Minneapolis: University of Minnesota Press.

Volk, Terese M. 1998. *Music, Education, and Multiculturalism: Foundations and Principles*. New York and Oxford: Oxford University Press.

Walker, David A., and James Haskins. 1986. *Double Dutch*. Hillside, NJ: Enslow Publishing.

Wallace, Michele. 1990. "When Black Feminism Faces the Music and the Music Is Rap." *New York Times* (July 29): 12.

Ward, Brian. 1998. *Just My Soul Responding: Rhythm and Blues, Black Consciousness, and Race Relations*. Berkeley: University of California Press.

Waterman, Richard. 1952. "Hot Rhythm in Negro Music." In *Acculturation in the Americas*, ed. Sol Tax, 207–18. Chicago: University of Chicago Press.

West, Cornel. 1989. "Black Culture and Postmodernism." In *Remaking History* (Discussions in Contemporary Culture, vol. 4), eds. Barbara Kruger and Phil Mariani, 87–96. Seattle: Bay Press.

Whiteley, Sheila. 1997. *Sexing the Groove: Popular Music and Gender*. London and New York: Routledge.

Williams, Raymond. 1983. *Keywords: A Vocabulary of Culture and Society,* rev. ed. New York: Oxford University Press.

Wilson, Olly. 1974. "The Significance of the Relationship Between Afro-American Music and West African Music." *Black Perspective in Music* 2(1) (Spring): 1–22.

———. 1985. "The Association of Movement and Music as a Manifestation of a Black Conceptual Approach to Music-Making." In *More Than Dancing: Essays on Afro-American Music and Musicians,* ed. Irene Jackson, 9–24. Westport, CT: Greenwood Press.

———. 1992. "The Heterogeneous Sound Ideal in African-American Music." In *New Perspectives on Music: Essays in Honor of Eileen Southern,* eds. Josephine Wright with Samuel A. Floyd, 327–38. Warren, MI: Harmonie Park Press.

Wong, Deborah. 2000. "The Asian American Body in Performance." In *Music and the Racial Imagination,* eds. Ronald Radano and Philip V. Bohlman, 57–94. Chicago: University of Chicago Press.

Zoloth, Laurie. 2001. "Passing Through: Jew as Black in the International Sweethearts of Rhythm." In *Jewish Locations: Traversing Racialized Landscapes,* eds. Lisa Tessman and Bat-Ami Bar On, 169–84. Lanham, MD: Rowman & Littlefield.

DISCOGRAPHY

Fugees. 1996. "Ready or Not." *The Score.* Ruff Ruffhouse Records/Columbia Record. CK 67147 (compact disc).

Get Your Ass in the Water and Swim Like Me! Narrative Poetry from Black Oral Tradition. 1976. Comp. and ed. Bruce Jackson. Rounder Records.

Jump Rope. 1955. Produced by Pete Seeger. Edgewood, IL. Folkways Records 7029.

Lee Andrews and the Hearts, performers. 1957. "Glad to Be Here" (sound recording). Written by Calhoun and Henderson. BMI/United Artists, UA136X.

Negro Folk Music of Africa and America. Produced by Harold Courlander. Folkways Records EFL-P500, 1951.

Old Mother Hippletoe: Rural and Urban Children's Songs. New World Records, NW291.

"Play and Dance Songs and Tunes, album 9." *Folk Music of the United States.* Produced and edited by Benjamin A. Botkin. Library of Congress AAFS-L9.

Public Enemy. 1990. *Fear of a Black Planet.* Compact Disc 45413. Def Jam Recordings/Columbia.

"Ring Game Songs and Others, v. 6." 1956. *Negro Folk Music of Alabama.* Produced by Harold Courlander. Folkways Records P417a.

Skip Rope. Thirty-three skip-rope games recorded in Evanston, IL. Folkways Records FC 7029.

Street and Gangland Rhythms: Beats and Improvisations by Six Boys in Trouble. Edited by E. Richard Sorenson. Folkways Records FD 5589.

Zap Mama, performers. 1994. *Sabsylma*. Time Warner, 945537-2.

FILM/VIDEOGRAPHY

I Was Made to Love Her: The Double Dutch Documentary. 2000. Directed by Nicole Franklin, Epiphany Inc. New York: Filmmakers Library (92 min.).

Hip Hop 101: The Game (documentary DVD). 2003. Directed by Gregory J. Cassagnol and Yves E. Salomon. New York: Win Media Corp. (www .hiphp101DVD.com).

Steppin' (documentary videorecording). 1992. Directed by Jerald B. Harkness. Written by M. J. Bowling and J. B. Harkness. New York: Cinema Guild (56 min.).

Pizza Pizza Daddy-O (documentary film). 1969. Bess Lomax Hawes, producer. Distributed by University of California, Berkeley.

A Question of Color: Color Consciousness in Black America (documentary videorecording). 1992. Produced, directed, and written by Kathe Sandler. San Francisco: California Reel (58 min.).

INTERVIEWS

Barbara (b. 1971, Chicago, Illinois). Interviewed November 12, 1994. Parents from Chicago, Illinois. Siblings: Two sisters. Occupation: Doctoral student in Psychology at the University of Michigan. Self-Designation: African American. Recorded on audiocassette.

Charlene (b. 1970, Pittsburgh, Pennsylvania). Interviewed February 1, 1995. Parents from North Carolina and South Carolina. Siblings: One older sister and three older brothers. Occupation: Doctoral student in Political Science at the University of Michigan. Self-Designation: Black. Recorded on audiocassette.

Doris (b. 1940, Detroit, Michigan). Interviewed January 27, 1995. Parents from Georgia. Siblings: Four older brothers, one younger brother. Occupation: Doctoral student in Public Health and staff member at the University of Michigan. Self-Designation: African American. Recorded on audiocassette.

Enid (b. date missing; Washington, D.C., raised in College Park, Maryland). Interviewed February 2, 1995. Parents from South Carolina and North Carolina. Siblings: One younger brother and one younger sister. Occupation: Doctoral student in Sociology at the University of Michigan. Sorority: Alpha

Kappa Alpha Sorority. since 1993. Self-Designation: Black. Recorded on audiocassette.

Faye (b. 1940, Alabama). Informally interviewed on November 11, 1994, and in May 1995. Occupation: Executive Secretary at the University of Michigan.

Felicia (b. 1973, Detroit, Michigan). Interviewed January 31, 1995. Parents from Memphis, Tennessee, and Detroit, Michigan. Siblings: none. Occupation: Undergraduate student at the University of Michigan. Self-Designation: Biracial (black and white). Recorded on audiocassette.

Greta (b. 1971, Highland Park, Michigan near Detroit). Interviewed February 8, 1995. Parents from Alabama and Louisiana. Siblings: One younger sister. Occupation: Doctoral student in Higher Education. Sorority: Detroit chapter of Delta Sigma Theta Sorority, since 1991. Self-Designation: African American. Recorded on audiocassette.

Jasmine and Stephanie, twins (b. 1985, Ypsilanti, Michigan). (No other biographical information; girls were adopted). Interviewed April 8, 1994. Recorded seven game-songs on audiocassette.

Laura (b. 1976, New York, New York). Interviewed October 6, 1995. Parents from New York City and Mississippi. Siblings: One older brother. Occupation: Undergraduate student at the University of Michigan. Self-Designation: Black (her father is black and her mother is white). Recorded on audiocassette.

Liese [pronounced "Lisa"] (b. 1962, Manhattan and raised in Queens, New York). Interviewed January 12, 1995. Parents from Philadelphia, Pennsylvania, and Cape May, New Jersey. Siblings: One older sister and two older brothers. Occupation: Doctoral student and staff at the University of Michigan. Self-Designation: Black American. Recorded on audiocassette.

Linda (b. 1948, Detroit, Michigan). Interviewed October 3, 1994. Parents from Detroit, Michigan. Siblings: Two brothers. Occupation: "Nontraditional" undergraduate student at the University of Michigan. Self-Designation: African American. Recorded on audiocassette.

Marietta [aka Ife] (b. 1938, Ann Arbor, Michigan). Interviewed September 9, 1994. Parents from Ann Arbor, Michigan. Siblings: One brother. Occupation: Blues and jazz singer. Self-Designation: African American. Recorded on audiocassette.

Marlys (b. 1956, Washtenaw County, Michigan). Interviewed November 11, 1994. Parents from Tennessee. Siblings: One older brother and a younger sister and brother. Occupation: Staff at the University of Michigan. College-educated. Self-Designation: African American. Recorded on audiocassette.

Melvin, Janice, current president of the American Double Dutch League. In-person conversation, June 15, 1995, World Invitational Double Dutch Championship held at Charleston Southern University in North Charleston, South Carolina.

Nancy (b. 1963, Philadelphia, Pennsylvania). Interviewed September 9, 1995. Siblings: Three older brothers, one older sister. Occupation: Biochemist at the University of Pennsylvania, University of Michigan Ph.D. Recorded game-songs on audiocassette.

Patricia (b. 1949, Baltimore, Maryland). Interviewed November 21, 1994. Parents from North Carolina and Maryland. Siblings: One sister. Occupation: Administrator at University of Michigan Graduate Library. Self-Designation: African American. Recorded on audiocassette.

Rashaunda M. [ruh-shawn-da] (b. 1969, Shreveport, Louisiana). Interviewed February 10, 1995. Parents from Shreveport, Louisiana. Siblings: Two sisters. Occupation: Doctoral student in Electrical Engineering. Sorority: Tuskegee chapter of Alpha Kappa Alpha Sorority since 1990. Self-Designation: African American. Recorded on audiocassette.

Ruqaiijah [ruh-kai-yah] (b. 1974, Detroit, Michigan, raised in Highland Park, Michigan, near Detroit, New Orleans, Louisiana, etc.). Interviewed March 16, 1995. Mother from Indianapolis, Indiana. Siblings: None. Occupation: Undergraduate student in Biology at the University of Michigan. Self-Designation: African American. Recorded on audiocassette.

Tosha D. (b. 1972, Memphis, Tennessee). Interviewed November 22, 1994. Parents from Mississippi and Tennessee. Siblings: None. Occupation: Public Health student at the University of Michigan. Self-Designation: African American. Recorded on audiocassette.

Walker, David, co-founder and former president of American Double Dutch League, president of the International Federation of Double Dutch. Telephone interview by author, May 14, 1995, Bronx, New York. Paraphrased written transcription and notes.

Index

2 Live Crew (musical group), 83
69 Boyz (musical group), 150

Abrahams, Roger, 50, 63
Abu-Jamal, Mumia, 120
Adams, De'Shone, 147
Adams, Nicki, 147
African American folk culture, 13
African American language, 24
African American music: academic instruction, 37; the body, 5–8, 9; call-and-response, 2, 8, 58; children's music, 61; in classrooms, 185; cross-rhythms, 8; dance, 6–8, 23; difference between children's and adult's music, 36; dominant characteristics, 58; embodied music-making, 23; embodiment, 25, 29; enculturation, 41–42; foreground features, 8; gender, 52, 187; improvisation, 58; individuality within collectivity, 8; kinetic orality, 57; lived identification with, 41–42; metrical ambiguity, 8; metronomic sense, 25, 30–31, 47, 77, 134; in multi-ethnic settings, 150; music schools, 43; musical identity, 41–44; oral-kinetic practices, 2; other ethnic identities, 43; patriarchy, 12; race, 52, 187; rhythm, 2, 25, 38, 58; rock 'n' roll, 75; roots of, 6; in schools, 37, 43, 185; somatic historiography of, 4, 60, 70, 126, 159–160, 183, 186; sound ideals, 31; syncopation, 2, 32; timbre, 8
African American popular culture: gender, 14, 111; girls' games, 58, 118; race, 14; signifyin', 131; thoughts of, 1
African Americans, 184–185
African music, 32

African Rhythm and African Sensibility (Chernoff), 64
Afrika Bambaataa (musician), 182
Agawu, Kofi, 61
Algorithms, 27–28
American Bandstand (TV show), 84, 126, 127
American Cultural Specialist and Hip-Hop Ambassador, 121
American Double Dutch League (ADDL), 15, 18, 139–155
Anderson, Laurie, 40
Andrews, Lee, 90–92
Answer/response records, 122–123
Anti-essentialism, 47, 60
Apollo Theater, 154
Archie Bell & the Drells (musical group), 47, 103
Artist Development Institute, 121
Athleticism, 15

"Baby Got Back" (song), 163
"Baby We Can Do It" (game-song), 86
Backstreet Boys (musical group), 44
"Ball the Jack" (game-song), 99–101
"Ballin' the Jack" (song), 101
Banned in the U.S.A. (album), 83
Baraka, Amiri (LeRoi Jones), 9, 46
Barris, Chuck, 104
Basketball, 140
Bass music, 83–84
Baumann, Max Peter, 10
"Bear Cat" (song), 122
Beat: cheers, 77, 81; handclapping games, 16, 24–30, 63; hip-hop, 19–20; in "Slide," 24–29; timbre, 30
Becker, Judith, 19

Beethoven, Ludwig van, 185
Belief, conditions for, 48
Bell, Archie (musician), 47, 103
Bell Biv DeVoe (musical group), 73
Berry, Chuck (musician), 68, 69
Berry, Fred (aka Rerun, dancer), 83
Between the Lions (TV show), 71
Big (film), 56, 96
Big Les (dancer), 106
"Bills, Bills, Bills" (song), 122
Biological determinism, 45–46
Birdwhistell, R. L., 60
"Bitches Ain't Shit (But Hos and Tricks)"
  (song), 120
Black femaleness, 58, 134, 157, 180
Black masculinity, 51–52, 114–115
Black music research, 8–12
Blacking, John, 61
Blackman, Toni (musician), 121
Blackness, 34–35, 38, 58, 60–61
Blige, Mary J. (musician), 155
Blues, the, 9, 64
Blues People (Jones), 9
Bluestein, Gene, 106
Body, the: African American music, 5–8, 9;
  black music research, 8–12; children's
  culture, 54; gyration, 95, 98, 168; "in-
  body formulas," 16; instruments, 59;
  language, 186; musical blackness, 59;
  somatic historiography, 60; as a technol-
  ogy, 57–62
Boone, Pat (musician), 170
Booty music, 83–84
Bop the (dance), 130
Boredom, 128
Borrowing, 89–110; from "Down, down
  baby," 91, 103–105, 184; by female hip-
  hop artists, 108–109, 184; in hip-hop
  music, 2–3, 19–20, 88, 93–97, 107, 121;
  and improvisation, 3; by Nelly, 95–97,
  101, 102, 108, 184
Bounce, the (dance), 103
Breakdancing, 113, 141–142
Broadway tunes, 162
Broonzy, Big Bill (musician), 68
Brown, Bobby (musician), 73
Brown, Delores, 147
Brown, H. Rap, 131
Brown, James (musician), 125, 126, 135,
  144

Browning, Barbara, 186
Burns, Jim, 101
Butler, Judith, 10
Butler, Melvin, 15

"C. C. Rider" (handclapping game, aka
  "See See Rider"), 68
Cabbage Patch, the (dance), 168–169
Calhoun, Wendell, 91
Call-and-response: African American
  music, 2, 8, 58; answer/response records,
  122–123; cheers, 77, 81–82; ethnic iden-
  tity, 70; "Jig-a-low," 80; race, 187; sex-
  ism, 187; from word to body, 1
Call-and-response records, 123
Campbell, Luther (aka Luke Skywalker,
  musician), 83
"Candy Girl" (song), 72–73
Carey, Mariah (musician), 43
Chants, 30, 137, 144–146, 151–152
Charles, Ray (musician), 68
Checker, Chubby (musician), 103
Cheerleaders, 85
Cheers, 56, 57, 76–88, 137
Chernoff, John Miller, 64, 90
Children's culture, 54
Children's music, 36, 61, 92–93
"Chocolate City (D.C.)", 151
Choreography, 2, 137
Christgau, Robert, 122
Chronic (album), 108, 120
Church music, 129
Ciphers, 112
Citron, Marcia, 10
Clark Sisters (musical group), 129
Classical music-making, 186
Cleveland, James (musician), 129
"C'mon Babe" (song), 83
Collins, Patricia Hill, 10
Color Purple (Walker), 109
Commercial music, 1, 2–3, 56, 92
Community, 93–94
Coolio (musician), 19
Coplan, David, 61
Country and western music, 162
"Country Grammar" (song), 88, 95–96,
  101
Courlander, Harold, 61, 68
"Criminal Minded" (song), 136
Cross-rhythms, 8, 29

Cultural DNA, 35
Cultural ethnographers, 184–185
Culture, transmission of, 102
Curtis, King (musician), 68

Dance: academic writing, 7; African American children's games, 74, 86; African American music, 6–8, 23; black culture, 103; black females, 177; breakdancing, 113; in classrooms, 185; in Detroit, 81; dominant characteristics, 58; hip-hop, 82–83; kinesthetic memories, 47; music, 25; rap music, 82–83, 122; somatic historiography, 126, 159–160; storytelling, 74
"Dancing Machine" (song), 81, 84
Dargan, Amanda, 138
Dating Game (TV show), 104
Davis, Miles (musician), 40
Death Row Records, 117, 119
Defamiliarization, 54
Destiny's Child (musical group), 122
Determinism, 45–46
Diamond, Beverly, 10
Diddley, Bo (musician), 75
Disco Four (musical group), 122
DNA, 35
Do Do Brown, the (dance), 83
"Do Do Brown" (handclapping game), 83
Dog, the (dance), 92, 103
"Dollar-bill" (song), 124
Doo-wop, 90
Dorsey, Lee, 75
"Double Dutch Bus" (song), 108
"Double-Dutch Cops" (nickname), 140
Double Dutch Divas (dance group), 18, 158–180
Double-Dutch Girls (dance group), 113, 159
Double-dutch jump rope, 133–180; athleticism, 15; author's childhood, 13; definition, 1; Double Dutch Divas, 18, 158–180; Double-Dutch Girls, 113; fusion double-dutch, 154–155, 162; hip-hop, 113, 137, 145–146; kinetic orality, 57, 152; linguistic play, 25, 145; music, 15, 133; patriarchy, 12; as a sport, 139–155 (*see also* American Double Dutch League); street double-dutch, 15, 134–137, 141–142, 148, 149, 150; studies of, 56; timelines, 135, 152, 167; tricks, 136, 146–147, 173
Double Dutch (Walker), 147
Double Forces (double-dutch team), 151–152, 153
"Down, down baby" (game-song, aka "Hot dog"), 94–102; borrowing from, 91, 103–105, 184; chant in, 137; musical transcription, 194–198
Dozens, the (cheer), 87, 131, 142
Dr. Dre (musician), 108, 120
Drumming, 30
DXT (DJ, formerly Grandmixer D.ST), 113
Dynamic Diplomats of Double Dutch (double-dutch team), 152, 154

Earth, Wind, and Fire (musical group), 72
"Eeny meeny pepsadeeny" (game-song), 89–90, 199–200
Electric Company (TV show), 71
Ellington, Duke, 167
Ellis, Shirley, 75, 108
Embodiment: African American music, 29; of algorithms, 27–28; black musical studies, 187; blackness, 60–61; disregard of, 87; ethnomusicologists, 25; gender, 53, 186; "Jig-a-low," 84; legitimizing, 87; literacy, 186; media, 76; musical blackness, 29, 58, 70–71; participation in music, 62; race, 53, 186; representations of, 34–35; significance, 59; social memory, 60; of syncopation, 29–30
Emceeing/emcees, 92, 112, 121
Emerson, Billie, 75
Eminem (musician), 39, 43, 118
Enculturation, 41–42, 53, 88. *See also* Socialization
Epperson, Jason "Jay E," 95
Essentialism, 35, 38
Ethnic identity: call-and-response, 70; fixed conceptions of, 47; gender, 52; girls' games, 14; kinetic orality, 8, 60; music, 184; musical behavior, 25, 41; musical blackness, 37
Ethnography, 86–88
Everly Brothers (musical group), 68

Fantastic Four (double-dutch team), 147, 148

"Fantastic Voyage" (song), 19
Femaleness, black, 58, 134, 157, 180
Feminine Endings: Music, Gender, and Sexuality (McClary), 10
Field recordings of games, 56
Fight, the (dance), 73
Flack, Roberta, 129
Floyd, Samuel A., Jr., 6, 9, 58
Folk music, 106–107
Folklore, 53–54, 87
Folksong, 87
Four Corners, the (dance), 168
Franklin, Aretha, 103, 167
Franklin, Kirk, 173
Franklin, Nicole, 160–161
Franti, Michael, 162
Freeman, Damita Jo, 81–82
Freestyle Union (FSU) (musical organization), 121
Frith, Simon, 75
Fugees (musical group), 155
Funk, 9, 73
Furious Five (musical group), 124
Fusion double-dutch, 154–155, 162

G, Warren (musician), 19
"Game" as metaphor in hip-hop, 17, 111, 115–118
Game-songs: double-dutch jump rope, 150; ethnomusicologists, 87; female artists, 108; musical blackness, 21, 61–62; the "real" popular, 102; types, 62
"Games Females Play" (song), 122
"Games People Play" (song), 122
Gangsta rap, 119–120
Gardner, Howard, 5
Gender: African American culture, 14, 111; African American music, 52, 187; black musical studies, 187; double-dutch jump rope, 138; embodiment, 53, 186; ethnic identity, 52; hip-hop, 93–94; kinetic orality, 8; language, 111; music, 184; musical blackness, 7, 9, 102; popular music, 92, 105; power, 114, 116–117; race, 51–52, 53; socialization, 14, 57
Gender and the Musical Canon (Citron), 10
Generation Ébène (double-dutch team), 151

Genes, 44–45
Gestures: cheers, 76, 78; "Eeny meeny pepsadeeny," 90; handclapping games, 25, 26, 64, 66–68, 76; hip-hop, 88; "Jig-a-low," 80–84, 190–193; "Miss Lucy," 67; "Miss Mary Mack," 66–68
"Get The Hell On (Get Gone)" (song), 122
Geto Boys (musical group), 117
Ghostface Killah (musician), 115–116
Gigolette (musician), 122
Gilroy, Paul: African American folk culture, 13; anti-essentialism, 47, 60; black identity, 39, 46, 70; black masculinity, 51–52; black social memory, 70; kinetic orality, 4–5; power of black music, 169
"Gin and Juice" (song), 19
"Glad to Be Here" (song), 90–91
Glassie, Henry, 143
Globalization of girls' games, 56
Goodwin, June, 139
Gospel music, 173
"Gossip Folk" (song), 108
Grandmaster Flash (musician), 122, 124
Grandmixer D.ST (DJ, later DXT), 113
Grateful Dead (musical group), 68
Gullah Gullah Island (TV show), 56
Gyration, 95, 98, 168

Hall, Edward T., 25
Hall, Stuart: on essentialism, 35; expropriation of black popular culture, 127; on identification, 110; "Notes on Deconstructing the 'Popular'", 107; popular culture, 102, 107, 109
Hamboning, 25, 63, 88, 130
Hampton, Barbara, 10
Hancock, Herbie, 113
Handclapping games, 19–36, 62–76; beat, 16, 24–30, 63; chants, 137; choreography, 137; "Do Do Brown," 83; handclapping bridges, 68–74, 94; previously recorded songs, 88; studies of, 56; "Tweedle deedle dee," 68, 80. See also "Miss Mary Mack"
Hanks, Tom, 56, 96
Harlem Globetrotters (basketball team), 167
Hawkins, Tremaine (musician), 173
Hearts (musical group), 90, 92
Henderson, Jocko (DJ), 90

Herder, Johan Friedrich, 87
Herndon, Marcia, 10
Higginson, Vy (radio host), 159
Hill, Lauryn (aka L-Boogie, musician), 108, 155–156
Hip-hop, 111–123; beat, 19–20; borrowing from girls' games/music, 2–3, 19–20, 88, 93–97, 107, 121; community, 93–94; dance, 82–83; Double Dutch Divas, 162; double-dutch jump rope, 113, 137, 145–146; emceeing/emcees, 92, 112, 121; female artists, 108–109, 121, 184; freestyling, 1, 112; fusion with R&B/funk, 73; future girls' musical play, 30; "game" as metaphor, 17, 111, 115–118; gender, 93–94; history of, 9; masculinism, 51, 109; misogyny, 19, 51, 73, 108, 118, 120–121; patriarchy, 12; rhyming, 19–20, 88, 92; rhythm, 19–20; sampling female music, 2–3, 14, 96, 121
Hip Hop 101: The Game ("how-to" DVD), 115–118
Hip-Hop Ambassador, America's, 121
Holiday, Billie (musician), 40
"Hollywood Swinging" (song), 182
hooks, bell, 47–48
"Hot Dog." *See* "Down, down baby"
Hot Peppers (double-dutch team), 149
Hot Steppers (double-dutch team), 144, 149
Hottentot Venus (a.k.a. Sara Baartmann), 163
"Hound Dog" (song), 122
House music, 162, 173
Houston, Whitney (musician), 175
Hungerford, James, 22

Ice T (musician), 119
Ideal (musical group), 122
"I'm a nut" (game-song), 188–189
Improvisation: African American music, 58; American Double Dutch League, 149–150; borrowing, 3; race, 187; rhyming, 112; sexism, 187
"In-body formulas," 16
Infinity Rappers (musical group), 113
International Federation of Double Dutch, 152
Intertextuality, 109–110
Intonation, 30

Jackson, Irene V., 10
Jackson, Janet (musician), 162
Jackson, Jesse, 170
Jackson, Michael (anthropologist), 48
Jackson, Michael (musician), 68–69, 80, 84, 94
Jackson Five (musical group), 73, 81
Jamaican Pepperseed, the (dance), 73
Jay-Z (musician), 103
Jerry Lewis, the (dance), 169
Jewel (musician), 68
"Jig-a-low" (cheer), 80–84, 190–193
Jingles, 85–86
Jive talk, 1
Johnson, Robert (musician), 51
Jones, A. M., 77
Jones, Bessie, 56
Jones, LeRoi (Amiri Baraka), 9, 46
Jordan, Michael, 13
Juba-patting, 21–23, 63, 88
Juba-rhyming, 21
"Juber Dance" (game-song), 22–23
Jump Energy (double-dutch team), 144
Jump Sister Jump (double-dutch team), 159
"Jump Sister Jump" (song), 158, 178–179

Kelley, Robin D. G., 120
Keyes, Cheryl, 10
Khan, Chaka (musician), 38–39
Kid Capri (DJ), 118
"Kill You" (song), 118
Kinesics, 60
Kinetic orality: African American music, 57; borrowing, 106–108; definition, 3–4, 5, 6, 62; description of, 164–179; double-dutch jump rope, 57, 152; ethnicity, 8, 60; gender, 8; Gilroy on, 4–5; hip-hop's sampling of female music, 14, 121; identity, 60; intertextuality between girls' games and black popular songs, 92; "Jig-a-low," 83; mnemonic rituals, 70; musical blackness, 3–4; onomatopoeia, 26, 98, 103; oral-kinetic etudes, 2, 11, 186; significance, 4–5; somatic historiography, 4, 60, 70, 126, 159–160, 183, 186; training, 59; West and, 5, 59
Kinetics, 59, 60, 61
Kool & the Gang (musical group), 38, 182
Koskoff, Ellen, 155

Kraftwerk (musical group), 182
KRS-One (musician), 118, 119–120, 136

L-Boogie (musician Lauryn Hill), 108, 155–156
Language: African American, 24; the body, 186; linguistic play, 25–26, 71–72, 78, 145
Leadbelly (Huddie William Ledbetter), 51, 68
Leppert, Richard, 10
Lincoln, Abbey (musician), 181
Lincoln Leapers (double-dutch team), 144
Lindsey, Melvin (radio DJ), 38
Linguistic play: cheers, 78; double-dutch jump rope, 25, 145; handclapping games, 25–26, 71–72; "Tutti Frutti," 90
Lipsitz, George, 75–76
Little Anthony and the Imperials (musical group), 97
Little Richard (musician), 90
"Little Sally Walker" (ring game), 68, 76
"Little Sally Walker" (song), 104
"Long Lonely Nights" (song), 90
Luke Skywalker (musician), 83
Lying Up a Nation: Race and Black Music (Radano), 11
Lyrics of game songs: "Ball the Jack" (game-song), 99–100; circulation among types of play, 68; "Down, down baby," 94–95; "Glad to Be Here," 90–91; handclapping games, 21; "Jig-a-low," 80; "Jump Sister Jump," 178–179; "Miss Mary Mack," 20–21, 63, 65, 66–67, 68, 74; "Walkin' the Dog," 104–105

Magrini, Tulia, 10
Mama, I Want to Sing (musical), 159
Marable, Manning, 181
Marshall, Penny, 96
Martinez, Angie (musician, radio personality), 118
"Mary Mack." *See* "Miss Mary Mack"
Masculinism, 50–52, 109, 155–156
Masculinity, black, 51–52, 114–115
Mass mediation, 56
Mathis, Johnny (musician), 43
Maultsby, Portia, 9
MC Lyte (musician), 108
McClary, Susan, 6, 9–10, 44

Medusa (musician), 121
Melo-rhythmic dynamics, 31
Melody, 31
Melvin, Janice, 145–146
Mendelssohn, Felix, 104
Merengue, 162
Merrill-Mirsky, Carol, 92
"Message" (song), 124
Metrical ambiguity, 8
Metronomic sense: African American music, 25, 30–31, 47, 77; double-dutch jump rope, 134
Misogyny: gangsta rap, 119; hip-hop, 19, 51, 73, 108, 118, 120–121
"Miss Lucy" (game-song), 23–24, 66–68
"Miss Mary Mack" (handclapping game), 63–68; lyrics, 20–21, 63, 65, 66–67, 68, 74; at music conference, 20–21; public domain, 105; recordings by male artists, 94; versions of, 15, 63–66; "Walkin' the Dog," 68, 103–105
Missy "Misdemeanor" Elliot (musician), 108
Mitchell-Kernan, Claudia, 131
Moisala, Pirrko, 10
Monk, David, 104
Monson, Ingrid, 52
Morrison, Toni, 13
Motown Records, 69
Moynihan Report (1965), 112
Multi-ethnic settings, 150
Multiculturalism, 41
Music: African American folk culture, 13; athleticism, 15; black females, 177; black women, 156; dance, 25; double-dutch jump rope, 15, 133; ethnic identity, 41, 184; gender, 184; sexual politics, 11; surface features, 25. *See also* African American music; Musical blackness
Music, Gender, and Culture (Herndon, Ziegler and Baumann), 10
Music and Gender: Perspectives from the Mediterranean (Magrini), 10
Music and Gender (Moisala and Diamond), 10
Music of Black Americans (Southern), 9
Music research, black, 8–12
Musical blackness, 3–9, 37–55; the body, 59; case histories of the development of, 123–131; embodiment, 29, 58, 70–71;

game-songs, 21, 61–62; gender, 7, 9, 102; identification with, 58; musical play, 14; somatic historiography, 60
Musical identity, 41–44
Musical intertextuality, 109–110
Musical play, 14, 30
Musical transcriptions, 188–200
"Musicking," 134
Musicology and Difference: Gender and Sexuality in Music Scholarship (Solie), 10
"My Girl" (song), 104
My Love Is Your Love (album), 175
"My Prerogative" (song), 73
"Mystery Date" (handclapping game), 69

'N Sync (musical group), 43, 44
"Name Game" (song), 75, 108
Nate Dogg (musician), 19
Nelly (musician): borrowing by, 95–97, 101, 102, 108, 184; "Country Grammar," 88, 95–96, 101
New Dance Show (TV show), 81
New Edition (musical group), 73
New jack swing, 73
New musicology, 10
New York City, 136, 138, 141, 147
New York City Rap Tour (1982), 112–113, 159
Newton, Wayne (musician), 68
"Night Game" (song), 75
"No Pigeons" (song), 122
"No Scrubs" (song), 122
Nonsense in girls' games, 98
Nonverbal communication, 25
North Charleston (South Carolina), 143, 144
"Notes on Deconstructing the 'Popular'" (Hall), 107
Novelty songs, 104
"Numbers" (handclapping game, aka "Slide"), 24–33
N.W.A. (musical group), 19
Nzewi, Meki, 31

Oakes, Robin, 147–148
O'Day, Bobby (musician), 69, 80
"Old MacDonald Had a Farm" (song), 104
Onomatopoeia, 26, 98, 103

"OO-lay-OO-lay" (cheer), 32–33, 77–80
Oral-kinetic etudes, 2, 11, 186
Orality, 59, 60, 61
Oreo jingle, 85–86
Oriental Peppers (double-dutch team), 144
Osbourne, Ozzy (musician), 40

Pantaleoni, Hewitt, 29
Parrish, Lydia, 99, 102
Party rap, 83
Patriarchy, 12
Pee Wee Herman, the (dance), 169
Pepper Steppers (double-dutch team), 144
Pepper Steppers, Jr. (double-dutch team), 144
Pitch, 24, 31
"Planet Rock" (song), 182
Play-party songs, 68
"Poison" (song), 73
Police Athletic League, 141
Polymeter, 28
Polyrhythm, 28–29
Popular culture: African Americans, 1; everyday and mass-mediated, 179; expropriation of black popular culture, 127; folklore, 53–54; folksong, 87; girls' influence on, 106; Hall on, 102, 107, 109, 127; the "real" popular, 102, 107
Popular music: being cool, 124; black popular music, 183; folk music, 106–107; gender, 92, 105; girls' games, 31, 118, 183–184; knowledge of, 57–58; women, 93
Power, 114, 116–117
Power of Black Music (Floyd Jr.), 6, 58
Public Enemy (musical group), 40

Queen Latifah (musician), 108
Queen Pen (musician), 108
Quik (DJ), 120
Quik is the Name (album), 120

Race: African American culture, 14; African American music, 52, 187; black masculinity, 114–115; call-and-response, 187; double-dutch jump rope, 138; embodiment, 53, 186; gender, 51–52, 53; improvisation, 187; rhythm, 187; as a social construct, 42; socialization, 14, 57; syncopation, 187

Race Music: Black Cultures from Bebop to Hip-Hop (Ramsey), 11, 184
Racial identity, 38
Radano, Ronald, 11
Rainey, Ma (musician), 68
Raitt, Bonnie, 43
Rammellzee (musician), 113
Ramsey, Guthrie, 11, 15, 57, 184
Rap-a-lot Records, 117
Rap City (TV show), 106
Rap music/rapping, 82–83, 113, 122
R&B music, 73, 90, 162
Real Little Ultimate Jazz Fake Book, 101
Red Hot Peppers (double-dutch team), 149
"Red Hot" (song), 75
Refusized (album), 38–39
Reggae, 162
"Regulate" (song), 19
Rerun (dancer), 83
Response/answer records, 122–123
Rhyming: double-dutch jump rope, 145; hip-hop, 19–20, 88, 92; improvisation, 112; juba-rhyming, 21
Rhythm: African American music, 2, 25, 38, 58; double-dutch jump rope, 135; handclapping games, 28–29; hip-hop, 19–20; learning to have, 46–47, 130; melody, 31; metronomic sense, 25, 30–31, 47, 77; polyrhythm, 28–29; race, 187; sexism, 187; in "Slide," 24–29; syncopation, 30; timbre, 30; West African, 33. *See also* Syncopation
Ring games, 76
Ring shouts, 6, 9
Riperton, Minnie (musician), 38
Robinson, Smokey (musician), 104
Robot, the (dance), 81–82, 84
Rock 'n' roll, 75, 90, 162
Rock Steady Crew (breakdancers), 113
"Rock Steady" (song), 103
"Rockin' Robin" (song), 68–69, 80
"Rockit" (song), 113
Rolling Stones (musical group), 104
Roots (musical group), 92
Rose, Tricia, 119
"Rubber Dolly" (song), 75
Running Man, the (dance), 73
Ruthless Records, 117

"Sally Walters" (handclapping game), 68

Salsa, 162
Salt-N-Pepa (musical group), 19
Same-sex play, 84–85
Sample, Joe (musician), 68
Sanford, Wilhelmina (Willie), 161, 163
Santana (musical group), 43
Saturday Night Fever (film), 177
Savoy Sultans (musical group), 68, 90
"Say Man" (song), 75
Scarface (musician), 117
Scatting, 1, 149
Scolds, 76, 111. *See also* Cheers
"See See Rider" (handclapping game, aka "C. C. Rider"), 68
Segar, Leslie (aka Big Les, dancer), 106
Serwadda, Moses, 29
Sesame Street (TV show), 56
Sexing the Groove (Whitely), 52
Sexism, 119, 120, 187
Sexual politics, 11
Sexuality, 7, 126–127
Shakur, Tupac, 119
Shim-Sham, the (dance), 91
Shimmy, the (dance), 97, 98–101
Shimmy Shimmy Coke-Ca-Pop! (Langstaff and Langstaff), 97
"Shimmy shimmy ko-ko bop" (song), 97, 101
"Shining Star" (song), 72
Shirley, George (opera singer), 20
"Shoop" (song), 19
Sight of Sound: Music, Representation, and the History of the Body (Leppert), 10
Signifyin', 131
Simone, Nina (musician), 129, 181
Singing the Master (Abrahams), 50
"Sir Duke" (song), 42
Sir Mix-a-lot (musician), 163
Slave Songs of the Georgia Sea Islands (Parrish), 99
"Slide" (handclapping game, aka "Numbers"), 24–33
Small, Christopher, 134, 148
Smith, Chris, 101
Smith, Frankie (musician), 108
Smithsonian Folk Festival, 161
Smurf, the (dance), 169
Snoop Doggy Dogg (musician), 19, 108
Social memory, 4, 60, 70
Social practices, 38

Socialization, 25, 57. *See also* Encultura-
tion
Solie, Ruth A., 10
Somatic historiography: the body, 60;
dance, 126, 159–160; Double Dutch
Divas, 159–160; kinetic orality, 4, 183,
186; musical blackness, 60; social mem-
ory, 4, 60, 70
Songs in the Key of Life (album), 42
SOS Band (musical group), 86, 182
Soul, learning to have, 46–47
Soul music, history of, 9
Soul Train (TV show), 81, 84
Source (magazine), 116
Southern, Eileen, 9
Southern rap, 83
Spearhead (musical group), 162
Spears, Britney (musician), 44
Spicer, Jimmy (musician), 122, 124
Spirituals, 9
Spivak, Gayatri, 35
Sporty Thievz (musical group), 122
Staton, Dakota (musician), 68
Stepping/steps, 76, 131
Storytelling, 70, 74
"Straight Outta Compton" (song), 19
"Summer Madness" (song), 38
Supremes (musical group), 84
Swing Shift: "All-Girl" Bands of the 1940s
(Tucker), 11
Syncopation: African American music, 2,
32; chants, 30; double-dutch jump rope,
135; embodiment of, 29–30; handclap-
ping games, 28; intonation, 30; learning,
25; "Miss Mary Mack," 64, 66; race,
187; rhythm, 30; sexism, 187; in
"Slide," 29–30; timelines, 32, 77, 90,
135, 152, 167

Tagg, Philip, 45
"Take Your Time (Do It Right)" (song), 86
"Take Your Time" (song), 182
"Teardrops" (song), 90
"Telephone" (children's game), 168
"Theorizing the Body in African-American
Music" (McClary and Walser), 6–7
Thomas, Rufus, 68, 88, 103–104, 122
Thompson, Ahmir "Brother ?uestion"
(musician), 92
Thornton, Big Mama (musician), 122

"Tighten Up" (song), 103
Timbre: African American language, 24;
African American music, 8; beat, 30;
"Eeny meeny pepsadeeny," 89–90;
handclapping games, 62–63; "Miss
Lucy," 67; "Miss Mary Mack," 66, 67;
rhythm, 30
Time Warner, 119
Timelines: double-dutch jump rope, 135,
152, 167; "Eeny meeny pepsadeeny,"
90; "OO-lay-OO-lay," 32, 77; syncopa-
tion, 32
TLC (musical group), 122
Tommy Boy Records, 182
"Tonite" (song), 120
Tootsie Roll: Hip-Hop Mix (album), 150
Tootsie Roll (dance), 150–151
"Tootsie Roll" (song), 150
Training, 59
Travolta, John, 177
Tucker, C. Delores, 119
Tucker, Sherrie, 11
"Tweedle deedle dee" (handclapping
bridge), 68, 80
Twice as Nice (double-dutch team), 150
Twist, the (dance), 103
Two Tons of Fun (album), 166
Tyson, Mike, 73

Urban play, 56

Vandross, Luther (musician), 129, 162
Vanilla Ice (musician), 43
Venus Hottentot, 163
Versioning, 15
View, The (TV show), 160
Visweswaren, Kamala, 41
Vowel sound words, 71–72

Walker, Alice, 109
Walker, David: American Double Dutch
League, 139–142; double-dutch as a
musical performance, 155; Dynamic
Diplomats of Double Dutch, 152, 154;
fusion double-dutch, 154, 162; International Federation of Double Dutch, 152;
rhyming in double-dutch jump rope,
145; tricks in double-dutch jump rope,
147
Walker, Hezekiah (musician), 167

"Walkin' the Dog" (song), 68, 88, 103–104, 105
Walser, Robert, 6, 40
Walters, Barbara, 160
Ward, Brian, 123
Wash, Martha (musician), 166
Waterman, Richard, 77
"We're at the Party" (song), 122
West, Cornel, 4–5, 59
What's Happening (TV show), 83
White, Barry (musician), 38
Whitely, Sheila, 52
Williams, Ulysses, 139–142, 143, 147
Wilson, Cassandra (musician), 181
Wilson, Nancy (musician), 129
Wilson, Olly, 7–8, 9, 25, 31
Winans (musical group), 129
Women: black femaleness, 58, 134, 157, 180; black women in secular music-making, 156; in Double Dutch Divas, 18; female hip-hop artists, 108, 121; gangsta rap, 119; on *Hip Hop 101: The Game,* 117; masculinism, 155–156; misogyny in hip-hop, 19, 51, 73, 108, 118, 120–121; popular music, 93, 183–184; power, 116–117; sampling by, 108–109; worldviews of black females, 177
Wonder, Stevie, 42
Wong, Deborah, 77
Woods, Arthur, 141
Wu-Tang Clan (musical group), 115

"Ya Ya" (song), 75

Zeitlin, Steven, 138
Ziegler, Suzanne, 10
Zulu Nation, 182

About the Author

Kyra D. Gaunt is an Associate Professor of Ethnomusicology at New York University who lectures nationally and internationally on black popular music. She is also a professional jazz vocalist, a singer-songwriter, recording artist, and a consultant for PBS children's shows *Between the Lions* and *Zoom* on WBGH-TV. She is committed to ending racism and sexism through her music and scholarship by 2020.